Science and the Beauty Business

The Beauty Salon and its Equipment

Second Edition
John V. Simmons
BSc (Hons) C Biol MI Biol
Member of the Society of Cosmetic Scientists

THOMSON
✷
™
LEARNING

Australia • Canada • Mexico • Singapore • Spain • United Kingdom • United States

Science and the Beauty Business: The Beauty Salon and its Equipment
Second Edition

For more information, contact Thomson Learning, Berkshire House, 168–173 High Holborn, London, WC1V 7AA or visit us on the World Wide Web at:
http://www.thomsonlearning.co.uk

British Library Cataloguing-in-Publication Data
A catalogue record for this book is available from the British Library

ISBN 1-86152-691-1

First edition 1989
Second edition 1995 Macmillan Press Ltd
Reprinted four times
Reprinted 2001 and 2002 by Thomson Learning

Printed by CTPS, China

Science and the Beauty Business

Newcastle-under-Lyme College
Staffordshire

Companion book by the same author
Science and the Beauty Business –
The Science of Cosmetics: Second Edition

Related Thomson Learning titles
Beauty Therapy – The Foundations by Lorraine Nordman
Professional Beauty Therapy: The Official Guide to Level 3 by Lorraine
Nordman, Lorraine Appleyard and Pamela Linforth
Manicure, Pedicure and Advanced Nail Techniques by Elaine Almond
The Complete Make-up Artist: Working in Film, Television and Theatre
by Penny Delamar
Aromatherapy for the Beauty Therapist by Valerie Ann Wood
The Complete Nail Technician by Marian Newman
Safety in the Salon by Elaine Almond
The World of Skin Care: A Scientific Companion by Dr. John Gray

Contents

Newcastle-under-Lyme College
Staffordshire

Preface

The scientific principles of Beauty Therapy divide quite naturally into two distinct areas: the science of the beauty salon and its equipment which is the subject of this volume, and the science of cosmetics and toiletries dealt with in Volume 1.

Together, the two volumes are primarily intended for students of Beauty Therapy studying for the major qualifications offered by the National Council for Vocational Qualifications – NCVQ, the Business and Technology Education Council – BTEC, the City and Guilds of London Institute and the professional beauty therapy organisations.

The content is however deliberately not limited by the examination syllabuses. Instead the two volumes examine the scientific principles of all aspects of the beauty industry and as such they will be valuable to all who seek a good general insight into the subject.

Although it is entitled *The Beauty Salon and its Equipment*, the larger part of this volume is concerned with the many pieces of equipment which are available to assist the therapist in treating the clients. By no means all of these are confined to the salon. Many therapists will have the opportunity to work in health centres, sports centres and health farms, and will have to treat clients in the pool or the gymnasium. In untrained hands many of these pieces of equipment have the potential to do untold damage to the client. The primary aim of this text is to highlight the necessity for the therapist to get to know the equipment well enough to be able to perform the treatments effectively, with confidence and above all in complete safety.

The equipment and the treatments

Beauty treatments using equipment are of five main kinds:

1 *Mechanical massage equipment* – is to simulate and extend the principles of manual massage. It includes various kinds of vibro-massagers and vacuum suction equipment.
2 *Electrotherapy* – is the passage of an electric current through the body for therapeutic purposes. It includes the use of direct current in galvanic therapy, pulsed currents for muscle stimulation in faradic and similar treatments, and high-frequency alternating currents in high-frequency and diathermy treatments.
3 *Actinotherapy or ray therapy* – is the use of heat radiations and ultra-violet for therapeutic purposes, heat rays for their soothing or stimulating warmth and ultra-violet for its ability to produce a suntan without real sunshine.
4 *Hydrotherapy* – is the use of water in treatment. It can be used for its warming, soothing and stimulating effects or as a most effective medium in which to perform exercise.
5 *Mechanical principles* – of movement and exercise equipment, in particular the use of gymnasium equipment to increase the effectiveness of and maintain the interest in exercise.

The sequence of the chapters

Much of the equipment is electrically powered. The first chapters attempt to explain the intricacies of the electricity supply and the electrical circuits within the salon. Next follows a consideration of the mechanical massage equipment and electrotherapy equipment. Before detailing the use of heat rays and ultra-violet in therapy, a look is taken at rays in general and light rays in particular.

Next the book deals with hydrotherapy and the mechanical principles in movement and exercise. Finally it deals with the working conditions and services to the salon: heating, ventilation, lighting, water supplies and fire safety. Following each chapter there are suggestions for further study and self-assessment questions.

IMPORTANT
Since the publication of the first edition, important new regulations have come into force regarding the installation and maintenance of services and equipment.

1 *Electrical installation*
   All installation work must comply with the 16th Edition of the regulations of the Institute of Electrical Engineers (IEE). This does not outlaw do-it-yourself work. However, the design and completed work must be approved by a qualified inspector and issued with a certificate of the National Inspection Council for Electrical Installation Contracting (NICEIC). Additionally the installation must be tested and re-certificated at intervals decided by the inspector.

2 *Gas installation and maintenance*
   Do-it-yourself work is *illegal*. All work *must* be done by a qualified engineer who is a member of the Confederation of Registered Gas Installers (CORGI).

3 *Water*
   Do-it-yourself is not illegal but work must comply with regulations and is liable to inspection by the water supply company. In particular, check valves must be fitted to prevent 'used' water being drawn back into fresh water pipes and all metal pipework must be bonded to the electrical 'earth' system. Modern unvented (mains pressure) hot water systems must be installed only by a qualified engineer.

4 *Inspection and servicing of electrical and mechanical equipment*
   To comply with the requirements of the extended Health and Safety at Work Act (HASAWA) which came into force in January 1993, all equipment must be checked for safety and correct operation annually by a qualified engineer and be certificated as such. Note that the Portable Appliance Test (PAT) is *not* adequate for this purpose.

Acknowledgements

I wish to express my gratitude to my many friends and colleagues in the Beauty Therapy Profession, the Cosmetics Industry and the Beauty Equipment Industry for their tremendous help in preparing the content of this volume. In particular I thank those companies who have very kindly supplied illustrations and technical information. My especial gratitude is due to beauty therapist Teresa Zajac for her assistance in preparing and checking the text and illustrations.

JOHN V. SIMMONS

1 The Basics of Electricity

Introduction to electricity in beauty therapy; the electric circuit; series and parallel circuits; conductors, insulators and resistance; mains and battery electricity; cells and batteries; alternating and direct currents – a.c. and d.c.; use of the cathode ray oscilloscope to illustrate an electric current

Introduction

Even the most basic salon will require a good working light. On all but the mildest of days heating will be needed to provide a comfortably warm temperature for the clients. When the air becomes hot and sticky, some form of forced ventilation will be needed to restore a pleasant atmosphere. A supply of hot water will be essential. Some, if not all of these services will be *electric*.

Sooner or later a salon will acquire *electrical equipment*. It may be a simple vibro-massager to assist facials or a heavy-duty vibrator, a 'G5', to take some of the hard work out of body massage. Then perhaps a heat lamp may be acquired: a galvanic unit, a faradic unit . . . . All these are *electric* too.

For greater convenience, extra or improved lighting may be installed. Extra power points may be required to enable the equipment to be operated. Is the supply to the salon able to cope with the extra load?

Later a sauna may be installed, together with its attendant shower, or perhaps a 'high-pressure' solarium. For these it is quite likely that an uprated supply *will* be necessary, possibly even a 'three-phase' supply.

Soon it becomes obvious that at least a basic knowledge of electricity could be a great advantage even if only to avoid seriously damaging the electricity system, the clients or oneself, or to spare the embarrassment of being 'blinded by science' by an electrical engineer.

To be able to use electrical equipment to its best advantage, it is also of great help to understand what is actually happening during the treatment – to appreciate the effect of adjusting the controls, or to know what might happen should a treatment go on too long or if the machine is set at too high an intensity.

The following chapters will reveal some of the mysteries of electricity, of electric circuits and the workings of electrical equipment. The aim is to progress *very* gently, a step at a time, so that hopefully the most unscientific reader will not be lost by the wayside and the therapist, through a better understanding, may work more effectively and, above all, more *safely*.

The electric circuit

Let us start with a very simple electric circuit. One may be made from a battery, a lamp, preferably in a lampholder, and some lengths of connecting wire. A switch is also useful in the circuit so as to be able to control the lamp (see Figure 1.1).

This is the arrangement to be found in a simple pocket torch. Note how for the circuit to work, the wires connect the components to form a continuous pathway for the electricity; hence it is an *electric circuit*.

When the lamp is '*on*', the circuit is '*made*' or '*complete*'. If the switch is switched off or if a wire is disconnected, the lamp will be '*off*' because the circuit has been '*broken*'. When a circuit is working it is *made*. When switched off it is *broken*.

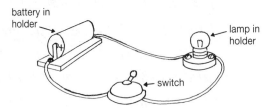

Figure 1.1 A simple electric circuit

In this simple circuit the battery is the *source* of the electrical *energy*. The lamp is the *appliance* which puts the electrical energy to use, in this case to produce *light* and heat!

Circuit diagrams

An electrician or an electronics engineer will use *circuit diagrams* to describe and illustrate his circuits. Even this simple circuit can be shown in the form of a diagram. The various components are shown by *symbols* and the wiring by straight lines, where possible running horizontally or vertically on the page. Figure 1.2 shows the symbols and the circuit diagram for the simple circuit.

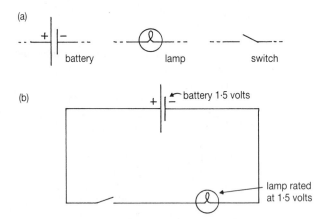

Figure 1.2 (a) Some symbols used in circuit diagrams. (b) Circuit diagram of the simple circuit used in figure 1.1

Series and parallel

A second lamp could be incorporated in the circuit. There are TWO ways in which it could be done:

1. In series
2. In parallel

In series

Figure 1.3 shows two lamps connected in series. This method of wiring them does however have serious drawbacks.

The first drawback is that the two lamps glow only dimly. Although each of the lamps in figure 1.3 requires only 1.5 volts, wired in this way the two will

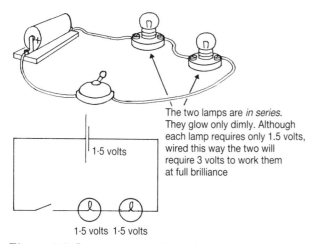

Figure 1.3 Lamps connected in series

The two lamps are *in series*. They glow only dimly. Although each lamp requires only 1.5 volts, wired this way the two will require 3 volts to work them at full brilliance

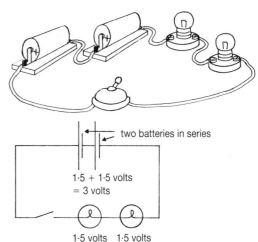

Figure 1.4 Adding a second battery restores the lamps to full brilliance

require 3 volts to work them at full brilliance. Figure 1.4 shows how a second battery, also wired in series, will provide the 3 volts necessary to restore the lamps to full brilliance. Be careful when connecting batteries in series to connect the $\oplus$ of one to the $\ominus$ of the next.

Even though both lamps now operate at full brilliance, there are still snags. If one lamp fails or is loose in its holder, the circuit is broken and both lamps will be 'off'. The lamps must be either all 'on' or all 'off'.

Connecting lamps or other appliances in *series* has only limited use. Strings of decorative lamps for Christmas trees are wired in series. Some heat lamps have two heat elements. When they are being operated as *infra-red* rather than as *radiant heat*, the two elements may be switched into series (see chapter 12).

In parallel

Figure 1.5 shows two lamps wired in parallel.

Lamps in *parallel* will both work at full brilliance even from the single battery. The two 1.5 volt lamps only need 1.5 volts to drive them both.

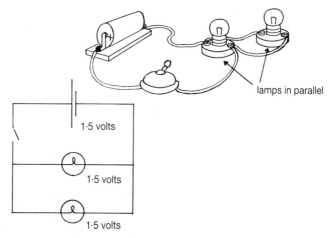

Figure 1.5 Lamps connected in parallel

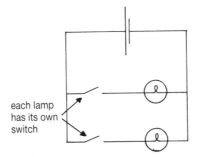

each lamp has its own switch

Figure 1.6 Each lamp in a parallel circuit can have its own switch

Should one lamp fail, the other will continue to work because its circuit is *not* broken.

Each lamp could have its own switch so it may be controlled independently (see figure 1.6).

When appliances are operated from a *mains supply*, they are connected in *parallel*.

Learn about electricity by doing experiments

You will have noticed that all the foregoing about electric circuits has been illustrated by *experiments*. These experiments are quite easy to do and, as long as the circuits are driven by 1.5 volt torch batteries, there is little chance of doing any damage either to the components or yourself.

The components required to do these experiments can be found in the physical science laboratories of most schools and colleges. Should a laboratory not be available, the bits and pieces required can mostly be bought quite cheaply from electrical shops or electronic hobby shops.

In most laboratories, the components are mounted in holders fitted with standard 4 mm sockets. The hook-up wires are fitted with a 4 mm plug at each end. This makes it a very quick and easy matter to set up these experimental circuits.

There are also available a variety of electrical and electronic kits which might be adapted to some of the experiments.

Conductors and insulators

When electricity flows round a circuit it flows through the metal centre of the connecting wires. The metal is acting as a *conductor* of electricity.

A *conductor* is a substance which allows electricity to pass through it.

The plastic coating on the connecting wires is to prevent the electricity straying from the metal conductor. This plastic coating is the *insulation*.

An *insulator* is a substance which does *not* allow electricity to pass through it.

To find out whether a substance is a conductor or an insulator, try this simple experiment. Set up the simple circuit as at the beginning of the chapter but do not include the switch. Instead leave the two wires unconnected (see figure 1.7).

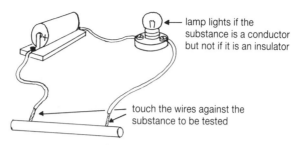

Figure 1.7 Finding if a substance is a conductor or an insulator

Touch the two wires against a variety of different substances. If the lamp lights, the substance is a conductor; if not, it is an insulator. Make a list of those substances which are conductors and one of those which are insulators.

Actually this method is not completely reliable. Some substances which are actually conductors – albeit not very good ones – will *not* light the lamp. A more reliable check is to use an *electrician's test meter* (see Figure 1.8). In figure 1.9 a test meter is being used for this purpose.

Figure 1.8 Electrician's test meter

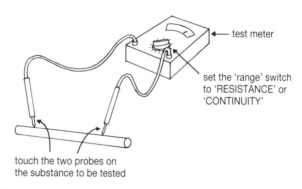

Figure 1.9 Using a test meter to test substances for electrical conductivity

Touch the two probes on a good conductor; the meter needle will swing right across the dial. On an insulator it will show no reading. On a poor conductor it will go part way across the dial. Try touching the 'lead' at each end of a pencil. It is made of *carbon* which although a conductor, is not a really good one.

Dip the probes in water. Distilled water will barely give a reading but tap water will. Salt water gives a good reading. Now moisten your fingers and grip the tip of a probe in each hand – you are a conductor!

Examples of conductors

Metals – Copper and steel are commonly used for connecting wires.

Carbon – Carbon is used for the 'brushes' in electric motors (see chapter 4). It is also included in the plastic used to make the plastic pad electrodes used with most 'faradic' muscle stimulation machines.

Water – Water is a conductor, particularly with *ionised* substances such as salts dissolved in it. Body fluids are like this. The body is a conductor.

Examples of insulators

Flexible plastics and rubber – are used for the insulating coating of connecting wires.

Rigid plastics and rubber – are used to make switches, lampholders, sockets, plugs, and many other components.

Wax and plastic resins – are used to coat many electronic components.

Electrical resistance

Even though electricity will pass through a conductor, it has to be *forced* through by the efforts of the battery or 'mains'. Any conductor offers a certain *resistance* to the passage of electricity through it.

Connecting wires have a *very low resistance*, so electricity passes easily with little wasted effort. Insulators though have an *extremely high resistance*, so virtually *no* electricity can pass through them.

Some conductors are deliberately chosen for their *fairly high resistance*, so that although electricity *can* pass through them it needs a lot of *energy* to force it through. The energy has to go somewhere and it turns into *heat*. The high resistance conductor gets *hot*. Some fairly high resistance conductors are:

Nichrome – the wire used for *heating elements*
Tungsten – the wire used for *lamp filaments*

Both have high melting points so that when they glow white hot, they do not melt.

Fuse wire is an alloy of tin, lead and copper. While its resistance is not particularly high, its *melting point* is very low so that should too much electricity flow through it, it will melt and break the circuit. A fuse is used to protect a circuit in the event of a fault or an overload. It is a deliberate 'weak link' in the circuit.

Some fuses consist of a length of fuse wire on a porcelain holder which fits in a fuse box (see figures 1.10 and 1.11).

Figure 1.10 A fuse box – fuse cover removed

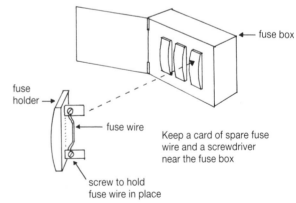

Figure 1.11 Fuse box with porcelain holders

In a plug it is usual to find a *cartridge fuse*. This also uses fuse wire but it is inside a glass or porcelain tube and soldered to a metal contact cap at each end (see figures 1.12 and 1.13). Always replace a 'blown' fuse with one of the correct value.

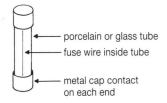

Figure 1.12 A cartridge fuse

- porcelain or glass tube
- fuse wire inside tube
- metal cap contact on each end

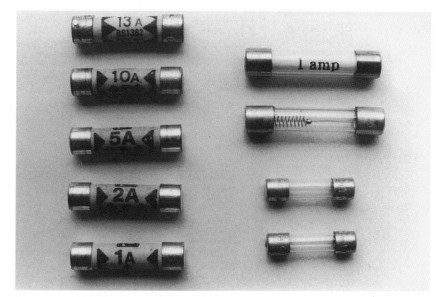

Figure 1.13 Selection of cartridge fuses

To show the heating effect of a wire of high resistance

Cut a 200 mm length of 26 s.w.g. *Nichrome* wire. Coil it and mount it on a suitable holder. Connect it to a suitable variable low-voltage laboratory power pack (see figure 1.14).

Now gradually increase the voltage. Note how the resistance wire gets hot – the *heating effect* – glows red, and then white giving *light* too. It eventually melts to break the circuit like a *fuse*.

An electric light bulb filament glows white hot and so gives out light but most of its output is actually heat (see figure 1.15). The glass envelope is to keep oxygen away from the hot filament to prevent it actually burning.

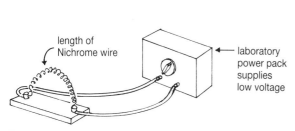

Figure 1.14 To show the heating effect of an electric current

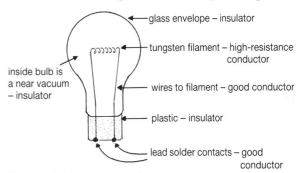

Figure 1.15 An electric lamp

- glass envelope – insulator
- tungsten filament – high-resistance conductor
- inside bulb is a near vacuum – insulator
- wires to filament – good conductor
- plastic – insulator
- lead solder contacts – good conductor

'Mains' and battery electricity

The simple circuits described so far in this chapter are shown operating from *batteries*. Not many electrical appliances in everyday life operate from batteries. They mostly run on *'mains'* electricity.

Batteries are quite satisfactory for portable equipment which uses very little electricity, but if more than a tiny amount of current is required batteries become prohibitive on the grounds of both their *bulk* and *cost*. Battery electricity is *thousands* of times more expensive than 'mains'.

Battery electricity

A battery produces electricity by a *chemical reaction*. A very simple battery can be made by putting strips of two *different* metals into an *ionised* solution – that is, a solution of a substance whose molecules have split into electrically charged particles called ions (see chapter 5).

As an example, a strip of copper and a strip of zinc can be put in a solution of dilute sulphuric acid. A copper nail and a galvanised (zinc coated) nail will do (see figure 1.16).

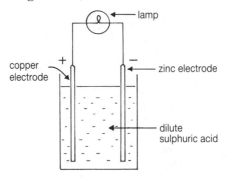

Figure 1.16 A simple battery or cell

This battery will drive a lamp but not very well. Chemical reactions between the metals and the acid produce the electricity. A simple battery like this is *not* very satisfactory. After working for a few moments only, it becomes 'blocked' with the products of the chemical reactions and needs a 'rest' for them to clear. It also carries on working when not connected, so it must be dismantled when not in use!

The most commonly available type of battery is the *dry battery*. Several types are available but the basic type consists of a zinc outer case containing ammonium chloride solution made into a paste with plaster of Paris; hence it is '*dry*'. Instead of copper it uses a rod of carbon in the centre (see figure 1.17).

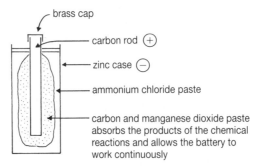

Figure 1.17 A dry battery

The whole battery is usually encased in tinplate or plastic to make it '*leak-proof*'. When it becomes exhausted, the contents may corrode their way out through the zinc and leak out. If this happens, they are corrosive enough to ruin the equipment.

Batteries should be removed as soon as they are exhausted. They must also be removed if the equipment is not to be used for some time. Even 'leak-proof' batteries might leak after long storage.

Once the chemical reactions are finished in this type of battery, it is exhausted and must be thrown away. A battery like this actually *makes* electricity. It is a *primary* battery.

Also available are *rechargeable* batteries. These can be connected through a *battery charger* to the mains and be charged with a 'fill' of electricity. This is stored within the battery to be released when it is used to operate equipment. In this type of battery the chemical reactions are reversed during the charging process. Rechargeable batteries cost much more than dry batteries and are economically viable only in equipment which discharges its batteries quickly – for example, an electric shaver.

ON NO ACCOUNT MUST A BATTERY BE CONNECTED DIRECT TO MAINS IN AN ATTEMPT TO RECHARGE IT. IT COULD EXPLODE.

Batteries in series

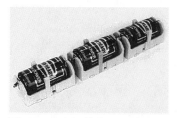

Figure 1.18 Cells connected in series

A single battery produces only a small *electrical force* of about 1.5 volts to drive a circuit. For many purposes this 1.5 volts is most inadequate. To obtain higher voltages, several batteries are connected together in *series*. For instance, four would give 6 volts (see figure 1.18).

The *power-pack* batteries used in transistor radios are made of several individual batteries or *cells* enclosed in a single casing. Depending on type, they deliver 6 or 9 volts. For higher voltages, batteries are impracticable. They are too heavy and costly.

A.C. and D.C. – alternating current and direct current

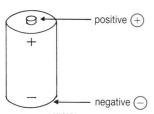

Figure 1.19 The polarity of battery terminals

A battery produces an electric current which flows round the circuit in *one direction*. This is called *direct current* or 'd.c.' for short.

Because direct current flows in *one* direction, it has *polarity*. The connections or terminals on the battery are labelled ⊕ for *positive* and ⊖ for *negative*. They may instead be colour-coded: *red* for ⊕ and *black* for ⊖ (see figure 1.19).

It is generally assumed that a direct current flows round the circuit from positive to negative, but a study of the way in which a current flows in a wire will show that the flow of *electrons* which constitutes the current is actually in the *opposite* direction! (see chapter 5).

Be careful when fitting batteries in electronic equipment such as radios, calculators and watches to put the batteries the *right way round*. If fitted wrongly, the equipment will not only not work but could be expensively damaged in the process.

Mains electricity is *alternating current* or 'a.c.'. It flows alternately in one direction then in the reverse direction in the circuit.

One complete back and forth alternation is a *cycle*. In most countries mains alternates 50 times each second. It has a *frequency* of 50 cycles per second.

The unit of measurement for *frequency* is the *Hertz*:

---

1 Hertz (Hz) is one alternation per second

Mains electricity therefore has a frequency of 50 Hz. Canada is, however, unique in having a mains frequency of 60 Hz.

Alternating current does not have polarity; there is *no* positive and negative. This is because they are continually changing over. The connections to the mains are termed *live* and *neutral*. The *live* connection is at mains voltage. In the UK this is 230 volts. The *neutral* is normally at zero volts, but do not rely on it being so!

The oscilloscope

Something as abstract as an electric current is very difficult to describe in words or to visualise in the mind. This is particularly so with some of the more complex currents used in electrotherapy.

Some kind of graphical illustration of an electric current is of immense value; indeed many manufacturers of electrotherapy equipment use such illustrations in their sales literature.

The *cathode ray oscilloscope*, CRO for short, is an electronic instrument which can instantly display a graphic representation of an electric current on a TV-type screen (see figure 1.20).

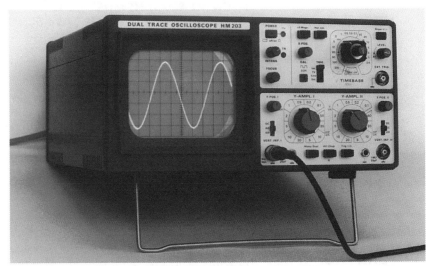

Figure 1.20 Cathode ray oscilloscope displaying an alternating current

The oscilloscope in effect draws a *graph* on the screen, using a moving spot of light. Movement of the spot *across* the screen from left to right along the *horizontal* or *x-axis* represents the passage of *time*.

When no electrical current is being fed into the oscilloscope, the light spot is usually adjusted to track across the centre of the screen.

When an electric current is fed in, the light spot is deflected *up* or *down* from the centre line to represent the *voltage* of the current at any moment in time. The up and down deflections are on the *vertical* or *y-axis*. It is usual to arrange the connections so that *upward* deflections represent voltages in the '*forward*' direction in the circuit and *downward* deflections represent voltages in the '*reverse*' direction. Hence the graph drawn by the oscilloscope is of *voltage* against *time*.

The graph of a direct current

Figure 1.21 shows the graph or *trace* produced on the oscilloscope screen by the *direct current* of a battery-operated circuit.

To show the direct current being switched on and off like this, the spot can be made to track *slowly* across the screen by adjusting the *timebase* control on the oscilloscope. The *sensitivity* or *volts/cm* control is adjusted to produce a suitable deflection of the spot from the zero line.

The graph of an alternating current

If mains was fed into the input of the oscilloscope, it would produce a trace like that shown in figure 1.22. If you want to try this, *do not* in the interests of

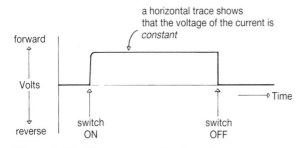

Figure 1.21 Direct current (d.c.) as shown on an oscilloscope screen

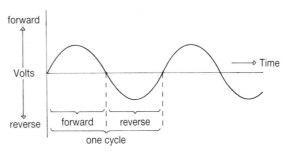

Figure 1.22 Alternating current (a.c.) as shown on an oscilloscope screen

safety take your current direct from the mains. Instead use the *low-voltage AC* output of a *transformer* or a *laboratory power pack*, and feed that into the oscilloscope.

This time the *timebase* control will be adjusted so a few distinct up and down waves show on the screen. Adjust the *trigger* control so the trace on the screen is steady.

In later chapters it will be seen how the oscilloscope can be used to illustrate the currents produced by various electrotherapy machines.

Things to do

1 If you do not have access to a laboratory, make a collection of the components used in the experiments.

2 Collect also a small tool kit, a small electrician's screwdriver, a wire stripper, a pair of small pliers with wire cutting blades, and a medium screwdriver with blades for slotted and cross-head screws. These will be useful for doing minor repairs in the salon.

3 If an oscilloscope is available, spend some time getting to know how to use it. It will be very useful experience later on.

Self-assessment questions

1 Draw diagrams of simple circuits to show two lamps connected (a) in series and (b) in parallel.

2 Give two reasons why electrical appliances are not usually connected in series.

3 What is meant by (a) a conductor of electricity and (b) an insulator?

4 What metal is used to make (a) the heating element of an electric fire and (b) the filament of a lamp.

5 What is a cartridge fuse?

6 What is the purpose of a fuse in a circuit?

7 Why should the batteries be removed from equipment that is not to be used for some time?

8 Distinguish between alternating current and direct current.

9 What is the voltage of the mains supply in the UK? What is its frequency?

10 Draw a diagram to show an alternating current as it would be displayed on an oscilloscope screen.

2 The Electricity Supply

The production of electricity; three-phase electricity;
distribution of electricity; the supply to a premises;
lighting and power circuits; sockets and plugs;
earthing and double insulation; fuses

The production of electricity

In the UK the electricity supply industry is run jointly by the electricity generating companies and the area electricity companies who distribute it to the consumers.

Dotted about the country are around eighty *power stations*. They have the joint capability, if all are working to their full capacity, to produce far more electricity than is needed to supply the biggest of peak demands. The extra capacity allows for stations to be shut down for overhaul or in case of breakdown without threatening power supplies.

In the UK there are power stations which run on

	coal
	oil
	nuclear energy
or	*water power*

In each power station are a number of *generators* to produce the electricity. Each generator is turned by a *turbine*. A turbine is in effect a very sophisticated paddle wheel driven by the pressure of water or steam impinging upon its blades.

A *hydroelectric power station* takes water from a reservoir in a mountain area high above the station. It is channelled at high pressure through the turbine and so turns the generator.

(a)

(b)

Figure 2.1 A hydroelectric power station, Rheidol, Mid Wales: (a) the 42 Megawatt Cwm Rheidol Power Station; (b) one of the three reservoirs supplying the station – note how it blends into the landscape (courtesy of the Central Electricity Generating Board)

There are only a few hydroelectric stations in the UK and these are quite small. The climate and geography of the UK are not suitable for large-scale hydroelectricity production. Do not confuse these with the huge new pumped storage schemes which 'store' off-peak electricity, using it to pump water to a high level lake. This water is used to regenerate electricity during periods of high demand.

Most power stations in the UK are driven by *high-pressure steam* from boilers. These may be fired by burning *coal* or *oil*, or they may be heated by the heat from a *nuclear reactor*.

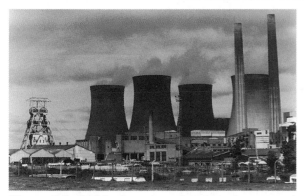

Figure 2.2 Coal-fired power station situated near a coal mine

Figure 2.3 A nuclear power station, Dungeness B, Kent (courtesy of the Central Electricity Generating Board)

Electricity cannot be stored in large amounts, so the generating companies must carefully monitor consumption at all times. They will then start up or shut down generators so that just enough is produced to satisfy the demand.

How a generator works

Most science laboratories will have a simple working model of a *generator*. It consists of a *magnet* mounted on a spindle so it can be rotated inside a *coil of wire* (see figure 2.4).

Connect the generator with two wires to a *galvanometer*. A galvanometer is a meter which can detect and measure electric currents. Now gently rotate the magnet on its spindle. Note how for half a turn of the magnet the galvanometer needle deflects *one* way on the dial; for the other half turn it deflects the *other* way. This indicates that the generator is producing a

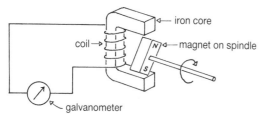

Figure 2.4 A simple model generator

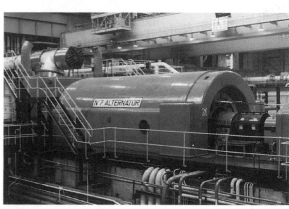

Figure 2.5 A power station generator or alternator

current which flows alternately in one direction, then in the reverse direction. That is an *alternating current*.

A power station generator produces *alternating current*. Its speed must be carefully controlled so the alternating current has a *frequency* of *exactly* 50 Hz.

Three-phase electricity

Power station generators actually have *three* sets of coils and so produce *three* alternating currents, each of which is out of step with the others. This is *three-phase current*. Figure 2.6 shows how the three currents would appear on an oscilloscope.

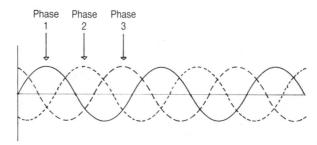

Figure 2.6 Three-phase current as it would appear on an oscilloscope

The cables carrying three-phase electricity are in threes. All three connections are *live* – *live 1*, *live 2* and *live 3*. A fourth wire is a combined *earth/neutral* connection.

Some beauty salon appliances which use large quantities of electricity may require a *three-phase* supply – for instance, *sauna stoves* and *'high-pressure' UV–A solaria*. Should you wish to install either of these pieces of equipment, you will have to arrange for a 410 volt *three-phase* supply to your salon.

Distribution of electricity

For convenience, modern coal and oil-fired power stations are situated close to the source of their fuel – coal-fired stations by coal mines, oil-fired stations by oil ports. Nuclear power stations tend to be in remote parts of the country.

To 'transport' the electricity to the consumers, it flows through overhead cables on the tall lattice pylons of the *national grid* (see figure 2.7).

As will be seen later in chapter 6, if the voltage of an electric current is to be stepped-up or stepped-down by a transformer, it *must* be an *alternating current*.

Electricity supply to a premises

In urban areas the final link in the supply to individual premises is by underground cables beneath the streets. The supply cable enters the building from underground and arrives at the *meter* and *fuse board*.

In modern houses, the meter and fuse board is to be found in a built-in box in an outside wall so the meter reader may read the meter without the need to disturb the occupants.

Here are to be found the *main fuses*, the *meter*, the *main switch* and the consumer's *fuses*. In modern systems the latter two are combined in a *consumer unit* (see figure 2.8).

The main fuse and the meter remain the property of the local electricity company. It is an offence for the consumer to interfere with these items.

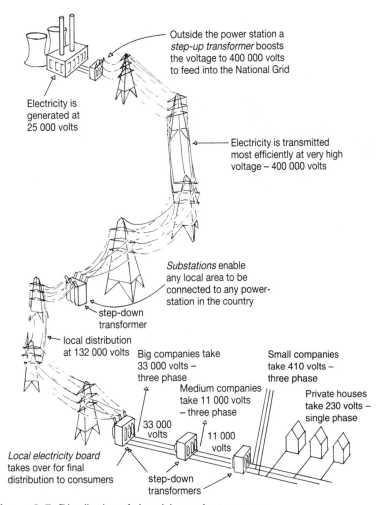

Outside the power station a *step-up transformer* boosts the voltage to 400 000 volts to feed into the National Grid

Electricity is generated at 25 000 volts

Electricity is transmitted most efficiently at very high voltage – 400 000 volts

Substations enable any local area to be connected to any power-station in the country

step-down transformer

local distribution at 132 000 volts

Big companies take 33 000 volts – three phase

Small companies take 410 volts – three phase

Medium companies take 11 000 volts – three phase

Private houses take 230 volts – single phase

33 000 volts

11 000 volts

Local electricity board takes over for final distribution to consumers

step-down transformers

Figure 2.7 Distribution of electricity to the consumers

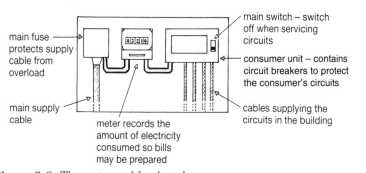

main switch – switch off when servicing circuits

main fuse protects supply cable from overload

consumer unit – contains circuit breakers to protect the consumer's circuits

main supply cable

cables supplying the circuits in the building

meter records the amount of electricity consumed so bills may be prepared

Figure 2.8 The meter and fuseboard

The consumer unit

The consumer unit provides the take-off point for the various electrical circuits in the premises. Each circuit is protected from overload by an appropriate circuit breaker in the live connection. In older installations circuits were protected by fuses.

15

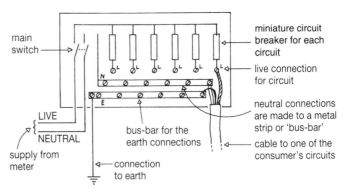

Figure 2.9 Consumer unit with main switch and RCB (left) and circuit breakers for each of the circuits in the building

Figure 2.10 The inside layout and connections in a consumer unit

The safety of the user of most electrical appliances is assured by the *earth connection*. The consumer unit provides a central point for the actual connection to *earth*. A wire from the consumer unit is taken to a long, copper-coated metal rod driven into the ground, which completes the connection. In modern units a Residual Current Circuit Breaker (RCB) further adds to user safety.

The *main switch*, you will notice, breaks both *live* and *neutral* connections, and so when switched off it completely *isolates* the consumer's circuits from the mains.

For safety's sake, *always* switch off the main switch when doing repairs or alterations to your circuits.

The electrical circuits of a premises

From the consumer unit run the cables of the various circuits in the building:

Lighting circuits – supply the permanently installed lighting fittings
Power circuits   – supply the POWER SOCKETS from which one will power portable plug-in appliances

Certain appliances which use large amounts of electricity are wired direct to the consumer unit by their own circuits:

Cooker   *Sauna stove*
Immersion heater for water heating   *Sunbed*
Electric shower unit

Each circuit is protected from damage due to overload by an appropriate value miniature *circuit breaker* in the consumer unit:

Lighting circuit   – 5 amps
Power circuit   – 30 amps
Cooker   – 30 amps
Immersion heater   – 15 amps
Shower unit   – 30 amps

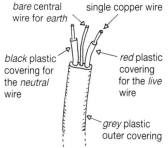

bare *central* wire for *earth*

single copper wire

black plastic covering for the *neutral* wire

red plastic covering for the *live* wire

grey plastic outer covering

Figure 2.11 Electrical installation cable – 'flat twin and earth'

Lighting circuits

The cable used for circuits is known as '*flat twin and earth*' (see figure 2.11). Different thicknesses of cable are used for:

Lighting circuits	– 1–1.5 mm² copper wires
Power circuits	– 2.5 mm² copper wires
Cookers, showers	– 6 mm² copper wires

When making additions to, or replacing circuits, it is *essential* to use the *correct* thickness of cable. Too thin a cable could cause a fire. When making connections all bared earth wires *must* be covered with green and yellow plastic sleeving.

The lights on a lighting circuit are wired in *parallel*. Figure 2.12 is a circuit diagram of a lighting circuit.

In older premises the lighting circuits actually look very similar to the diagram in figure 2.12. The *neutral* wire colour-coded *black* links from one lamp holder to the next. The *live* wire coded *red* links from one switch to the next. Then *grey* coded wires link each switch to the lamp or lamps it operates. Modern lighting circuits like that shown in figure 2.13 are required to have an *earth* wire. They are wired with a suitable 'flat twin and earth' cable.

The *ceiling rose* is a junction box for the cables. Figure 2.14 shows how the connections are made inside it.

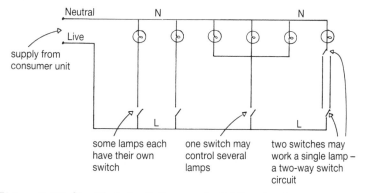

Figure 2.12 Simplified circuit diagram of a lighting circuit

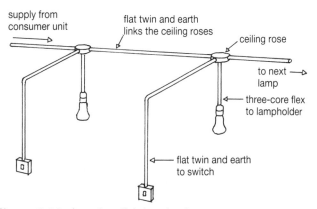

Figure 2.13 A modern lighting circuit

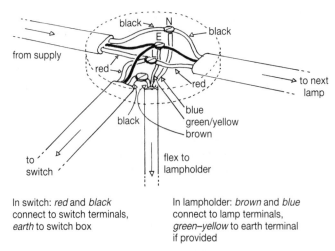

In switch: *red* and *black* connect to switch terminals, *earth* to switch box

In lampholder: *brown* and *blue* connect to lamp terminals, *green–yellow* to earth terminal if provided

Figure 2.14 Wiring a ceiling rose with 'flat twin and earth'

A two-way switch circuit

It is often convenient to be able to switch a light on or off by two separate switches:

> at top and bottom of stairs
> at either end of a passage way
> by each of two doors to a room
> by a bedroom door and by the bed

Special *two-way* switches are used. They have *three* connections instead of the normal two, labelled *common*, *live 1* and *live 2*. Operating the switch transfers the connection from one *live* to the other.

In a two-way switch circuit, the two switches are connected as shown in figure 2.15.

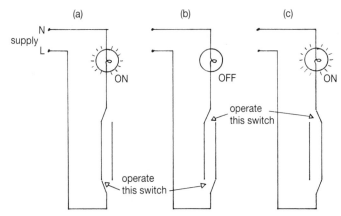

Figure 2.15 The working of a two-way switch circuit

Power circuits

In the early days of electricity, power circuits too were wired in *parallel*. However, it was necessary to wire each socket or perhaps two sockets on a *separate* circuit. Each circuit was protected by a 15 amp fuse in the main fuse box.

This required a lot of cable and so was expensive. The fuse in the box was the only fuse protecting the circuit. There was *no fuse* in the *round pin* plugs to protect the appliance and its flex.

A modern power circuit is wired on the *ring main system* (see figure 2.16). This system is much more economical in its use of cable. Each circuit will normally supply up to *eight* sockets. The circuit itself is protected by a 30 amp miniature circuit breaker in the consumer unit. A fuse in each plug protects the appliance and its flex.

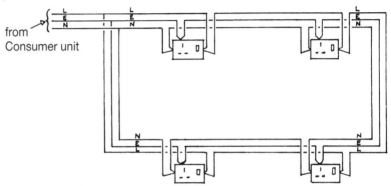

from Consumer unit

Figure 2.16 A ring main power circuit showing four sockets

Notice how the cable links from one socket to the next and joins back on itself. This means that in effect there are two paths for the electricity to each socket. Should one wish to position a socket well away from the run of the ring main, it can be connected by a length of cable from one of the sockets of the ring main. Such an arrangement is known as a *spur*.

The 13 amp socket and plug

The sockets used on a ring main take plugs with *rectangular* pins. Each socket can supply a maximum current of 13 amps. When no plug is in the socket, the *live* and *neutral* holes are closed by a shutter. This is opened by the *longer* earth pin as the plug is pushed into the socket (see figure 2.17).

Because the switch on the socket breaks *only* the live connection, it is *essential* to *unplug* an appliance when it is not in use or it is being serviced. This is an important *safety* point.

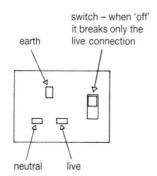

switch – when 'off' it breaks only the live connection

earth

neutral   live

Figure 2.17 A 13 amp power socket

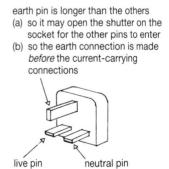

earth pin is longer than the others
(a) so it may open the shutter on the socket for the other pins to enter
(b) so the earth connection is made *before* the current-carrying connections

live pin   neutral pin

Figure 2.18 A 13 amp plug

Wiring a plug

Although manufacturers *should* now supply electrical appliances with a 13 amp plug already fitted, some might not. You may therefore have to fit the plug yourself. In the interests of *safety* it is *essential* to do this correctly. Figure 2.19 shows a correctly wired plug.

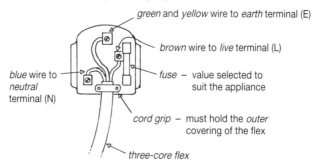

green and *yellow* wire to *earth* terminal (E)

brown wire to *live* terminal (L)

blue wire to neutral terminal (N)

fuse – value selected to suit the appliance

cord grip – must hold the *outer* covering of the flex

three-core flex

Figure 2.19 A correctly wired 13 amp plug

Before actually fitting the plug, it is necessary to prepare the end of the flex. First carefully remove sufficient of the *outer* covering to expose about 5 cm of the inner wires. Then lay the flex in the plug so the end of the outer covering is just past the cord grip. Bend the inner wires along the direction they should take, then trim them back to be 1.25 cm longer than needed to reach their terminals. With wire strippers, carefully remove 1.25 cm of insulation from each wire (see figure 2.20a).

Most plugs have terminals with a hole for the wire and a clamping screw. Twist the bared end of the wire then bend it back in half. It can then be easily pushed in the hole and the screw can be tightened (figure 2.20b).

Some plugs have screw terminals with nuts and washers. Trim the ends of the wires in the same way but this time twist the bared end and bend it into a hook shape which will fit *clockwise* round the terminal. Put on the washer and screw down the nut (figure 2.20c).

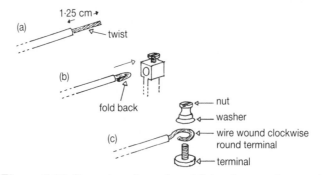

1·25 cm

(a)

twist

(b)

fold back

nut

washer

(c)

wire wound clockwise round terminal

terminal

Figure 2.20 Preparing wire ends and fixing them to plug terminals

Colour coding of flexes

An appliance may be fitted with a *three-core flex* with three wires in it, or it may have a *two-core flex*. So that the flex may be wired correctly to its plug, the wires are colour coded. Table 2.1 shows *two* colour codes which are used in flexes.

Table 2.1 Colour coding for flexes

Connection	'New' colours	'Old' colours
Live	Brown	Red
Neutral	Blue	Black
Earth	Green–yellow	Green

The 'new' colours were intended to be a world standard. The colours were chosen to be easily recognisable even by people who suffer colour blindness. Many men particularly have some degree of red–green colour blindness.

The 'old' colours are the former British standard. There are however many stalwart appliances still in use which have flexes with this colour code.

Appliances with a *two-core* flex may have a colour-coded flex, in which case *connect brown* to *live* and *blue* to *neutral*. A few appliances have two-core flex without colour coding. Connect one wire to *live*, the other to *neutral*. It does not matter which is which.

The earth wire

The earth wire is a *safety* device. Should a fault develop in an appliance, the outer casing could become electrically *live*. Anyone using or touching the appliance might receive a *shock* – which could be fatal. The *earth* wire is to take this 'stray' electricity *safely* to earth.

> **IF AN EARTH WIRE IS PROVIDED IT *MUST* BE CONNECTED**

If an appliance is fitted with a *two-core* flex, it does not have an earth connection. It has been designed and constructed in such a way that there is no possibility of 'stray' electricity passing to the user. Such an appliance is *double insulated*. It bears the symbol

The Residual Current Circuit Breaker – RCB

Even with the earth wire there is still a great risk that a faulty appliance could give the user an electric shock. For instance, a damaged cable or loose connection could sever the earth connection but leave the live connected. A residual current circuit breaker is an electronic device which will detect the smallest leakage of current from the circuit and cut off the supply within a few thousandths of a second. RCBs are available either to install in the consumer unit (see figure 2.9 on page 16) or as plug-in devices to protect individual appliances.

The fuse in the plug

When purchased, a plug is usually fitted with a 13 amp fuse. This protects the socket from being overloaded. However, the function of the fuse is also to protect the appliance *and its flex* from damage due to overload in the event of a fault.

To do this effectively, it may be necessary to replace the 13 amp fuse with one of a lower value. In the next chapter you will see how to calculate the correct value to use, but here in table 2.2 are some examples as a rough guide.

Table 2.2 Choice of fuse for the plug of an appliance

13 amp	5 or 7 amp	2 or 3 amp
Electric fire	Hairdryer	Mains radio
Fan heater	Vacuum cleaner	Television
Convector	Vacuum suction machine	Hi-fi
Kettle	Heat lamp	Faradic unit
Washing machine	Heavy-duty vibro	High frequency
Portable steam bath		Galvanic unit
Portable sauna		

Things to do

1. Most power stations have open days. Some are open on a more regular basis. Pay a visit to a power station.

2. Collect information literature on the electricity generating industry from National Power or Powergen.

3. Collect information literature from your local electricity showroom on the safe and economic use of electricity.

4. Learn the correct way to wire a 13 amp plug.

Self-assessment questions

1. What is a three-phase electricity supply?

2. What is the voltage of a three-phase supply?

3. Why must mains electricity be alternating current?

4. What is the National Grid?

5. What is the purpose of the main fuse in your electricity supply?

6. What is an alternative to a fuse in a circuit?

7. What is 'flat twin and earth'?

8. What is a 'two-way' switch circuit?

9. Electric socket outlets are usually wired on what system?

10. Give two reasons why the earth pin of a three-pin plug is longer than the other two.

11. What is the colour of (a) the live connection, (b) the earth connection in a three-core flex?

12. What is the purpose of the earth connection to an appliance?

3 Electrical Measurements & Calculations

Volts, the measure of electrical force or potential; amps, the measure of rate of flow of electricity; ohms and Ohms law; electrical power, watts and kilowatts; overloading and supply ratings; consumption and costs, the electricity meter

Electrical measurements are important

Already you will have noticed the use of various units of measurement. The *voltage* of a mains supply is 230 volts. The maximum *current* which may be taken from a power socket is 13 amps.

Let us now find out the significance of these *units of measurement* and the importance of the *calculations* involving them.

Do not be frightened off at the mention of calculations. The 'sums' involved are quite easy and straightforward.

Voltage

The *voltage* is the *force* produced by a battery or a generator to 'push' the electric current round the circuit. More correctly it is called the *potential difference*.

The voltage is measured in units called *volts*, named after Volta, the Italian inventor of the battery. The voltage may be *measured* with a *voltmeter*.

Current

The *current* is the *rate of flow* of electricity round a circuit. The units of current are *amps* or *amperes* named after the French electrical pioneer, Ampère. The current may be measured with an *ammeter*.

Measuring volts and amps

A suitable voltmeter and ammeter may be used to measure the voltage and current of a simple circuit like the ones described in chapter 1. Better still, if they are available, use a 12 volt car bulb and operate it from the d.c. output of a laboratory power pack (see figure 3.1).

Turn up the power pack until the voltmeter shows a reading of 12 volts. Then read the ammeter. It might show a reading of, say, 2 amps.

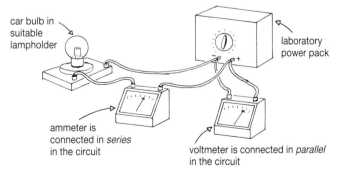

car bulb in suitable lampholder

laboratory power pack

ammeter is connected in *series* in the circuit

voltmeter is connected in *parallel* in the circuit

Figure 3.1 Voltmeter and ammeter in circuit

You may notice that to give a voltmeter reading of 12 volts you will have turned up the power pack to between 13 and 14 volts on its dial. Nothing is wrong! If you disconnect the lamp, the voltmeter will then show 13–14 volts.

The higher voltage under 'no load' is the *electro-motive force*. The lower voltage 'under load' is the *potential difference*.

Resistance

In chapter 1 we have already seen that conductors of electricity, and in particular electrical appliances, offer *resistance* to the flow of the current. Hence the need for the voltage to push the current along.

The *resistance* to the flow of electricity is measured in units called *ohms*, after Gustaf Ohm, another pioneer of electricity.

Ohms cannot be measured directly. They have to be *calculated* from the *volts* and *amps*. The relationship between volts, amps and ohms is *Ohm's law*:

$$\text{Ohms} = \frac{\text{Volts}}{\text{Amps}}$$

For example

The voltage of the lamp in the experiment in figure 3.1 is 12 V
The current flowing is 2 A

To find the resistance of the Lamp:

$$\text{Ohms} = \frac{\text{Volts}}{\text{Amps}}$$
$$= \frac{12}{2}$$
$$= 6$$

Resistance of lamp is 6 Ω

Note the abbreviations used: V for volts
                                     A for amps
                                     Ω (omega) for ohms

Now try these 'mains' examples:

1 Find the resistance of an electric fire which works off 230 V mains and takes a current of 10 A.

2 Find the resistance of a heat lamp which works off 230 V mains and takes a current of 2 A.

3 How many amps flow through a 46 Ω element when it is connected to a 230 V supply?

You will need to rearrange the relationship for question 3 so that

$$\text{Amps} = \frac{\text{Volts}}{\text{Ohms}}$$

Can you work out how this is done?

Here are the answers: 1.   23 Ω   2.   115 Ω   3.   5 A

Using an electrician's test meter to measure resistance

Actually, to say that one cannot measure resistance directly is not quite true. The resistance of a component which is *not* connected in a circuit can be measured with an electrician's *test meter* (see figure 3.2). When the meter is set to *resistance*, the meter sends an exact voltage from its internal battery through the component under test and indicates the *current* which flows on the dial. The dial also shows the resistance in *ohms*.

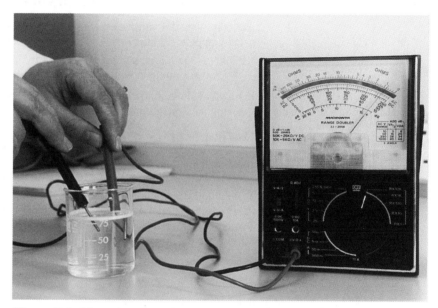

Figure 3.2 Measuring the resistance of a solution with an electrician's test meter

Electrical power – watts and kilowatts

How much electricity an appliance uses depends on how much work it is designed to do – that is, its *power rating*. The *power* of an appliance is measured in *watts* and *kilowatts*, named after James Watt of steam engine fame.

1000 watts (W) = 1 kilowatt (kW)

Watts cannot be measured with a meter. They too have to be *calculated* from volts and amps, this time by multiplying them together:

Watts = Volts × Amps

For example, for the lamp in the experiment in figure 3.1:

Voltage – 12 V
Current – 2 A

W = V × A
  = 12 × 2
  = 24

The power of the lamp is 24 W

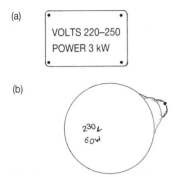

(a)

VOLTS 220–250
POWER 3 kW

(b)

230 V
60 W

Figure 3.3 (a) The specification plate such as is fitted to an electric fire. (b) The printed label on an electric lamp

Now try these 'mains' examples:

1   An electric fire working on 230 V mains takes a current of 8 A. What is its power?
2   A solarium working on 230 V mains takes 13 A. What is its power?
3   An electric lamp takes 0.26 A when working on 230 V. What is its power?

Here are the answers:

   1.   1840 W   2.   2990 W   3.   60 W

The labelling of electric appliances

Actually, it is not often necessary to work out the *power* of an appliance. It usually appears on the label! Each appliance is marked with:

The voltage it is designed to work from
The power rating in watts or kilowatts

Figure 3.3 shows the plate that would be fitted on an electric fire and the label that might be printed on an electric lamp.

The importance of electric power calculations

What is *not* usually stated on the label of an appliance is the number of *amps* it takes. There are a number of reasons why we might need to know this:

1   To find the correct value of fuse for the plug.
2   To check the possibility of overloading a socket.
3   To find out if the number of appliances in use might overload the salon supply.

To find *amps* knowing *volts* and *watts*, the relationship

Watts = Volts × Amps

must be rearranged to give

$$\text{Amps} = \frac{\text{Watts}}{\text{Volts}}$$

Choice of fuse for a plug

The previous chapter concluded with a general guide to selecting a suitable fuse for the plug of an appliance and with the promise that this chapter would explain how to *calculate* the correct value.

Let us assume that fuses available are 13 amp, 5 amp and 2 amp. There is another series – 13 amp, 7 amp and 3 amp (so much for standardisation!).

In these examples we will also assume the mains is 230 volts.

Example 1

What value fuse should be fitted in the plug of a 690 watt hairdryer?

$$\text{Amps} = \frac{\text{Watts}}{\text{Volts}}$$

$$= \frac{690}{230}$$

$$= 3$$

Hairdryer takes 3 amps – fit 5 amp fuse

Example 2

What value fuse should be fitted in the plug of a 2750 watt washing machine?

$$\text{Amps} = \frac{\text{Watts}}{\text{Volts}}$$

$$= \frac{2750}{230}$$

$$= 12.0 \text{ (to 1 place of decimals)}$$

Washing machine takes 12 amps – fit 13 amp fuse

Now calculate the amps taken by each of these appliances and select the appropriate fuse. Remember, fit a fuse of the next value *above* the calculated amps.

1. A 750 watt heavy vibro
2. A 2¼ kilowatt kettle
3. A 2 kilowatt fire
4. A 350 watt heat lamp
5. A 25 watt high-frequency unit
6. A 3000 watt solarium

Answers: 1. 3.3 A (5 A fuse).   2. 9.8 A (13 A fuse).
3. 8.7 A (13 A fuse).   4. 1.5 A (2 A fuse).
5. 0.1 A (2 A fuse).   6. 13.0 A (13 A fuse).

The possibility of overloading a socket

However many power sockets have been installed in a building, it is frequently necessary to operate two or more appliances from *one* socket using an *adaptor*.

A socket can supply a maximum *safe* load of 13 amps. When using more than one appliance at a time from a socket, it *is* possible to exceed the 13 amps.

Although the adaptor, if it is a modern one, will probably be fitted with its own 13 amp fuse, the fuse will not actually blow until well above 13 amps is flowing through it. The socket could therefore be supplying well above 13 amps and probably getting dangerously *hot* in the process.

To check if overloading is occurring, add up the 'wattages' of the appliances, then find the total amps.

Example

In your sitting room you are running a 2 kilowatt fire and 300 watt colour TV from the single socket using an adaptor. Is this safe?

$$\text{Total watts} = 2000 + 300$$

$$= 2300$$

$$\text{Total amps} = \frac{\text{Watts}}{\text{Volts}}$$

$$= \frac{2300}{230}$$

$$= 10$$

This is less than 13 amps – so it is safe

Now try these:

1   In the kitchen a 2.5 kilowatt kettle and a 1 kilowatt iron are operated from one socket using an adaptor. Is this safe?
2   In the salon a 60 watt magnifier lamp and a 20 watt epilation unit are operated together from one socket. Is this safe?

Answers: 1. 15.2 A. Unsafe. The fuse would probably not blow.
             2. 0.3 A. Safe.

While most portable appliances are designed to take less than 13 amps, there are a few items of equipment which *cannot* be operated from a 13 amp socket. An example in many households is the electric cooker which must have its own 30 amp supply direct from the consumer unit.

If in your beauty salon, you wish to instal a *sauna*, it will have to be wired direct from the consumer unit. The smallest stoves for a 2-person sauna are rated at 3 kilowatts. They would take a current of just under 13 amps.

A stove for a sauna for four to six persons would be rated at 7 kilowatts. To find its amps:

$$\text{Amps} = \frac{\text{Watts}}{\text{Volts}}$$

$$= \frac{7000}{230}$$

$$= 30.0 \text{ (to one decimal place)}$$

A 7 kilowatt sauna stove takes 30 amps

Rating of the mains supply

When such demanding electric equipment as *saunas* and their attendant *showers* is to be installed, one must then ask – can the mains supply cope? – or will it be overloaded? The local electricity company is *not* amused if the consumer overloads the supply and blows the main fuse! They will, however, provide an *uprated* supply should it be necessary.

Example
A salon has a supply rated at 60 amps. The owner wishes to instal a *sauna* with an 11 kilowatt stove and a *shower* with a 6 kilowatt heater. Existing equipment uses 40 amps. Can the supply cope?

Extra power   = 11 000 + 6000 watts

              = 17 000 watts

$$\text{Amps} = \frac{\text{Watts}}{\text{Volts}}$$

$$= \frac{17\ 000}{230}$$

$$= 74$$

The extra load = 74 amps

The *total* load = 74 + 40

              = 114 amps – that is, *well* above the 60 amps available

An uprated supply *will* be necessary

The consumption of electricity

Electricity is *not* a substance, so one cannot measure its consumption by the *tonne* like coal, or by the *litre* like oil.

The 'amount' of electricity has to be measured in terms of what it will do. Its quantity is measured in *kilowatt-hours* (kWh). These are commonly called *'units'*.

An appliance of power 1 kilowatt run for 1 hour uses 1 *kilowatt-hour*.

To find the consumption of electricity used by an appliance, multiply its power in kilowatts by the number of hours for which it is used:

Consumption (kWh) = kW × hours

Example
A 2 kW electric fire run for 6 hours uses

$$2 \times 6 = 12 \text{ kWh}$$

If the power of the appliance is stated in *watts*, then find the consumption this way:

$$\text{Consumption (kWh)} = \frac{\text{Watts}}{1000} \times \text{hours}$$

Example
A 500 W heat lamp run for 4 hours uses

$$\frac{500}{1000} \times 4 = 2 \text{ kWh}$$

To give an idea what 1 *'unit'* of electricity will do, *one kilowatt-hour* will run

---

a 1 kilowatt, single-bar fire for 1 hour
a 2 kilowatt, two-bar fire   for ½ hour
a 4 kW sauna   for 15 minutes
a 100 W lamp   for 10 hours

The cost of running an appliance

When you are deciding what to charge for a beauty treatment, it may be *very* necessary to include the *cost* of the electricity to run the machines you intend to use. Some machines like *faradic* and *high frequency* use a negligible amount of electricity. Its cost may be ignored. But how much electricity will a steam bath use? What will it cost?

Example
The *steam bath* has a 2 kW element. For the treatment it will run for 1 hour including the 'warming-up' time needed to start the water boiling.

$$\begin{aligned} \text{Consumption} &= 2 \text{ kW} \times 1 \text{ hour} \\ &= 2 \text{ kWh} \end{aligned}$$

The approximate cost of electricity for small businesses (1994) is 9p per unit. Two units will therefore cost 18p. An allowance will have to be made in the cost of the treatment for the 18p-worth of electricity.

A *sauna* will have to be run *all day*, however many people use it, particularly if it is to be available for 'casual' clients. The treatment charge will have to cover the electricity cost, even if only a few people use it.

Example

A medium sized *sauna* might have an 11 kW stove. If it is run for a 12 hour day, how much will the electricity cost?

Consumption =   11 kW × 12 hours
            = 132 kWh

At 9p per unit, it will cost

132 × 9 = 1188p
        = £11.88

The electricity cost for the sauna will be around £12 per day.

The electricity meter

The electricity meter keeps a record of the total consumption of electricity in the premises so that the Electricity Board may prepare the quarterly *electricity bill*.

Four times a year, at 13-week intervals, an Electricity Board official will call to read the meter. If you wish to lessen the 'surprise' when you receive the bill, you can easily read the meter too and work out the bill for yourself.

Reading the meter

Two types of electricity meter displays are used. Modern meters have an easy-to-read *digital display* as shown in figure 3.4.

The meter in the photograph shows a reading of 99788 units. There are still some older meters in use with a *dial display* like that in figure 3.5.

Figure 3.4 Modern digital electricity meter

Figure 3.5 Old dial type electricity meter (courtesy of the Electricity Council)

Reading this type of meter is more difficult. Note that adjacent dials are numbered in opposite directions. Because of the gears that drive the pointers they rotate in opposite directions. The pointers move continuously so you *read the figure* the *pointer last pointed to*. This is not necessarily the one it is nearest to.

Try reading the meter in figure 3.5. The reading is 44927. Can you see why?

10 000s dial – pointer has passed 4 but not reached 5. Read it as 4.
1000s dial – pointer has passed 4 but not reached 5. Read it as 4.
100s dial – pointer has passed 9 but not reached 0. Read it as 9.
10s dial – pointer has passed 2 but not reached 3. Read it as 2.
units dial – pointer has passed 7 but not reached 8. Read it as 7.

The reading is 44927.

The electricity bill

On the electricity bill the electricity company will state the *present reading* of the meter and the *previous reading*.

Subtracting the *previous* reading from the *present* reading gives the '*units used*'. From this the electricity company calculates the *cost* by using one of a number of different *tariffs*.

The ordinary *private house tariff* is in two parts:

1 Standing charge – which is the same however much electricity is used.
2 Cost of units used – which is number of units multiplied by the cost per unit.

The tariff for a business premises is much more complex. It too includes a standing charge, but certain numbers of units are charged at different rates, depending on the 'size' of the business.

If, however, you look at an electricity bill, you can work out an *actual* average cost per unit:

> Turn the final total into *pence*
> Divide the pence by the units used

In 1994 this would give approximately 9p per unit.

You can now work out how much your bill is likely to be before it comes. When the official calls to read your meter, go and read it yourself:

Let us imagine the reading is 45762

Now find your last bill and look for the 'present reading':

Let us imagine it is 42971
Units used = 45762 − 42971
= 2791

Your bill will be approximately

2791 units × 9 pence per unit = 25119 pence
= £251.19

Things to do

1 Work out the number of amps of electric current required by each of the electrical appliances in the salon, then check if the fuse fitted in each plug is the correct one.

2   Read the electricity meter at the same time as the electricity company meter reader calls. You can then work out your own bill. The real one when it arrives will not be such a surprise!

3   Work out the cost of using each of the electrical treatment machines for a treatment. This information is useful in working out the charge for the treatment.

Self-assessment questions

1   What is measured in (a) volts, (b) amps, (c) ohms, (d) watts?

2   How should (a) a voltmeter, (b) an ammeter, be connected in a circuit?

3   What is another name for a kilowatt hour?

4   What is the relationship between volts, amps and ohms?

5   What is the relationship between volts, amps and watts?

6   How many amps is taken by a 690 watt heat lamp working on 230 volt mains?

7   What is the resistance of the heating element of the heat lamp in question 6?

8   How much does it cost to run this heat lamp for a 20-minute treatment plus its 10-minute warming up time? Assume electricity is 9p per unit.

Answers: 6. 3 Amps.   7. 76.7 ohms.   8. 3.11 pence.

4 Electrical Massage Equipment

The physical, physiological and psychological effects of massage; aids to massage; magnets and magnetism; electromagnets; vibro-massagers; electric motors; sound-wave vibrators; vacuum suction massage; air pressure; barometer

Massage

The kneading, slapping and cupping movements of manual massage are hard work. It is often said that the one who gains most from a massage is the masseur or masseuse!

The *vibrators, vacuum suction machines* and other mechanical aids are intended to take some of this hard work out of massage. Before dealing with the machines, let us consider the value of *manual massage*. This will make it easier to understand what each massage machine can do.

Manual massage

In manual massage, there are *three* basic movements:

> *Effleurage* – light pressure, stroking, flowing movements
> *Petrissage* – compression movements: kneading, knuckling, lifting, rolling, pinching
> *Tapotement* – percussion movements: tapping, hacking, whipping

The effects of massage

The effects of a treatment fall into *three* main areas:

1 The *physical effects* are the direct effects of the massage movement on the part of the body being treated.
2 The *physiological effects* are the body's own response to the physical effects.
3 The *psychological effects*. Between them the physical and physiological effects should, hopefully, make the client *feel better*; to use the well-worn cliché – a 'feeling of well-being'.

The importance of the *psychological effects* must not be underestimated. It is essential that the therapist should work purposefully and methodically and really believe in what he or she does. This confidence will then inspire a feeling of 'this *must* be doing me good' in the client. With this psychological feeling in the client, the treatment most likely *will* do good!

The physical and physiological effects of massage

The immediate effect of massage is that of touch. The stimulation of the sensory nerves is a psychologically satisfying experience.

Massaging with creams or oils will have an emollient effect, imparting a smooth feel and an increased softness to the skin. They will also help to remove ingrained grime and assist desquamation, the shedding of loose skin cells.

The *petrissage* and *tapotement* movements of massage are very energetic. The *friction* of these movements will result in this *energy* being transferred to the body, mostly as *heat*. The body will then respond physiologically to this localised *heating* of the area being treated. A reflex action *dilates* the capillaries and arteries in the area. The increased blood flow then dissipates the heat elsewhere in the body. The increased blood flow results in a *reddening* of the area. This reddening in response to heat is termed *hyperaemia*.

Also to counter the heating effect is the stimulation of the activity of the *sweat glands*. Water brought by the blood passes via the glands on to the surface of the skin where it can *evaporate* to *cool* the skin. The sebaceous glands too are activated by the heating, and the sebum output is increased.

Warming the tissues increases the *metabolism*. The metabolism is a complex *chemical* process, and chemical processes go faster at higher temperatures. The result should be speedier growth and repair of the tissues. The effects resulting from warming the tissues are summarised in figure 4.1.

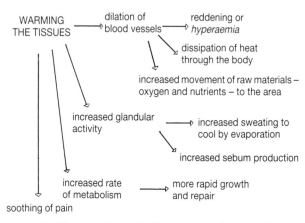

Figure 4.1 The physiological effects of warming the tissues

In muscles the increased metabolism creates a demand for more oxygen and nutrients, which causes the capillaries inside them to dilate thus attracting an increased blood supply. This will ease the pain and assist the recovery of fatigued and damaged muscles, and will improve the tone and responsiveness of muscles in general.

A further effect of the *energy* of massage is to cause 'damage' to certain tissues. The kneading and pummelling movements are intended to break the rather delicate cells of the subcutaneous fatty layer. This releases their fatty contents and so assists the dissipation of fat from the treatment area. Used in conjunction with a 'calorie-controlled' diet, the hope is that it will be *this* fat that is used up and so the area will be 'spot-reduced'.

One must not be too heavy-handed with petrissage movements or the blood vessels within the tissues may be damaged, resulting in *bruising*. The colour of a bruise is due to blood which has leaked from damaged vessels into the surrounding tissues.

The *effleurage* movements of massage are to assist the dissipating of waste products and mobilised fat from the treatment area through the *venous* and *lymphatic* systems. The therapist must know about these systems in order to direct the effleurage movements in the way of venous and lymphatic drainage from the area. By doing so, the therapist is assisting the *myo-fascial pumping* action of the veins and lymph vessels (see figure 4.2).

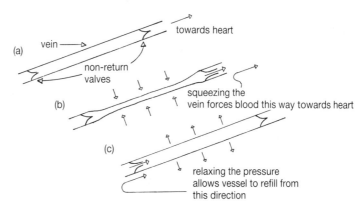

Figure 4.2 The myo-fascial pumping action for movement of blood through the veins

The vessels have frequent non-return valves to prevent back flow. The forward movement of fluid through them is produced by alternately squeezing and relaxing the vessels. Normally the contractions of muscles in the area result in the squeezing of the vessels. Effleurage movements produce the same result.

Massage creams and oils

Without the use of a cream or oil to *lubricate* the skin during a massage, the *friction* would generate so much *heat* that burns to the skin would be a distinct possibility.

In general, a massage *cream* is used for facial massage. A high-oil-content cream of the cold-cream type is most commonly used (see Volume 1, chapter 10). Here is a possible formulation:

White beeswax	– 5	
White soft paraffin	– 30	
Mineral oil	– 20	Oil phase
Lanolin	– 5	
Arachis oil	– 15	
Borax	– 0.3	Water phase
Water	– 24.7	

The formulation may be made by the method described in Volume 1, chapter 6.

For *body massage* it is often preferable to use an *oil*, being easier to distribute over the larger treatment area. It is usual to use a *vegetable oil* such as olive oil, corn oil, sunflower oil or peanut oil, though *mineral oil* is equally suitable especially if lightly perfumed, such as a baby oil.

Vibro-massagers

To take the hard work out of massage, a selection of *vibro-massagers* is available. Suitable for the 'easier' areas of the face and neck is the *percussive vibro-massager*. For deeper penetration there is the *audiosonic* or *sound-wave vibrator*. While for the really heavy work of massaging the lower body there is the *gyratory vibrator* typified by the legendary 'G5'.

All these machines are driven by *electric motors*. An electric motor depends for its action on *magnetism*.

Magnets and magnetism

Magnetism is the attraction and repulsion forces that occur between certain metals. Only *steel*, *cobalt* or *nickel* and alloys thereof may be made into *permanent* magnets. *Iron* can be made *temporarily* magnetic.

A bar of steel may be made into a *permanent magnet* by two means:

1 by stroking it with a magnet as shown in figure 4.3;
2 by winding a coil of insulated wire around it and passing a *direct current* of electricity as in figure 4.4

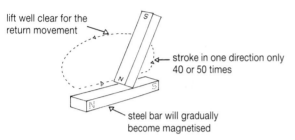

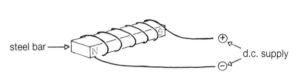

Figure 4.3 Magnetising a steel bar by stroking with a magnet

Figure 4.4 Magnetising a steel bar with a direct current of electricity

Properties of magnets

If a fine string is tied round a bar magnet and it is hung so it can swing freely as shown in figure 4.5, it will come to rest in a *north–south* direction. This is the principle of a compass.

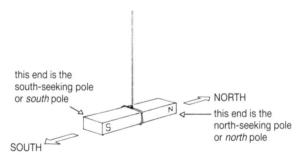

Figure 4.5 A magnet hung to swing freely will stop in a north–south direction

If two magnets are placed near each other with the north pole of one near the south pole of the other, they will *attract* each other (see figure 4.6). *Unlike poles attract.*

If one is turned round so either the two north poles or the two south poles are together, they will repel each other (see figure 4.7). *Like poles repel.*

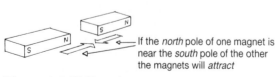

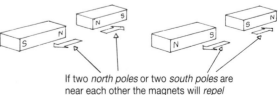

Figure 4.6 Unlike poles attract

Figure 4.7 Like poles repel

36

Magnetic field

If you are able to try the experiments, you will have already noticed that the magnets do not have to be in *contact* to attract or repel.

The magnetism is detectable over quite a large area around the magnet. This is the *magnetic field*.

The magnetic field of a magnet may be 'mapped' by laying over it a sheet of paper, and then sprinkling on iron filings. Note how, if you tap the paper gently, the filings form a pattern of curved lines – *lines of force* – linking the north and south poles (see figure 4.8).

Now try mapping the magnetic fields when two magnets are placed next to each other, first with unlike poles together then with like poles together (see figure 4.9).

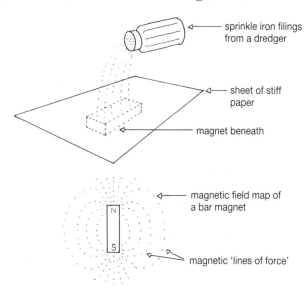

Figure 4.8 Mapping a magnetic field with iron filings

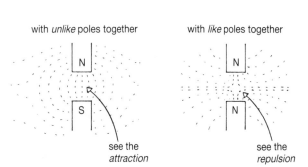

Figure 4.9 The magnetic fields of attracting and repelling magnets

The electromagnet

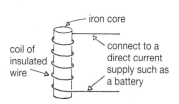

Figure 4.10 An electromagnet

The big problem with a *permanent* magnet is that it cannot be turned on and off. It will attract but it will not let go!

An *electromagnet* is a magnet that *can* be turned on and off. It consists of a piece of *iron* known as the core with a coil of wire wound round it (see figure 4.10).

If you switch *on* the current through the coil, the *iron* core becomes *magnetised*. Switch *off* the current and the magnetism is lost.

Passing an alternating current through an electromagnet

Because an alternating current is an intermittent current, the magnetism it produces in the iron core is also intermittent. An iron bar held nearby will be alternately attracted and released. It will *vibrate* (see figure 4.11).

This is in effect all there is to the 'works' of a *vibro-motor* such as drives a *percussive vibro-massager* and many makes of electric shavers and electric hair-clippers. Figure 4.12 shows the vibro-motor in a typical percussive vibro-massager.

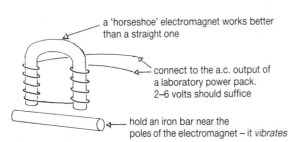

a 'horseshoe' electromagnet works better than a straight one

connect to the a.c. output of a laboratory power pack. 2–6 volts should suffice

hold an iron bar near the poles of the electromagnet – it *vibrates*

Figure 4.11 An electromagnet operated on an alternating current

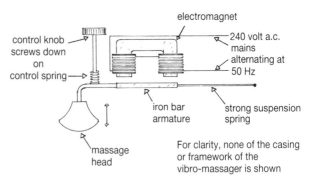

electromagnet

control knob screws down on control spring

240 volt a.c. mains alternating at 50 Hz

iron bar armature

strong suspension spring

massage head

For clarity, none of the casing or framework of the vibro-massager is shown

Figure 4.12 The vibro-motor in a percussive vibro-massager

Alternating at 50 Hz, mains current consists of 100 pulses of current each second. This causes the magnetism in the electromagnet to be created and destroyed 100 times each second. The iron armature is thus attracted and released 100 times each second. The massage head is made to *beat* up and down on the skin 100 times per second.

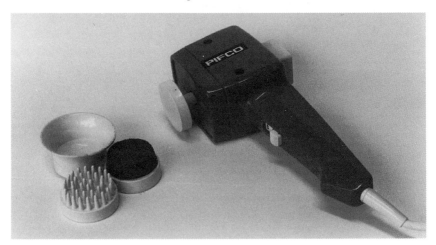

Figure 4.13 Percussive vibrator and attachments

The control knob is to adjust the intensity of the vibration. Screwing it down tightens the control spring to lessen the intensity. Slackening it releases the control spring, allowing the massage head to vibrate more vigorously and increase the intensity.

A percussive vibro-massager produces a *tapotement* type of massage which is stimulating and causes a local heating of the skin and the benefits derived therefrom. The tapping-type of movement cannot be too strong otherwise the area being treated might be badly *bruised*. This means that a percussive vibrator can only be used to advantage on the less bulky tissues of the face, the neck and perhaps the shoulder area.

Gyratory vibro-massager

On the bulkier areas of the body, the relatively shallow penetration of a percussive vibrator can have little effect. These areas require the kneading type vibration of a *gyratory vibro-massager*. Examples are shown in figures 4.15 and 4.16.

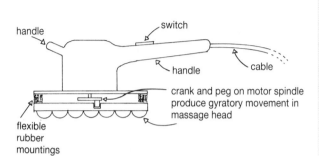

Figure 4.14 A gyratory vibro-massager

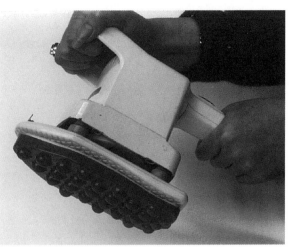

Figure 4.15 Self-contained heavy gyratory vibro-massager

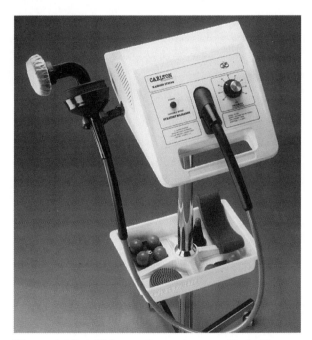

Figure 4.16 A G5 heavy vibrator (courtesy Taylor Reeson Laboratories Ltd)

A gyratory vibrator is driven by a conventional rotary electric motor such as is described below. A crank and peg on the motor spindle engages a hole in the back of the flexibly mounted massage head to produce the eccentric or 'gyratory' movement (see figure 4.14). This movement can confer a deeply penetrating vibration massage on the tissues without the fear of bruising which would result from a powerful-enough percussive vibration.

While the term 'G5' was originally the manufacturer's model number for a particular machine, it is now used to describe any heavy vibro-massager with a stand as in figure 4.16. In some machines the motor is on the stand and drives the massage head through a flexible drive.

The electric motor

Two types of rotating electric motors are used in electrical appliances.

One type works by the attractions and repulsions between the poles of a stationary magnet called the *stator* or *field magnet* and the poles of a rotating electromagnet, the *armature* (see figures 4.17 and 4.18).

Current to energise the rotating electromagnet is passed to the armature by the carbon *brushes* and the '*split-ring*' of the *commutator*.

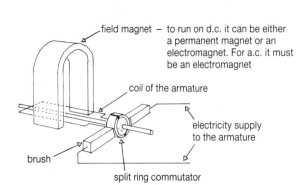

Figure 4.17 A commutator-type electric motor

Figure 4.18 A model electric motor with commutator and brushes

The motor spindle runs in bearings with 'sealed-for-life' lubrication so an electric motor will run for years with no attention. The only 'servicing' such a motor might require is to replace the carbon brushes when they are worn out, but this only occurs after many years of use.

The other type of motor is the *induction motor*. This very simple motor is commonly used in 'mains' appliances. It must have an a.c. supply. No electricity has to be passed to the armature so there are no brushes to wear out (see figures 4.19 and 4.20).

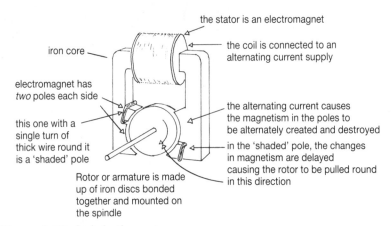

Figure 4.19 An induction motor

Figure 4.20 Induction or 'shaded-pole' electric motors

The body-belt vibrator

The body-belt vibrator is for self-treatment. The belt is connected to a crank at each end of the motor shaft. When you lean back in the belt, it vibrates with a side-to-side movement on the area being treated. Figure 4.21 shows the machine in use.

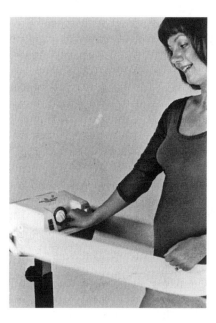

Figure 4.21 A body-belt vibrator (courtesy of Nordic Saunas Ltd)

Sound-wave or audiosonic vibrator

A sound wave or audiosonic vibro-massager is superficially very like a percussive vibrator both in its general appearance and its operation.

Inside though, the construction of its *vibro-motor* is somewhat different. The static part is an *electromagnet* with a *hollow centre*. It is called a *solenoid*. Inside it, suspended on springs, is the armature which in this case is a *permanent magnet*. The massage head is mounted on this armature (see figure 4.23).

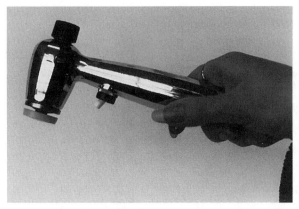

Figure 4.22 An audiosonic or sound wave vibrator

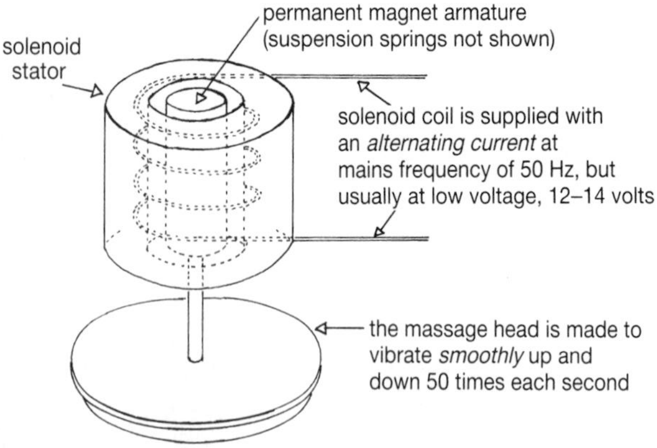

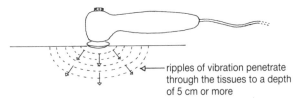

Figure 4.23 The working parts of a sound-wave vibrator

solenoid stator

permanent magnet armature (suspension springs not shown)

solenoid coil is supplied with an *alternating current* **at mains frequency of 50 Hz, but usually at low voltage, 12–14 volts**

the massage head is made to vibrate *smoothly* **up and down 50 times each second**

The coil of the electromagnet is supplied with a *smoothly alternating current* at the 'mains' frequency of 50 hertz, though it is usually converted to a low voltage of 12–14 volts by a *transformer* supplied with the vibrator. The smooth alternating current causes the *permanent magnet armature* to vibrate *smoothly* up and down 50 times each second.

The *massage head* is mounted on the armature, so it too vibrates smoothly up and down. When placed on the skin, the vibrations penetrate through the skin rather like ripples across a pond (see figure 4.24). The massage head does not beat the skin like a percussive vibrator. It remains in *contact* with the skin. Despite the apparent 'gentleness' of the audiosonic vibrator, its vibrations penetrate quite deeply through the underlying tissues. It is reputed to penetrate usefully to 5 cm or more with no danger of bruising the skin.

ripples of vibration penetrate through the tissues to a depth of 5 cm or more

Figure 4.24 Penetration of sound-wave vibrations into the tissues

Why 'audiosonic'?

The answer is that the vibration produced, a *smooth* vibration of 50 Hz, is a *sound* – a musical note. Place the massage head on a table top and listen to the low-pitched hum.

The vibration is of a frequency within the range of audible *sound* – just! The *range of sound frequencies* is from about 30 hertz of the lowest notes to 20 000 hertz for the highest pitched whistle – if you can hear it!

Some experiments with sound

Most well equipped physics laboratories will have an *audiofrequency signal generator*. To do these experiments you will need one of these plus a good quality *loudspeaker* and an *oscilloscope*. Consult the instructions or *ask* how to connect the loudspeaker and oscilloscope to the signal generator and how to operate the set-up. It varies from one make to another. A typical set-up is shown in figure 4.25.

Figure 4.25 An audiogenerator connected to an oscilloscope

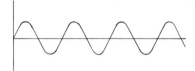

Figure 4.26 Sine-waves as displayed on an oscilloscope screen

For the first experiment, set the signal generator to give a *sine-wave* or ∿ and set it to 50 hertz. Listen to the smooth low hum from the loudspeaker. It is the same as from the *audiosonic vibrator*. The *sine-wave* can be seen displayed on the oscilloscope screen (see figure 4.26).

Turn up the volume so it is quite loud. You will feel the sound waves vibrating your body. You have probably experienced this at a disco or a pop-concert. Smooth sine-waves *are* penetrating.

Now switch the signal generator to *square-wave* or ⊓⊔, or to *saw-tooth wave* or ∧∧∧. Note how the sound changes to a sharp *buzz* and how it loses its penetrating quality. It is now more akin to the vibration produced by a *percussive vibrator*. See the change in the shape of the sound on the oscilloscope screen (figure 4.27).

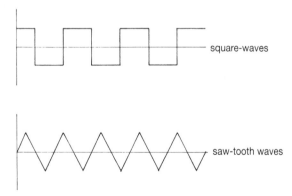

square-waves

saw-tooth waves

Figure 4.27 Square-waves and saw-tooth waves

Switch back to sine-wave and turn down the frequency to say 5 hertz. You will not now hear a sound but if your loudspeaker does not have a grille or cloth covering it, you will see that its cone is still vibrating back and forth quite *smoothly*.

Now for a rather 'unsociable' experiment to test the range of your hearing! Slowly turn up the frequency control. You will notice that at about 30–40 hertz the vibrations become a musical note, a very low one.

Turn up the control increasing the frequency. The pitch of the sound rises.

Note as you do so how on the oscilloscope screen the waves become shorter and more numerous. Keep increasing the frequency. You may have to 'change range' on the generator. The sound becomes a whistle which becomes higher and higher until it eventually disappears. For young ears in good condition this happens at 18 000 to 20 000 hertz. Older ears or ones damaged by loud discos may hear only up to 12 000 hertz or even less.

Vacuum suction massage

In manual massage there is a movement called *cupping* in which the centre of a downward-facing hand is raised into a cupped shape. With the sealing effect of the massage cream or oil, this creates a *suction* beneath the hand.

Vacuum-suction machines simulate and extend this cupping movement. The machine consists basically of a vacuum pump connected via a flexible tube to a glass or plastic cup which is placed on the skin (see figure 4.28). The degree of suction is set by a control valve and indicated by a *vacuum gauge* on the machine. It will be described in more detail later.

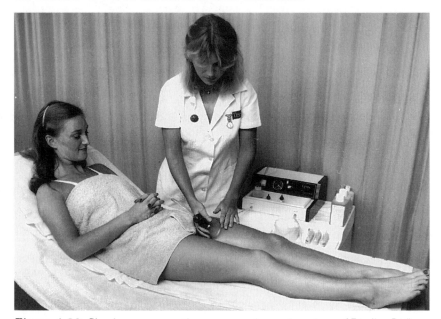

Figure 4.28 Simple vacuum suction massager in use (courtesy of Depilex Ltd)

Therapeutic effects

Beneath the cup, the *air pressure* which normally presses in on the body is *reduced*. This causes the skin and underlying tissues to be *lifted* and *stretched*. This results in:

1 *Dilation* of vessels in the area:

   Dilation of arteries increases fluid flow to the area. The skin reddens
   Dilation of veins and lymph vessels causes them to fill with fluid

2 *Increased secretion* from sweat and sebaceous glands as the suction draws out the contents of the pores. A 'deep cleansing' effect.

3 *The break-up of fatty cells* of the subcutaneous layer as they 'burst' under the reduced pressure so releasing their fatty contents to be dispersed in the lymph. Here vacuum suction massage has an effect equivalent to the kneading movements of *petrissage*.

The cup does not remain static but is slid over the skin. The use of massage cream or oil not only provides a seal between the cup and skin but allows the cup to *glide* easily without excessively stretching the skin.

As the cup glides from the area, the tissues are lowered and contract. The veins and lymph vessels contract driving their fluid contents from the area, thereby completing the increased fluid flow *through* the area.

The sliding movements of the cup are directed in the direction of lymphatic flow, so increasing its effectiveness. This is *effleurage*. In this way, mobilised fat is taken away. Used in conjunction with an *energy-controlled diet*, the treatment can be valuable for *spot-reducing* in figure-correction.

Precautions

Vacuum suction must be used with great care. The degree of suction must not be too high or it will cause capillaries to burst, resulting in *bruising*. Particular care must be taken not to pass over areas with broken veins or capillaries. *Stretch-marked* areas should also be avoided. The skin here has lost its full elasticity and may easily suffer further.

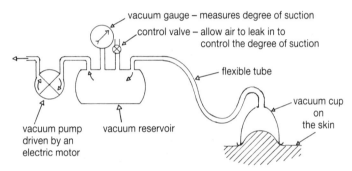

Figure 4.29 The components of a simple vacuum suction massager

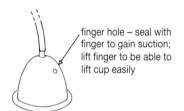

Figure 4.30 A vacuum suction cup

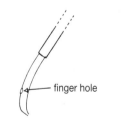

Figure 4.31 A comedone extractor

Figure 4.29 shows the working of a basic vacuum suction unit used in conjunction with a single cup.

Before switching the unit on, open the control valve fully. After switching on, place the cup on your own skin and *slowly* close the valve until the required degree of suction is obtained. In this way you will avoid using too great a degree of suction on the client.

The *vacuum cups* are of various sizes: small ones 2–3 cm diameter for facial use, and larger ones up to 10 cm diameter for use on 'bulkier' areas such as the buttocks and thighs (see figure 4.30). To ease lifting the cup at the end of a stroke, it may have a small hole in its side over which to place a finger. A special tubular probe is available to extract acne comedones (see figure 4.31).

A vacuum pump can 'blow' as well as 'suck'. On many machines the air outlets can be used to drive sprayers which may be used to spray various cosmetic lotions as shown in figure 4.32.

Multicup pulsating vacuum massage units

A basic vacuum suction unit works with a *single* cup which as it is slid manually over the skin alternately lifts and lowers the tissues.

Units are available which can operate up to *six* cups simultaneously – valuable for treating the 'larger' areas of the body such as the buttocks and thighs. However, without six hands they cannot all be *moved* simultaneously!

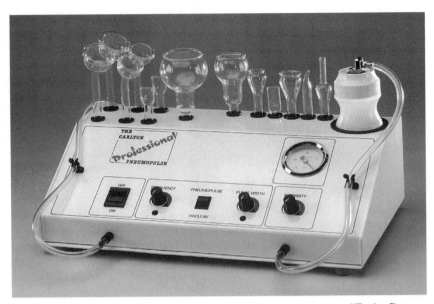

Figure 4.32 A spray unit on a vacuum suction massager (courtesy of Taylor Reeson Laboratories Ltd)

So instead the vacuum suction is *pulsed* – alternating every few seconds between a *higher* degree of suction which lifts the tissues and a *lower* degree which lets the tissues beneath the cup relax back again. This is done by an *automatic pulsation* valve inside the unit. Figure 4.33 shows such a multicup pulsating machine.

These machines require an amount of practice to acquire the necessary skill to operate them competently. Great care is needed to adjust the higher and lower degrees of suction. The higher level must not be so high that the client is bruised, and the lower level must allow the tissues to contract back but not be so low that the cups fall off.

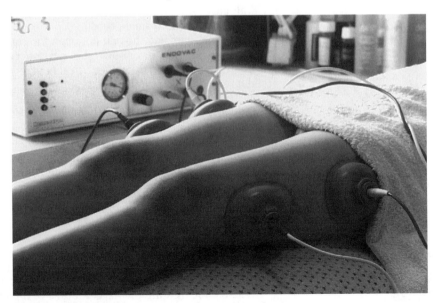

Figure 4.33 Multicup vacuum suction massager in use

Operating a multicup unit

The tube to each cup has its own vacuum shut-off valve. Before switching on the machine, make sure all these valves are shut. Take the first cup. Place it on the skin and open its valve. Adjust the main vacuum control so the cup lifts the tissues well. Switch on the *pulsation* and adjust its control so the lower degree of suction is still sufficient for the cup not to fall off.

Now you can place each of the other cups on the skin and open its valve. During the treatment each cup may be slid in turn to a new area. At the end of the treatment each cup may be removed after closing its valve.

Air pressure

Actually, calling the treatment *vacuum* suction is a misnomer. To subject parts of the body to a true vacuum would cause a great deal of damage. It is better to call it just 'suction' or the use of 'reduced air pressure'.

Although we are used to it and do not notice it, our bodies are all the time subjected to the quite substantial *pressure of the air* around us.

The Earth is covered by the *atmosphere* – a layer of air which extends to a height of several hundred miles and is held down by the Earth's *gravity*. Like any other matter, the air *presses down* on the Earth. Its *pressure* at sea level is on average:

10.1 newtons (1030 grams force) per cm^2
or about 15 lbs per square inch

Because air is a fluid, it presses not only down but also inwards and upwards on objects. The total force pressing in on the 2 square metres of skin of an 'average' person amounts to many *tonnes*. Create a true vacuum and remove all the air from round the body and it would *explode*! This is why astronauts who 'walk in space' must wear very strong space suits and be very careful not to puncture them!

Changes in air pressure

The air of the atmosphere is constantly moving. The *winds* are *convection currents* caused by the heat of the *sun*. This means the air pressure *varies* (see figure 4.34).

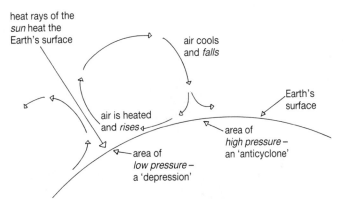

heat rays of the *sun* heat the Earth's surface

air cools and *falls*

Earth's surface

air is heated and *rises*

area of high pressure – an 'anticyclone'

area of low pressure – a 'depression'

Figure 4.34 Changes in air pressure and the weather

These variations in air pressure affect the *weather*:

> *Low pressure* – is associated with cloudy, wet weather; mild in winter but
>   cool in summer
> *High pressure* – means clear skies and fine weather; cold in winter, hot in
>   summer

Barometer

Because of the effect of changes in air pressure on the weather, many people own a *barometer*. This is an instrument to *measure* the air pressure and help one forecast the weather.

The original kind of barometer was the *Mercury barometer* (see figure 4.35).

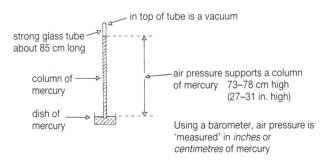

Figure 4.35 A mercury barometer

The instrument in your home is probably an *aneroid barometer* (see figure 4.36). This contains no mercury but its dial still shows its reading as *inches* or *centimetres*. The aneroid barometer works by the effect of air pressure on a sealed metal box which is squeezed or relaxed by changes in air pressure. The minute movements in the box are magnified by levers and shown by a pointer on the dial. Figure 4.37 shows the inner workings of an aneroid barometer.

Figure 4.36 An aneroid barometer

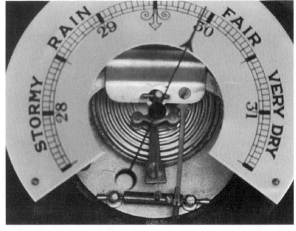

Figure 4.37 The mechanism of an aneroid barometer

48

Vacuum gauge

A vacuum suction unit is fitted with a vacuum gauge to indicate the degree of suction. It too gives its reading in *inches* or *centimetres* of mercury. This time it is the number of inches or centimetres by which air pressure is *reduced* by the vacuum suction unit from its normal value (see figure 4.38).

For a total vacuum the gauge would show around 76 cm or 29 inches on its dial. In vacuum suction therapy, nothing like that degree of suction is used, usually 10–20 cm or 4–8 inches is sufficient. Any more than this and superficial blood vessels will burst. The result will be *bruising*.

Figure 4.38 Vacuum gauge on vacuum suction unit

Things to do

Collect manufacturers' literature on mechanical massage equipment: various types of vibro-massagers, audiosonic vibrators and vacuum suction machines.

Self-assessment questions

1   What is the normal physiological reaction of the skin to the warmth generated by the friction of massage?

2   Explain briefly what is meant by the myo-fascial pumping action.

3   If two magnets are positioned so that they repel each other, they will have . . . . poles together.

4   What is a magnetic field?

5   What metal is used to make the core of an electromagnet?

6   Why is the audiosonic vibrator so called?

7   What is the range of sound frequencies which can be heard by young undamaged ears?

8   Which two massage movements does a vacuum suction massager simulate?

9   What instrument is used to measure air pressure?

10   What is the likely effect of using too great a degree of suction in vacuum suction massage?

5 Introducing Electrotherapy

What electrotherapy is; safety and contra-indications;
the nature of an electric current; atomic structure;
molecules; solutions as conductors of electricity; ionisation;
electrolysis; movement of ions

Electrotherapy

Electrotherapy is the use of an electric current actually passed *through the body* for therapeutic purposes. Because of this, client *safety* is of prime importance.

Three main types of electric current are employed in electrotherapy:

1 A continuous and smooth-flowing *direct current* is used to produce the *chemical* effects of *galvanic therapy*.
2 A low-frequency *pulsed* or *alternating current* brings about the contraction and exercising of muscles in *electronic muscle stimulation* (EMS).
3 A high-frequency *alternating* current produces the warming or heating effects of *high-frequency therapy* and *diathermy*.

Safety

Although electricity through the body is potentially lethal, it is most unlikely that an electrotherapy client could receive a fatal electric shock from the treatment. The current intensity is far too low.

However in the hands of an ill-trained or incompetent operator the client could be in for a very uncomfortable experience and could even be scarred for life or receive a very serious internal injury.

It is therefore of the utmost importance that the operator knows *exactly* what he or she is doing and appreciates the discomfort or harm which could result from incompetence or carelessness.

General safety precautions

Attempting to use faulty equipment for client treatment could lead to serious injuries such as burns, or even result in an electric shock which could prove fatal either to the client or the therapist.

Before every use, any electrical appliance *must* be checked:

1 For general condition.

Are any parts obviously broken or missing?
Are all screws securely in place?
Is the mains lead in good condition?
Is the plug correctly attached?
Are all other leads, plugs, electrodes, etc. in good order?

2 For correct operation. When switched on

Does the appliance actually work?
Do indicator lamps and meters operate normally?
Are there any unusual noises or smells?

If anything is abnormal, switch off *at once* and do not attempt to use the appliance until the faults have been identified and put right. It could invalidate your insurance to knowingly use faulty equipment.

Contra-indications

As part of the consultation prior to a course of treatment, the therapist should establish whether or not the client suffers from any medical condition which might *contra-indicate* electrotherapy treatment. If a client is not certain, he or she should consult his or her general practitioner before receiving the treatment.

Many beauty therapists tend to learn exhaustive lists of contra-indications but have little or no idea *why* the conditions contra-indicate treatment. If some of these lists were followed to the letter, very few clients would qualify for treatment! There are, however, some *important* contra-indicating conditions.

Heart disease

A heart in poor condition may be unable to cope with the extra load placed upon it by the treatment:

Strenuous exercise demands a much increased *pulse rate* to provide the increase in blood flow needed to satisfy the greater demand for oxygen. A diseased heart might not cope.

Constriction of the blood vessels which may occur with any increase in body tension will increase blood pressure.

Dilation of the blood vessels such as will occur in any relaxing, warming treatment may mean the heart is incapable of maintaining the blood pressure. This could lead to *fainting*, particularly when the client rises from the couch.

Whether the heart is diseased or not, electronic muscle stimulation treatments should be kept away from the vicinity of the heart. They could upset the rhythm of the heartbeat.

Blood vessel disorders

The most frequently encountered disease of the arteries is *arteriosclerosis* or hardening of the arteries. This results in an inability of the main arteries to 'open up' to allow an increased flow of blood in response to demand.

As a result, *strenuous exercise* may 'overload' a heart struggling to maintain the required flow of blood through the diseased arteries.

Similarly in response to the *dilation* following heat treatments, the required blood flow may not be possible again leading to fainting.

Diabetes

Diabetes is an inability of the body to control the level of sugars in the blood. It arises through a fault in the production of the hormone *insulin* by the *pancreas*. Any treatment which *constricts* or *dilates* the blood vessels or which causes any great loss of water from the body by perspiration will disturb the effective sugar concentration in the blood, and could set off the faintness or even the coma of a diabetic attack.

Nervous disorders

The 'correct' current intensity for an electrotherapy treatment is often found by asking the client to report the *sensation* he or she *feels* as the intensity control is gradually turned up.

If the area being treated had no 'feeling', this feedback would not be possible. Should a treatment such as *galvanic therapy* be attempted on an anaesthetised area, serious injury could result from an excessive current.

The nature of an electric current

Because in electrotherapy, the current is being passed *through* the body, it is an advantage to know what an electric current is and how it brings about its effects.

To explain the nature of an electric current, it is first necessary to consider the structure of the *atoms* and *molecules* of the matter through which the current will pass. A more detailed account is to be found in chapter 3 of Volume 1.

The structure of the atom

It has been known for a long time that atoms are *not* the smallest particles of matter. Atoms are composed of smaller particles.

Research into *atomic structure* is still going on and from time to time 'new', hitherto unknown atomic particles are discovered. However, for our purposes, we will assume that the atom is made of *three* types of particles:

> *Protons* – Each proton carries a *positive* electric charge
> *Neutrons* – A neutron has *no* electric charge
> *Electrons* – Each electron has a *negative* electric charge

Figure 5.1 shows in very much a diagrammatic form how these particles make up an atom.

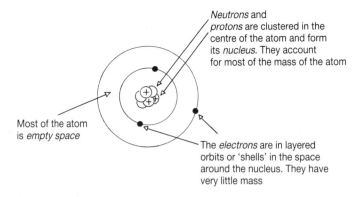

Neutrons and *protons* are clustered in the centre of the atom and form its *nucleus*. They account for most of the mass of the atom

Most of the atom is *empty space*

The *electrons* are in layered orbits or 'shells' in the space around the nucleus. They have very little mass

The numbers of *protons* and *electrons* in an atom are *equal*. An atom has *no* nett electrical charge

Figure 5.1 The structure of an atom

Atoms and elements

Matter is made of over a hundred basic substances called *elements*. The atoms of each element are all alike. The atoms of the different elements differ from each other in the *numbers* of protons, neutrons and electrons of which they are made. Figure 5.2 shows some examples.

Now let us consider two elements which are important to us when dealing with the passage of electricity through the body. These are element No. 11, sodium, and element No. 17, chlorine, which constitute sodium chloride – common salt. They are shown in figure 5.3.

An atom would be much more stable if the outer electron shell could contain a full complement of *eight* electrons.

If a *chlorine* atom could *gain* an electron it could have a full outer shell.

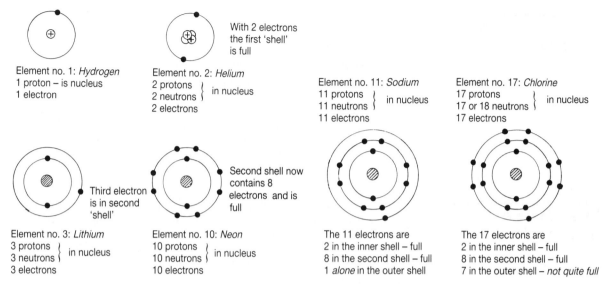

Element no. 1: *Hydrogen*
1 proton – is nucleus
1 electron

With 2 electrons
the first 'shell'
is full

Element no. 2: *Helium*
2 protons } in nucleus
2 neutrons }
2 electrons

Element no. 11: *Sodium*
11 protons } in nucleus
11 neutrons }
11 electrons

Element no. 17: *Chlorine*
17 protons   } in nucleus
17 or 18 neutrons }
17 electrons

Third electron
is in second
'shell'

Second shell now
contains 8
electrons and is
full

Element no. 3: *Lithium*
3 protons } in nucleus
3 neutrons }
3 electrons

Element no. 10: *Neon*
10 protons } in nucleus
10 neutrons }
10 electrons

The 11 electrons are
2 in the inner shell – full
8 in the second shell – full
1 *alone* in the outer shell

The 17 electrons are
2 in the inner shell – full
8 in the second shell – full
7 in the outer shell – *not quite full*

Figure 5.2 The atoms of some elements

Figure 5.3 The atoms of sodium and chlorine

Chlorine is a *non-metal* element. The atoms of non-metals have between four and seven electrons in the outer shell and can best reach the 'magic' *eight* by *gaining* electrons. How, will be seen later.

A *sodium* atom can best reach the stable *eight* in its outer shell by *losing* the odd electron. Sodium is a *metal* element. Metals have one, two or three electrons in the outer shell and they reach the stable state by *giving away* the outer electrons.

In a piece of metal, the atoms are *closely packed* together and the 'odd' electrons in the outer shells are able to 'wander' from atom to atom. They are called *free electrons*.

A metal as a conductor of electricity

The ability of a metal wire to pass an electric current makes use of the *free electrons*.

Figure 5.4 shows what happens when an *electric force* or *voltage* is applied to a piece of wire.

Note how the flow of electrons is from *negative* to *positive*. We usually imagine that electricity flows from positive to negative!

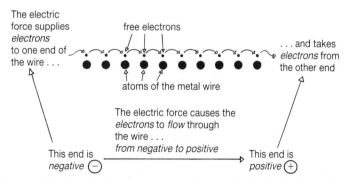

The electric
force supplies
electrons
to one end of
the wire . . .

free electrons

. . . and takes
electrons from
the other end

atoms of the metal wire

The electric force causes the
electrons to *flow* through
the wire . . .
from negative to positive

This end is
negative ⊖

This end is
positive ⊕

Figure 5.4 An electric current through a metal wire is the flow of free electrons

Non-metals are insulators

In a non-metal atom, the many electrons in the outer shell are more strongly held by the atom and cannot 'wander' like those of a metal. *Non-metals* are *insulators*. They do not allow the passage of electricity.

There are, however, *two* notable exceptions:

Carbon – The four electrons in the outer shell of the carbon atom *can* 'wander'. Carbon *is* a conductor.

Silicon – has rather special powers to conduct electricity in a very controlled way. It is a *semiconductor* and is the basis of the *transistors*, *diodes* and '*chips*' in modern electronic equipment. The new generation of *electrotherapy* equipment contains many of these electronic devices.

The atoms in a molecule

When atoms link together to form *molecules*, the *bonds* between them are formed by the electrons of the outer shells. In an attempt to get *eight* electrons in the outer shell, atoms may *share* electrons with each other and so join themselves together. An example is the joining of a *sodium* atom and a *chlorine* atom to form a molecule of *sodium chloride* – common salt. This is illustrated in figure 5.5.

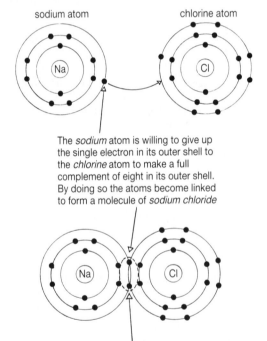

The *sodium* atom is willing to give up the single electron in its outer shell to the *chlorine* atom to make a full complement of eight in its outer shell. By doing so the atoms become linked to form a molecule of *sodium chloride*

The shared electrons form the bond joining the two atoms – an *electrovalent bond* or '*salt linkage*'. It will be seen later that this bond has special properties . . .

Figure 5.5 Sodium and chlorine atoms form a sodium chloride molecule

The body as a conductor of electricity

The human body is made very largely of *water*. About two-thirds of the body is water. Most of us are aware that very often *water* and *electricity* 'do not mix'. If an electrical appliance gets wet where it should not, electricity will 'go astray', with often very expensive consequences. If a person should touch 'live' connections at mains voltage, the effect could be *lethal*.

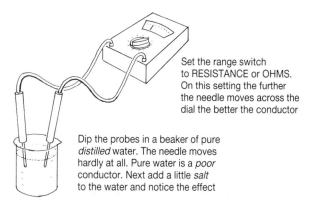

Set the range switch to RESISTANCE or OHMS. On this setting the further the needle moves across the dial the better the conductor

Dip the probes in a beaker of pure *distilled* water. The needle moves hardly at all. Pure water is a *poor* conductor. Next add a little *salt* to the water and notice the effect

Figure 5.6 Using a test meter to demonstrate the conductivity of water

Water can be a conductor of electricity – but it is much better if it has something dissolved in it! Try this experiment with an *electrician's test meter*. Set the 'range' switch to *'resistance'* and dip the probes in a beaker of water as shown in figure 5.6.

Now add a little salt to the water. Stir it to dissolve the salt. Then dip in the probes again. Salt water gives a good reading. It is quite a *good* conductor.

Hard tap water has salts dissolved in it. It too is a *good* conductor. So too is the water in the body. Body fluids are quite strong solutions of salts in water.

Lick your fingers and grip a probe in each hand. You are a conductor of electricity. The needle will swing well across the dial.

Why does *salt* make water a better conductor? We must look again at the molecules of salt and at what happens to them when they are dissolved in water. The molecules split apart, but not into atoms. They split instead into electrically charged particles called *ions*. The process is called *ionisation*.

Ionisation

When sodium chloride is dissolved in water, its molecules split into sodium *ions* and chloride *ions*, as shown in figure 5.7.

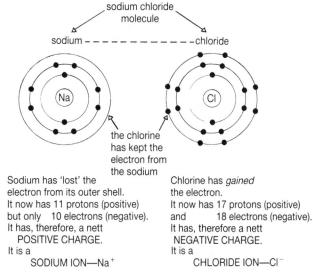

sodium chloride molecule

sodium – – – – – – – – – –chloride

Sodium has 'lost' the electron from its outer shell. It now has 11 protons (positive) but only 10 electrons (negative). It has, therefore, a nett POSITIVE CHARGE. It is a SODIUM ION—Na$^+$

the chlorine has kept the electron from the sodium

Chlorine has *gained* the electron. It now has 17 protons (positive) and 18 electrons (negative). It has, therefore a nett NEGATIVE CHARGE. It is a CHLORIDE ION—Cl$^-$

Figure 5.7 The ionisation of sodium chloride

The passage of electricity through solutions

If the molecules in a solution have *ionised*, the solution will be a *conductor* of electricity. A solution which can conduct electricity is called an *electrolyte*.

To pass electricity through a solution, it is connected into a circuit with a pair of *electrodes*. The electric current will then pass through the solution by causing the *ions* in the solution to *move* and 'hitching a lift' with them.

When a *direct current* is passed through the solution, the ions each move in one direction, the positive ions towards the negative electrode and the negative ions towards the positive electrode. The movement of ions is called *electrophoresis* or by Beauty Therapists – *iontophoresis*. When the ions arrive at their respective electrodes, *chemical reactions* occur. These chemical reactions at the electrodes are called *electrolysis* (see figure 5.8).

An *alternating current* causes the ions just to *vibrate* back and forth in the solution and because there is no 'arrival' of ions at the electrodes, there are *no* chemical reactions.

Should you try doing the reaction in figure 5.8 as an experiment, you will *not* be able to see the movement of the ions, but you will be able to see some of the chemical effects of the electrolysis. You can show the acidity and alkalinity by dipping in a piece of pH paper close to each electrode. If you include an *ammeter* in the circuit, it will show that an electric current is flowing (see figure 5.9).

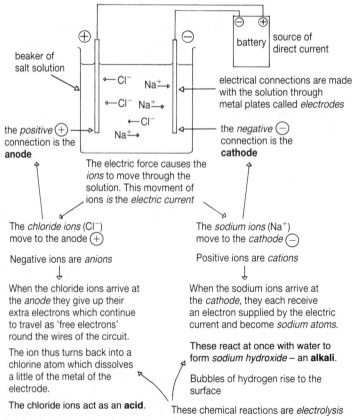

Figure 5.8 The chemical effects of passing a direct current through a salt solution

You *can* show the movement of ions by doing a similar experiment with *ionised dyes*. Many dyes *ionise* when dissolved in water:

> *Eosin* – is an *acid* dye – its *pink* colour is its *anion*
> *Methylene blue* – is a *basic* dye – its *blue* colour is its *cation*

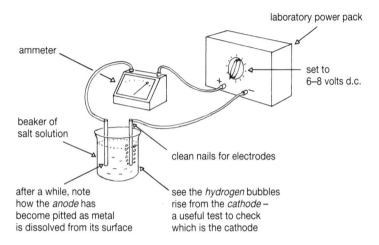

laboratory power pack

ammeter

set to
6–8 volts d.c.

beaker of
salt solution

clean nails for electrodes

after a while, note
how the *anode* has
become pitted as metal
is dissolved from its surface

see the *hydrogen* bubbles
rise from the *cathode* –
a useful test to check
which is the cathode

Figure 5.9 Showing the effect of passing a direct current through a salt solution

Dissolve a few crystals of *eosin* in a few cm^3 of water. Pour just enough into a shallow, flat-bottomed glass dish to cover the bottom. Half a Petri-dish will do. Dip in the electrodes and turn up the d.c. voltage to 20–25 volts. In a few seconds you will see how the colour congregates round the anode $\oplus$ and clears from around the *cathode* $\ominus$ (see figure 5.10).

Now do the experiment with *methylene blue*. This time the coloured cations congregate around the *cathode* and clear from the *anode*.

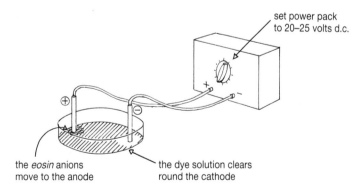

set power pack
to 20–25 volts d.c.

the *eosin* anions
move to the anode

the dye solution clears
round the cathode

Figure 5.10 Eosin dye shows the movement of ions

As will be seen in the next chapter – chapter 6 – the movement of ions and the chemical reactions at the electrodes which are the result of passing *direct current* through the body, are the essential features of *galvanic therapy*.

1 What two main types of particles constitute the nucleus of an atom?

2 In what way does electricity flow through a metal wire?

3 What happens to the molecules of salt when it is dissolved in water?

4 What is an electrolyte?

5 Why is a solution of salt in water a better conductor of electricity than pure water?

6 Distinguish between an anode and a cathode.

7 Distinguish between an anion and a cation.

8 Briefly describe the chemical reactions which occur at the cathode when a direct current of electricity is passed through a salt solution.

9 Describe briefly how one can ascertain which electrode is the cathode and which is the anode.

10 Why does defective skin sensation contra-indicate electrotherapy treatment on that part of the body?

6   Galvanic Therapy

Direct current in therapy; galvanic current; transformers; rectifiers; capacitors for 'smoothing'; galvanic therapy unit; the electrodes; the physical and physiological effects of galvanic therapy; safety with galvanic treatments

Direct current in therapy

The therapeutic effects of galvanic treatments are brought about by passing a *direct current* of electricity through the body. Figure 6.1 shows a galvanic treatment in progress on a client.

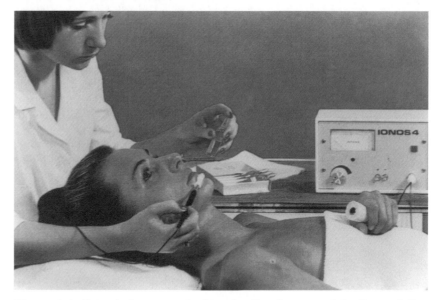

Figure 6.1 Galvanic therapy on the face of a client (courtesy of the George Solly Organisation)

The *movement of ions*, which *is* the direct current, is employed in

    through-body galvanism
    and *iontophoresis*

In through-body galvanism, the movement of ions stimulates the metabolism in the tissues being treated. In iontophoresis, the 'active ions' of special cosmetics are forced into the skin by the electric current.

The *chemical reactions* which occur at the electrodes are also used in galvanic treatments, particularly the *alkaline* effects around the *cathode*. These treatments are often referred to as *cathodermy* – sometimes spelled 'cathiodermy':

> *Disincrustation* – is the removal of excess sebum from the skin
> *Skin-peeling*   – is the removal of layers from an excessively thick *Stratum corneum*

The original method of electrical epilation called galvanic epilation uses these chemical reactions to destroy hair follicles. This electrical–chemical destruction is *electrolysis*. Hence the term *'electrolysis'* is commonly used to mean electrical epilation. The more modern method, *short-wave diathermy* does *not* use chemical electrolysis but *'blend'*, which combines galvanic and short-wave currents, does destroy follicles chemically.

The galvanic current

For galvanic therapy, a *smooth direct current* is required. It must flow smoothly without interruptions, pulses or ripples which would probably stimulate the 'motor points' of muscles and cause them to twitch or contract. The direct current from a battery would be ideal.

However, because the *Stratum corneum*, the horny layer of the epidermis, has a low water content and is coated with a layer of greasy sebum, it has a *high resistance*, so a fairly *high voltage* is necessary to pass sufficient current through it. Once through the *Stratum corneum*, the current flows quite easily in the body.

In old-fashioned galvanic therapy units, a *battery* was used to supply the electricity. At the time, earlier in the century, batteries were available producing 60, 90 or 120 volts. They were intended for use in 'valve'-type radios before the days of transistors. The demise of valve radios as transistors took over in the early 1960s means that these batteries are no longer made.

Each battery contained sufficient of the *'dry cells'* described in chapter 1, connected in *series* to give the required voltage. A 120 volt battery would contain *eighty* of these 1.5 volt cells.

Galvanic current from the mains

Modern galvanic units operate from the *mains*. Inside them, the mains *alternating current* at 230 volts is converted into a *smooth direct current* at up to 100 volts.

This is done in *three* stages by three electronic devices contained within the unit:

> A *transformer* – reduces the voltage of the a.c. mains
> A *rectifier*   – changes the alternating current to direct current
> A *capacitor* – smooths any irregularities in the direct current

The transformer

The main purpose of a *transformer* is to *change the voltage* of an alternating current from one value to another. It can either reduce the voltage ('*step-down*') or increase it ('*step-up*').

A transformer consists of an *iron* core with *two* coils of wire wound round it. The coils are known as 'windings' (see figures 6.2 and 6.3).

The incoming alternating current in the *primary coil* produces a rapidly changing *magnetism* in the iron core, which in turn *generates* a new alternating current in the *secondary coil*.

How much the transformer *changes* the voltage depends on the *ratio* of the number of turns of wire in the primary and secondary windings. Each winding

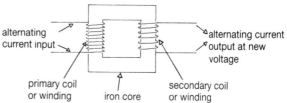

Figure 6.2 A transformer

Figure 6.3 A transformer

actually consists of hundreds of turns of wire, but for clarity let us imagine each is only a few turns. For example, see figure 6.4.

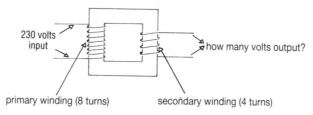

Figure 6.4 How a transformer changes the voltage of an alternating current

Ratio of secondary turns to primary turns
= 1:2 or ½
So output volts = ½ input volts
½ of 230 volts = 115 volts
Output voltage = 115 volts

Note that a transformer will work in this way *only* on *alternating current*. It cannot be used to change the voltage of direct current.

As will be seen in chapter 7, in a faradic therapy unit a transformer supplied with *pulses* of direct current performs an electronic 'trick' with them to produce the rather unusual faradic current.

The transformer as an isolating device

You will notice that there is *no* electrical connection between the primary and secondary windings. This means that the *output* is completely separate from the *input*. They are *isolated* from each other.

For mains operated equipment, it means that beyond the mains transformer, the electrical circuits of the equipment are not connected to the mains at all and so there is *no* possibility of the equipment giving a *'mains' electric shock*. This is an important *safety* feature. The output is *'mains free'*.

The autotransformer

But *beware*, some mass-produced electrical appliances may use a transformer which *does not isolate*. It uses a *single* winding with four connections or 'tappings' on it. It is called an *autotransformer* and is much cheaper to make. For safety's sake a *autotransformer* should *not* be used in *electrotherapy* equipment.

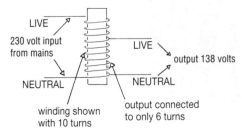

Figure 6.5 An autotransformer

The output voltage is calculated in the same way as for an ordinary transformer:

Ratio of turns = 6:10 or 6/10
Output volts = 6/10 × 230
        = 138 volts

Experiments with a transformer

In most college physics laboratories there will be a *demountable transformer*. It consists of an iron core which can be fitted with a variety of windings with different numbers of turns.

For the experiments you will also need a laboratory power pack which can supply low-voltage a.c., an a.c. voltmeter (or a test meter set to a.c. volts) and an oscilloscope.

Set up the transformer with windings of, say, 600 and 300 turns. Connect the 600 turn coil to the a.c. supply set at, say, 6 volts. With the a.c. voltmeter measure the voltage from the 300 turn coil. It should measure 3 volts (see figure 6.6).

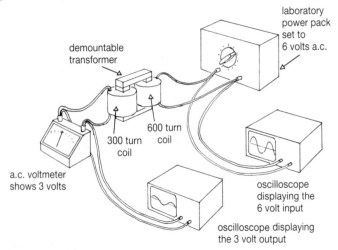

Figure 6.6 A demountable transformer shows the effect of a transformer

You can also connect the input a.c. of 6 volts, then the output a.c. of 3 volts, to the oscilloscope. The waves for the 6 volts will be twice as high as those for the 3 volts.

The rectifier

current flows in this direction only

Figure 6.7 A diode as shown in circuit diagrams

A rectifier is a device for changing alternating current to direct current. A rectifier consists of one or more *diodes*. A diode is a device which will allow an electric current to flow through it in *one* direction but not in the reverse direction. A diode is shown in a circuit diagram as in figure 6.7.

An oscilloscope will show the effect of connecting a diode in an a.c. circuit (see figure 6.9). Note how the d.c. produced is an *uneven d.c.* The 'reverse half' of each wave has been lost. The current flows in a series of 'jumps' or pulses. This is called *half-wave rectification*.

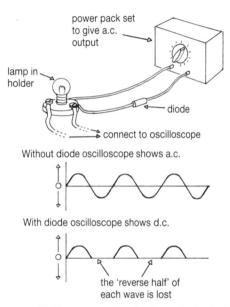

Figure 6.9 Half-wave rectification by a single diode

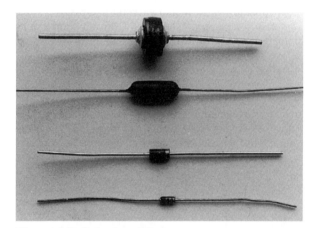

Figure 6.8 Selection of diodes

The bridge rectifier

A more efficient rectifier is built up from *four* diodes connected as shown in figure 6.10. The 'reverse half' of each wave is 'turned round' so it too flows in the 'forward' direction rather than being lost. This is *full-wave rectification*.

An experimental bridge rectifier may be built up from four diodes and its effect can be shown on an oscilloscope. Connect the diodes in a 'square' like in figure 6.10. Make sure they are the right way round! Connect the input 'corners' to a low-voltage a.c. supply from the power pack. Connect a suitable lamp to the d.c. output corners; a rectifier will 'rectify' only if it has a load connected to it.

Connect the oscilloscope to the input a.c. The trace on the screen will be as in figure 6.11a. Then connect it to the output. The trace will then be as in figure 6.11b.

Notice how the reverse half of each wave is turned round to become 'forward'. Notice too that the output d.c. is still uneven. It is *unsmoothed d.c.*

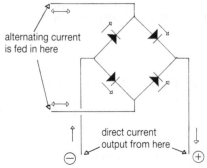

(a) Connect the oscilloscope to the a.c. supply . . .

(b) then to the d.c. output of the rectifier

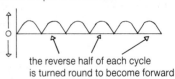

the reverse half of each cycle
is turned round to become forward

Figure 6.10 A bridge rectifier for full-wave rectification

Figure 6.11 Full-wave rectification by a bridge rectifier

The capacitor

The capacitor, or 'condenser' as it is often called, is rather like electricity's version of a spring. It can be used to *smooth out* the 'bumps' in the d.c. output from a rectifier.

Figure 6.12 shows how a capacitor is shown in a circuit diagram.

If a suitable capacitor is connected in *parallel* across the output connections of a rectifier, the smoothing effect can be shown on an oscilloscope (see figure 6.13).

Should you try this with your experimental bridge rectifier, you may have to try different values of capacitors to find one which gives the best smoothing effect.

The values of capacitors are measured in units called *microfarads*, μF for short. These units are named after that early pioneer of electricity, Michael Faraday, who also gave his name to the faradic current.

Figure 6.12 Circuit diagram symbol for a capacitor

Figure 6.13 A smoothed direct current as displayed on an oscilloscope

The galvanic therapy unit

We have already established that the output of a *galvanic therapy unit* must be a *smooth direct current* so inside it contains a transformer, a rectifier and a capacitor.

It also contains a *variable resistance* operated by the *intensity control* knob. This is to adjust the amount of current flowing through the client during the treatment.

Early galvanic units required a lot of skill to operate them correctly so that the client was not damaged by passing an excessively high current. Modern units contain electronic refinements which can detect any tendency for the current flow to change, and by automatically increasing or decreasing the voltage, restore it to the correct level. This minimises the chance of an excessive current flow and makes the galvanic unit as 'idiot-proof' as possible. Figure 6.14 shows a modern galvanic unit.

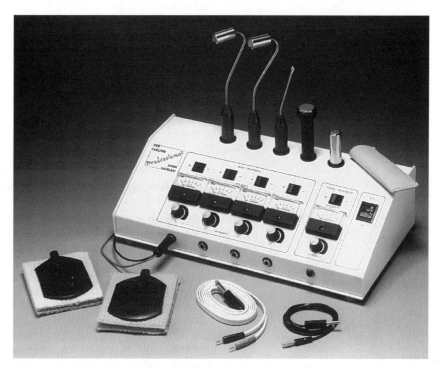

Figure 6.14 A galvanic therapy unit (courtesy of Taylor Reeson Laboratories Ltd)

A galvanic unit is instantly recognisable from the features on its front panel. In addition to the *intensity* control, there will usually be a *milliammeter* to indicate the flow of current through the client during the treatment.

One milliamp (mA) is one-thousandth of an amp

The *output sockets* into which the electrode leads are plugged are also quite characteristic. There are two alternative arrangements. There will be either two separate sockets labelled ⊕ and ⊖, or a non-reversible two-pin socket with, nearby, a current reversing switch labelled ⊕ and ⊖.

The electrodes

To form a complete circuit for the flow of electricity through the client, *two* electrodes are needed. One, the *anode*, connects to the ⊕ outlet socket. The other, the *cathode*, connects to the ⊖ outlet socket on the galvanic unit.

In most treatments, one electrode is used at the site of the treatment of the skin. This is termed the *active* electrode. The other electrode is just to complete the circuit. It is referred to as the *indifferent electrode*.

As *active* electrodes, one might use a carbon or metal ball electrode or a 'tweezer' electrode wrapped in lint or cotton wool soaked in *salt* solution or an *iontophoresis* lotion (see figure 6.15).

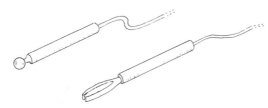

Figure 6.15 Ball and tweezer electrodes for galvanic therapy

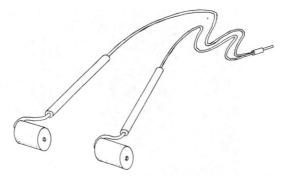

Figure 6.16 Roller electrodes for galvanic therapy

Metal roller electrodes may also be used, either uncovered or covered with special *viscose* covers. Often the roller electrodes are used in *pairs*, both connected to the same outlet terminal on the machine (see figure 6.16). A third electrode, the indifferent electrode, is required to complete the circuit.

As *indifferent* electrodes or as electrodes for use in 'through-body galvanism' it is normal to use *metal plate* electrodes. The metal plate must be covered with *lint* or *viscose* to a thickness of at least ½ inch (1.25 cm) to prevent the electrolysis reactions at the electrode affecting the skin. This used to involve covering the electrode with *nine* layers of surgical lint soaked in salt water and squeezed out. Nowadays *viscose* covers are used. The plate is slid inside one viscose cover and another is placed between the electrode and the skin (see figure 6.17).

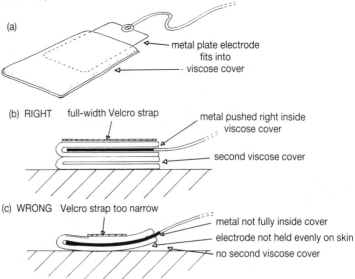

(a)

metal plate electrode
fits into
viscose cover

(b) RIGHT full-width Velcro strap

metal pushed right inside
viscose cover

second viscose cover

(c) WRONG Velcro strap too narrow

metal not fully inside cover
electrode not held evenly on skin
no second viscose cover

Figure 6.17 (a) Galvanic electrode inside viscose cover. (b) Electrode correctly attached to skin. (c) Electrode incorrectly attached to skin

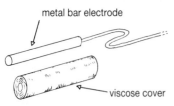

metal bar electrode

viscose cover

Figure 6.18 The bar-type indifferent electrode and its viscose cover

These electrodes *must* be firmly and evenly attached to the skin. The securing straps must hold the whole area of the electrode in contact with the skin. The straps usually have '*velcro*' fastenings. Figure 6.17 shows the correct and incorrect methods of securing the electrode.

An alternative type of indifferent electrode is a metal or carbon bar covered by a viscose tube to be held by the client in his or her hand. This is shown in figure 6.18.

The effects of the galvanic current

The physical–chemical effects of the galvanic current are of *two* kinds. The chemical reactions we call electrolysis which occur *at the electrodes* are the *polar effects*. The physical movement of *ions* within the body is the *interpolar effect*.

These effects are summarised in a flow diagram in figure 6.19.

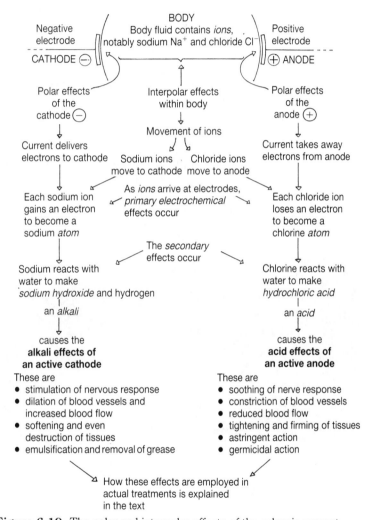

Figure 6.19 The polar and interpolar effects of the galvanic current

Use of the polar effects in treatment

Treatments which use the *alkaline* reactions beneath an *active cathode* are sometimes referred to as *cathodermy*. Traditionally the lint or cotton wool around the electrode is moistened with *salt* solution (sodium chloride) so the *physical* effects of the treatment are due to the production of *sodium hydroxide* alkali at the cathode (see chapter 5). Nowadays the salt or a similar substance is disguised in the form of special fluids or gels supplied in individual vials or sachets, but their action is essentially the same.

Disincrustation

This is the removal of excess sebum from a greasy skin. The sodium hydroxide emulsifies and removes the sebum. The treatment must not be repeated too frequently or the sebaceous glands are stimulated into greater production! This would make the treatment counterproductive.

Skin-peeling

This uses the sodium hydroxide to dissolve away layers of keratin squames from an excessively thick *Stratum corneum* or horny layer. Such a skin may have become thickened and coarsened by a life *out-of-doors* and an excess of ultra-violet from sunshine. Thinning it makes it softer and more supple.

A skin affected by the *blackheads of acne* can also benefit from skin-peeling. By removing the outermost layers, the blackheads should be loosened and made easier to remove.

Galvanic epilation

In the original method of electrical epilation, the hair follicle is destroyed *chemically* by the action of a *direct current*. The cabinet of the epilation unit contained one of those 90 volt or 120 volt batteries already described. The indifferent electrode is connected to the *positive* of the battery. The active electrode is a fine *needle* connected via a *variable resistance* to the *negative* battery terminal.

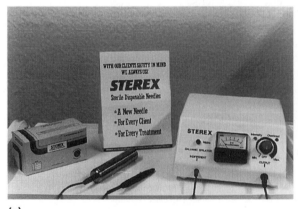
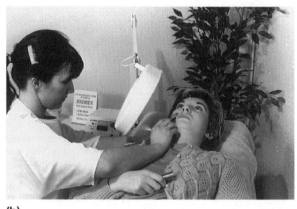

(a) **(b)**

Figure 6.20 (a) A modern, mains operated galvanic epilation unit. (b) Galvanic epilation in progress. Note client holding indifferent electrode (courtesy of E.A. Ellison and Co Ltd)

How galvanic epilation is done and how the direct current brings about the destruction of the hair follicle is described in figure 6.21. The process is very slow compared with the modern methods (see chapter 10). It takes up to fifty seconds to treat each follicle.

Electrotonus

Electrotonus is a term used to encompass the *stimulating* and *soothing* effects of the galvanic current. These work by the effect of the current on the transmission of nerve impulses along a nerve.

Transmitting the impulse works by causing the *discharge* of electrical charges along the nerve fibre. After passing the impulse, the nerve has to be

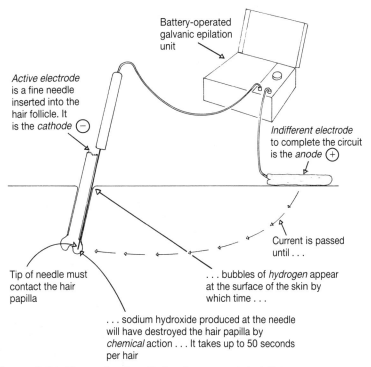

Figure 6.21 How galvanic epilation destroys a hair follicle

recharged before it can transmit the next impulse and it is this which is affected by the galvanic current (see figure 6.22).

Under an *active cathode* ⊖, sodium ions will accumulate and so assist the recharging of the nerves. Hence the nerves are *stimulated*.

Under an *active anode* ⊕, sodium ions are driven away and will be depleted, inhibiting the recharge of the nerves. Hence the *soothing* effect. Care must be taken not to overdo this or the nerves might become completely *anaesthetised* and the area will temporarily lose all feeling.

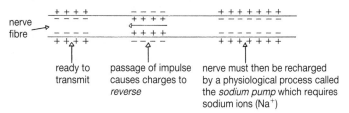

Figure 6.22 The transmission of a nerve impulse

Erythema

If during the treatment the skin becomes *reddened* and *irritated*, it means it is becoming *distressed*. Should this occur, the treatment should be discontinued. The current should be *reversed* for a short time. This will *neutralise* any remaining chemical residues in the skin and alleviate the irritation.

Iontophoresis

To accompany galvanic therapy units, many companies produce a range of special *cosmetic lotions* or *gels* for use in treatments. The lotions, usually supplied in individual sealed glass vials, are to be soaked on to the lint cover of the active electrode before the treatment. The gels, often in sealed sachets, are applied direct to the skin in the treatment area. A gel is basically similar to a lotion but it has been thickened with a thickening agent such as methyl cellulose. This makes the product more controllable on the skin but does not affect its conductivity or its chemical action.

The active materials in these cosmetics are *ionised* and in *iontophoresis* the current is used to *propel* these ions into the skin on the principle of '*like charges repel*'.

Each lotion or gel is labelled with a large $\oplus$ or $\ominus$. This shows the polarity of the active electrode to be used. Make sure that the correct electrode is used.

A lotion or gel marked $\oplus$ will have active *cations* $\oplus$; for example, the aluminium ions (Al^{3+}) of an astringent. These will be propelled into the skin by an *active anode* $\oplus$. This process is called *cataphoresis*.

A lotion or gel marked $\ominus$ will have active *anions* $\ominus$; an example is a peroxide skin bleach (O_2^{2-}). An *active cathode* $\ominus$ will drive these into the skin. This is called *anaphoresis*. It gets very confusing. Do take care.

The intensity of the current and the timing of the treatment are both critical. Too little of either will not push the ions far enough. Too much for too long will push them clean through the skin and they will be dispersed in the bloodstream. Read the *instructions* and follow them to the letter.

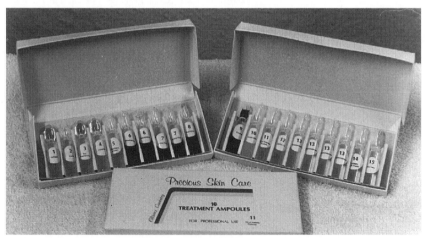

Figure 6.23 A range of iontophoresis lotions in ampoules (courtesy of E. A. Ellison and Co Ltd)

Through-body galvanism

Through-body galvanism is the use of the movement of ions to *stimulate* the *metabolism* in the tissues. This movement of ions 'stirs up' the cell contents and assists the passage of substances in and out of cells through cell membranes. Stimulating the metabolism gives a 'feeling of well-being' in the treatment area (see figure 6.24). This stimulation plus the stimulation of the nervous system makes galvanic a valuable preliminary to faradic muscle stimulation. There are machines available which combine both treatments. A galvano–faradic machine is shown in figure 6.25.

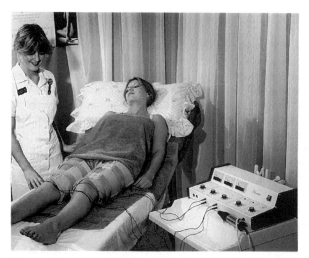

Figure 6.24 Through-body galvanic treatment on the thighs (courtesy of Depilex Ltd)

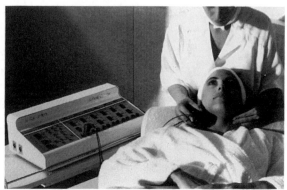

Figure 6.25 A galvano-faradic therapy unit (courtesy of the George Solly Organisation)

Safety with galvanic therapy

Galvanic therapy is a deceptively simple treatment, but in the hands of an untrained or incompetent operator who is not using sophisticated modern equipment, it is capable of doing untold and permanent damage to the client. It is *very* important to observe the precautions if the client is to experience an effective, pleasant and *safe* treatment.

Preparation of the client

In addition to the usual contra-indications, one must check the *sensitivity* of the area to be treated by a simple *pin-prick* test. It is essential that the client is able to report back the sensation felt during the treatment. This means that the treatment should *not* be done on any area which lacks feeling – that is, an *anaesthetised area*.

The treatment area should be inspected for signs of cuts, grazes or blemishes. The damaged epidermis could possibly have a higher *water* content and therefore a *higher conductivity* than the surrounding skin, causing an excessively high current to be channelled through the affected area. Such injuries should be *insulated* by smearing over them a little soft paraffin or petroleum jelly.

As a preliminary to through-body galvanism, the areas of skin on which the electrodes are to be placed should be carefully *washed* and dried. This is to remove sebum and even-out any variations in the skin's resistance. This should also be done before applying an indifferent electrode.

This is not essential, though, before *cathodermy* because one of the effects of the *active cathode* is to cleanse away the sebum. However, it should be remembered that as it does so the skin's resistance will *fall* and so the flow of current through it will tend to *increase*. It could rise above the safe level, so keep an eye on the *milliammeter*. Modern machines will most probably have a current-stabilising device which controls the current flow automatically.

Particularly when working on the *face*, warn clients about the *taste*. If they have any fillings, the current will dissolve them *very* slightly but sufficient to produce a *metallic taste* in the mouth. Do reassure your client that his or her fillings are *not* about to disintegrate, but should the taste become intolerable be prepared to stop the treatment.

Preparing the electrodes

The electrodes should be prepared *exactly* as required for the treatment. For *facial* treatments, the *active electrode* must be covered with *lint* soaked either in *salt* solution or an *iontophoresis* lotion. After thorough wetting, the lint should be squeezed out, and applied to cover the electrode *evenly*. No metal of the electrode should be allowed *accidentally* to touch the skin, or current might be *concentrated* through that point and could cause a *burn*.

Do not forget the importance of the *half-inch* thickness of covering required on *indifferent electrodes* and *through-body electrodes*. It is essential that the covering is applied *evenly* with no tucks or folds, and the electrode is well strapped to the skin so as to spread the flow of current over its entire contact area (see figure 6.17 on page 66).

Current intensity limits

For safety, the current should be limited to a *maximum* of

> 0.3 milliamps per square centimetre of electrode contact
> (2 milliamps per square inch)

The *total* current for

> *facial treatment* should not exceed   3 milliamps
> *body treatment* should not exceed   8 milliamps

With the *correct* current flow, the client should be able to report a not-unpleasant tingling sensation from under the electrodes.

Modern machines now usually have an *automatic current control* circuit which is set to limit the current to these maxima. In any case the *milliammeter dial* has 'red line' markings to indicate these levels.

Always start a treatment with a *lower* than maximum current until the resistance of the skin has stabilised itself. Then increase it to the 'working' level.

The *penalty* for passing an excessively *high* current could be *burns*. *Alkali burns* beneath the electrodes are very nasty and very slow to heal. They could scar for life.

Worse still are '*bone burns*'. An excess current passing through a bone can actually *char* it. A bone burn is very painful and even slower to heal.

At the end of the treatment

As the treatment draws to its close, the current should be *reduced gradually* to allow the chemical effects to be completed and not leave chemical residues in the skin. Alternatively, *reverse* the current for the last few moments to *neutralise* these chemical residues.

Finally, should a client find the treatment is causing unbearable irritation to the skin, *stop* the treatment and *reverse* the current to neutralise the cause of the irritation.

Things to do

Collect manufacturers' information literature on galvanic therapy equipment.

Self-assessment questions

1   What type of electric current is required for galvanic therapy?

2   What is the purpose of a transformer?

3   What is the relationship between the number of turns on the input and output coils of a transformer and the input and output voltages?

4   What is an autotransformer and why is this type not recommended in a piece of electrotherapy equipment?

5   What is the function of rectifier?

6   Distinguish between half-wave and full-wave rectification.

7   What is the function of a smoothing capacitor?

8   Why should the electrode for through-body galvanism be separated from the skin by at least 1.25 cm (½ inch) of lint or viscose?

9   Distinguish between the active and indifferent electrodes in galvanic therapy.

10   Describe briefly the chemical reactions which occur at the active electrode during a disincrustation treatment.

11   Describe briefly how galvanic epilation works to remove unwanted hair permanently.

12   Explain briefly how a galvanic current can soothe and even anaesthetise an area of skin.

13   In iontophoresis which electrode is used to apply a positive charged lotion or gel? Why?

14   What should be the maximum current flow through the person (a) in a facial galvanic treatment, (b) in a body galvanic treatment?

15   What action should be taken if a galvanic treatment starts to irritate the client's skin?

7 Electronic Muscle Stimulation

Muscle stimulation by electric currents; sinusoidal therapy; the potentiometer as an intensity control; electrical stimulation of muscles; faradic therapy; electromagnetic induction; production of the faradic current; modified faradic current; modern electronic muscle stimulation machines; the electrodes; padding-up for treatment; extra features on modern electronic muscle stimulation machines

Muscle stimulation by electric currents

Should a short sharp *pulse* of electric current pass through the body, muscles in its path will 'twitch' in response. An electric current flowing as a *series of pulses* in not too rapid succession will make the muscles *contract* and *hold* contracted for as long as the current flows.

Two types of current could be used:

1   An *alternating current* flows as a series of pulses (see chapter 1). Passed through the body for this purpose it is called a

   sinusoidal current

2   An interrupted *direct current* in the form of a succession of short, sharp pulses directed through the body is a

   faradic current

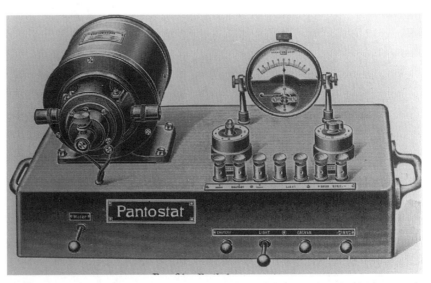

Figure 7.1 A sinusoidal therapy unit. This early 20th Century combined therapy unit used a motor-driven generator (left) to convert the d.c. mains of the time into the sinusoidal therapy current (courtesy of Pantostat)

Sinusoidal therapy

The use of alternating current for muscle stimulation therapy has long been a thing of the past. However unintentional muscle stimulation by an alternating current is the principle of the *mains electric shock*!

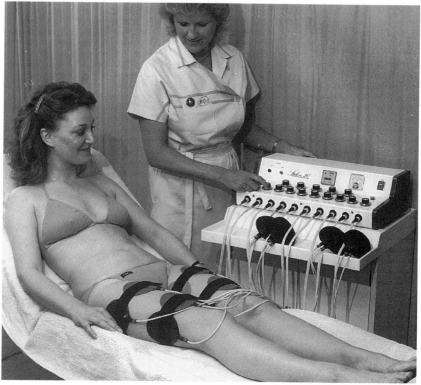

Figure 7.2 A modern faradic therapy unit (courtesy of Depilex Ltd)

Mains electricity is alternating current, but it is most inappropriate for therapeutic purposes for two reasons. First, at 230 volts, its voltage is *too high*. It would produce muscle contractions which are far too violent and uncomfortable.

Second, given the opportunity, it will pass right through the body to *earth, contracting all* the muscles in its path including those of the chest, stopping the breathing, and those of the heart, stopping the heartbeat. These are the symptoms of a *mains-to-earth* electric shock.

For sinusoidal therapy purposes, the voltage is *reduced* to around 100 volts by a *transformer*. At the same time the transformer *isolates* the therapeutic current from the mains supply, making it *'earth free'*. How a transformer performs these functions is described in chapter 6.

The potentiometer as an intensity control

The voltage of the treatment current is further reduced and controlled by a *potentiometer* or potential divider – often referred to as a 'pot'.

This is a variable control which can 'tap-off' as much of the available voltage as is required. Potentiometers are used in many pieces of electrical equipment as intensity controls (see figures 7.3 and 7.4).

In chapter 6, we saw the use of a *variable resistance* as an intensity controller for galvanic therapy. Here we have a *potentiometer* apparently doing the same thing. The difference between them is that a *variable resistance* adjusts the flow of *current*, a *potentiometer* adjusts the *voltage*.

Figure 7.3 A potentiometer

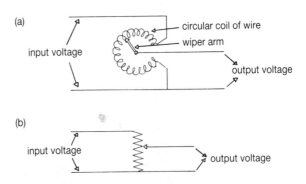

Figure 7.4 (a) Inside a potentiometer.
(b) Circuit diagram symbol for a potentiometer

Sinusoidal muscle stimulator

A sinusoidal machine is basically very simple, consisting of a *transformer* and a *potentiometer*. The circuit diagram in figure 7.5 shows just how simple it is.

The *output* of the machine is a straightforward *alternating current*, and displayed on the *oscilloscope* would look as shown in figure 7.6.

Each half-wave of the a.c. output is a *pulse* of electricity. Mains alternates with a *frequency* of 50 Hz, so there are 100 of these pulses each second. Remember, each cycle of the alternating current consists of two pulses – one 'forward' and one 'reverse'.

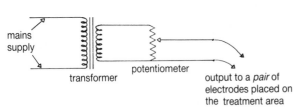

Figure 7.5 Circuit diagram of a sinusoidal muscle stimulator

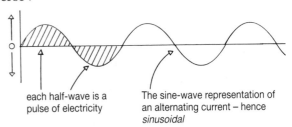

Figure 7.6 The output of a sinusoidal muscle stimulator as shown on an oscilloscope

How the sinusoidal current contracts a muscle

When we decide consciously to move, the brain sends electrical messages through *motor nerves* to those muscles which will contract to bring about the movement. The *electrical messages* from the brain consist of a succession of *electrical pulses*.

So if 'outside' electrical pulses of the same order of frequency – up to 100 pulses per second – are fed into the body, they too should be picked up by the *motor nerves* and bring about muscle contraction.

However, *nature* tries hard to prevent this. By giving skin a high resistance it prevents our brains controlling each other's bodies when people are touching each other! Also each nerve is *insulated* by a fatty *myelin sheath*.

This means that first, the *outside* pulses must have a fairly high voltage to get them through the skin, and second, they must be directed to the *motor-point* of the muscle so they will be picked up by it. The *motor-point* is the point on the muscle where its motor nerve enters. The electrodes have to be carefully positioned so that the current flow through the body is through this motor-point.

So long as the current passes, the muscle will contract and hold contracted. Turn down the current and the muscle can relax. The muscle can be made to contract and relax alternately by turning the current up and down. This is known as *surging*.

Because of the *high resistance* of the skin, passing sufficient current through it to be effective in treatment causes a considerable sensation. This is too much for many clients who would feel discomfort or even pain. For this reason, *sinusoidal therapy* is no longer used. *Faradic therapy* is far more comfortable and pleasant.

Faradic therapy

Faradic therapy is named after Michael Faraday, one of the pioneers of science who is credited with inventing the *transformer*.

A *faradic therapy machine* uses a *transformer* in what might seem an unusual way – a way invented by Faraday. He fed it a *direct current*. In chapter 6 it was said that a transformer will not work off direct current. It will, but not in the 'normal' manner.

Electromagnetic induction

We have already seen that a *transformer* works by electricity making magnetism, then magnetism making electricity once more. This is called *electromagnetic induction*.

This can be shown by a series of experiments. These experiments in effect show the development of a faradic therapy unit and explain how it works. If the apparatus is available, you might care to try them.

For the first experiment we need a *very* sensitive *galvanometer*. This is an instrument which *detects* and measures electric currents. These experiments require a galvanometer with a *centre zero* so that it can detect currents in either direction. Lay out the circuits as in figure 7.7.

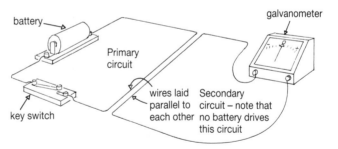

Figure 7.7 A basic experiment to show electromagnetic induction

Press the key switch to *switch on* the primary circuit. The galvanometer should detect a momentary current in the secondary circuit – then nothing.

Release the key switch to *switch off* the primary circuit. The galvanometer will again detect momentary current in the secondary circuit – perhaps a little 'stronger' and in the *opposite* direction. These currents in the secondary circuit are called *induced currents*.

Do not worry if the experiment does not work. It means that your galvanometer is not sensitive enough. To improve the response, we will now use two *coils* of wire and an *iron core*. The parts of a demountable transformer will do. It is more convincing if the coils have similar numbers of turns of wire – say 300 turns each. You will now *not* need such a sensitive galvanometer or you might do it irreparable damage! (see figure 7.8).

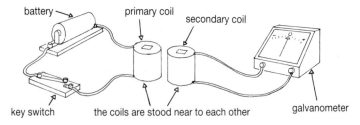

Figure 7.8 To show electromagnetic induction between coils of wire

Press the key switch to *switch on* the current to the *primary coil*. The galvanometer indicates a pulse of current in the *secondary coil* – a much stronger pulse than in the first experiment. Now release the key to *switch off* the primary current. The galvanometer needle kicks even more sharply in the opposite direction.

Now stand the coils on top of each other and slide in an *iron core* (see figure 7.9). Press the switch then release it. The galvanometer will show even *stronger* pulses this time.

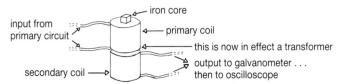

Figure 7.9 Electromagnetic induction through a transformer

An *oscilloscope* will show the pulses of current better than the galvanometer. Disconnect the galvanometer and replace it with an oscilloscope. Then repeat the experiment. You will need to set the *timebase* control of the oscilloscope so the lightspot tracks quite slowly across the screen. Then adjust the *sensitivity* or *volts/cm* control for the best effect. You should obtain a 'trace' looking like figure 7.10.

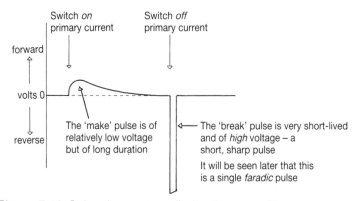

Figure 7.10 Induced currents as displayed on an oscilloscope

Explanation

When the primary current is turned *on* it takes a moment or two to build up, so the magnetism it produces also takes a moment to build up. In the secondary circuit the output pulse is relatively gentle and prolonged.

When turned *off* the primary current stops *instantly*, so its magnetism is destroyed instantly. In the secondary circuit, it produces a *very* short-lived but *very* intense pulse.

Now an experiment to really convince your 'best friend'! Ask him or her to *hold* the output leads from the secondary coil and tell them to say if they feel anything. Switch on . . . nothing! . . . wait . . . then switch off . . . 'ouch!' It will really make him or her jump!

Who said you could not get a shock from a torch battery? This is basically one of Faraday's original experiments, and also the basis of Galvani's 'frog-leg-kick' experiment you may have seen in your school biology. The *single* pulse will make the muscles *momentarily contract*.

In faradic therapy, a rapid succession of these pulses is passed to the muscle. We can produce this rapid succession of pulses by switching the primary current alternately *on* and *off* very rapidly. Alternatively, we can let an electric *buzzer* do it for us. In the experiment, replace the key switch with the buzzer. An electric bell with the gong removed will do. Such a bell usually needs 3 volts or 4.5 volts to operate it, so we will need two or three batteries in *series* to drive it (see figure 7.11).

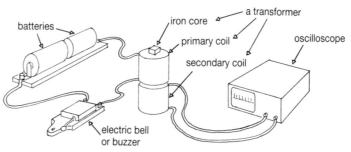

Figure 7.11 Apparatus to produce experimental faradic current

Switch on the circuit and display the *output* on the *oscilloscope* screen. The buzzer serves to *make* and *break* the input current in rapid succession, producing an *interrupted direct current*. The oscilloscope will show the output to be in effect a series of short, sharp electrical pulses. This is the *faradic current*, the output of a transformer working on d.c.

If you have a *twin-beam oscilloscope* you will be able to display the primary and secondary currents simultaneously. In theory, they should look as in figure 7.12.

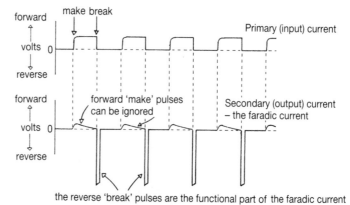

Figure 7.12 The experimental faradic current as shown on a twin-beam oscilloscope

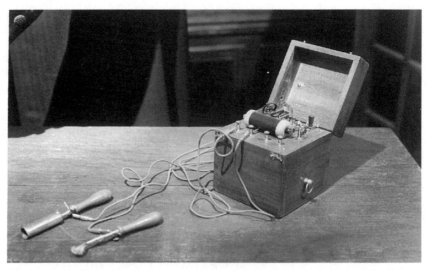

Figure 7.13 Early faradic unit or interrupted current unit (courtesy of The Science Museum)

The *first faradic machines* were literally just like this experiment. With a pair of electrodes the current was directed to the *motor-point* of the muscle to be treated, and it *remained contracted* for as long as the current flowed or until it became *fatigued*. The classic faradic current was a *continuous* current. One of these early machines is shown in figure 7.13.

The modified faradic current

With the experimental circuit still running, gently slide the *iron core* in and out of the coils. Note how when you slide the core out, the *intensity* of the pulses falls and when you slide it in, it increases again. Sliding it in and out causes the current to *surge* (see figure 7.14).

A *modified faradic machine* had a hole through its cabinet to enable the *iron core* to be slid in and out (see figure 7.15). Slide it in and the strong pulses

Changing over the leads to the oscilloscope will make it show the 'break' pulses above the zero line on the screen instead of below it

Figure 7.14 The modified faradic current as shown on an oscilloscope

Figure 7.15 An early modified faradic unit – the Bristow coil (courtesy of The Science Museum)

made the muscle contract; slide it out and the muscle could *relax*. To cause the muscle alternately to contract and relax, the operator had to slide the core in and out like a violin bow and probably at the same time hold an electrode over the motor-point of the muscle!

Present-day faradic machines

The faradic machine has come a very long way since then. Faradic units are now probably the most advanced and sophisticated pieces of electrotherapy equipment (see figure 7.16).

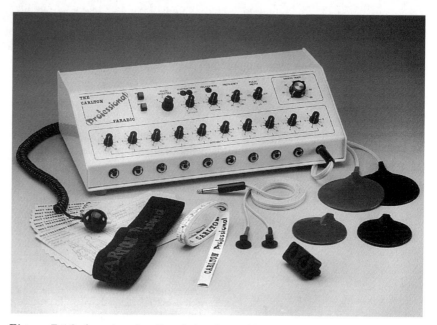

Figure 7.16 A modern faradic unit (courtesy of Taylor Reeson Laboratories Ltd)

In modern machines the surging is done *automatically* by an electronic timing device. In most machines, the current is not surged as such but is turned alternately *on* and *off*. During the 'on' period or *stimulation period*, the current flows and the muscle *contracts*. During the 'off' period or *interval*, the muscle *relaxes*. Connect the output of the machine to an oscilloscope and the stimulation periods and intervals will be displayed (see figure 7.17). Set the *timebase* control so the light spot tracks very slowly across the screen.

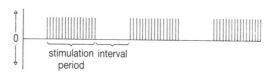

Figure 7.17 A modern faradic current as displayed on an oscilloscope

Figure 7.18 A silicon 'chip' microcircuit

In these modern machines, the '*make and break*' to create the pulses of the faradic current, and the '*stimulation period* and *interval*' timer are both likely to be sophisticated electronic devices based on the '*silicon chip*' (see figures 7.18, 7.19 and 7.20).

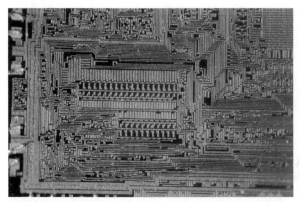

Figure 7.19 Microscope photograph of the electronic circuit on a 'chip' (courtesy of David Harris)

Figure 7.20 Chips in a faradic therapy unit

A basic faradic therapy unit

A basic faradic machine to operate from a mains electricity supply consists of the following main components (see also figure 7.21):

1 A *mains unit*–transformer, rectifier and capacitor to produce *smooth direct current*.
2 A stimulation period and interval *timer* to *surge* the current.
3 A *'make and break'* vibrator to produce an *interrupted direct current*.
4 A special *transformer* to generate the *faradic pulses*.
5 A *potentiometer* to control the intensity.

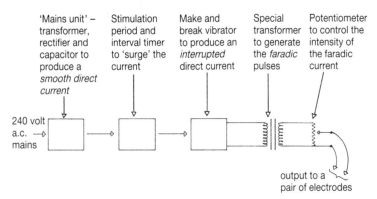

Figure 7.21 The main components of a faradic muscle stimulator

Some units are *battery* operated and would therefore not include the mains unit. Faradic units use very little electricity so battery-portable units are quite feasible. These will run for many hours on an easily obtainable transistor radio battery.

The electrodes

To complete the circuit through the client, the faradic current is applied through a *pair* of electrodes. The old-fashioned faradic units used a *'mushroom-stick'* electrode together with an indifferent electrode to complete the circuit.

82

The mushroom-stick electrode

The 'mushroom-stick' is a disc of tin, lead or zinc, covered with several layers of lint gauze and mounted on a wooden handle (see figure 7.22). It is held in contact with the skin over the *motor-point* of the muscle to be exercised. Mushroom-sticks are available in several sizes; smaller ones of 1 inch (2.5 cm) diameter are for use on the face; larger ones are for body treatments.

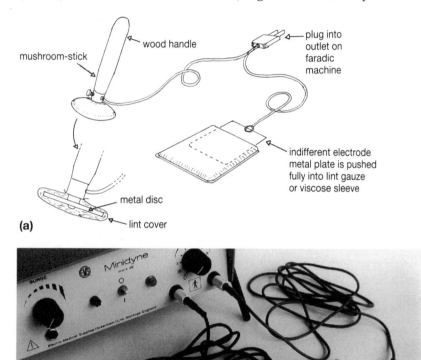

(a)

(b)

Figure 7.22 (a) Diagrams and (b) photograph of the mushroom-stick electrode and indifferent electrode

An indifferent electrode, consisting of a metal plate in a lint-gauze sleeve, is strapped conveniently to the body elsewhere to complete the circuit. To be conductive to electricity, the lint covers of both electrodes are soaked in *salt* water and wrung out just before use.

The manual method of applying faradic current using the mushroom is useful when learning faradic treatment in that it enables the student to locate just where the motor-points are. A modern alternative for facial work is the two-button facial electrode (see figure 7.23).

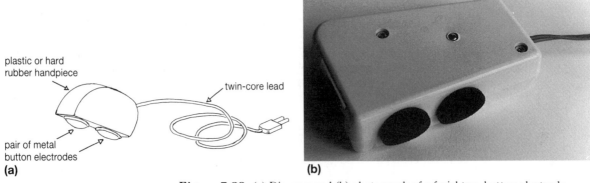

plastic or hard
rubber handpiece

twin-core lead

pair of metal
button electrodes

(a)

(b)

Figure 7.23 (a) Diagram and (b) photograph of a facial two-button electrode

Pad electrodes

The familiar image of a client receiving faradic treatment is of a 'spaghetti' of wires leading to *pad electrodes* strapped to the body as shown in figure 7.24.

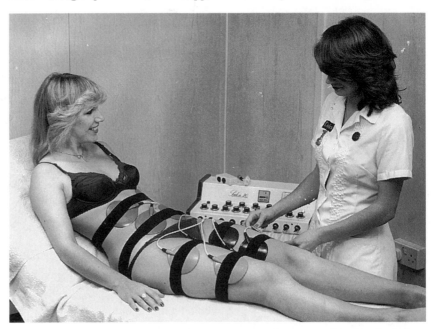

Figure 7.24 Client padded up for faradic treatment (courtesy of Depilex Ltd)

Figure 7.25 Carbon-impregnated plastic electrodes

Pad electrodes used to be made of discs of thick metal foil covered in lint-gauze. Later they were covered in thin plastic foam. The electrodes needed wetting with salt water to make them conductive. Each of the pair could be placed on a separate motor-point so two muscles might be exercised at the same time.

Salt is very damaging to the metal of the electrodes. However thoroughly they are washed and dried after use, they soon corrode and deteriorate to become unusable. Modern pads are made of a flexible *carbon-impregnated plastic* which is electrically conductive without the need for salt or water (see figure 7.25).

Padding-up the client

Most faradic machines are 'multi-outlet' machines which can operate several pairs of electrodes simultaneously. The electrodes *must* be used in their pairs to obtain complete circuits. There are, however, a number of methods of applying the pairs of pads:

In *duplicate motor padding*, the pair of electrodes is placed on the motor-points of two adjacent muscles. The current has only a short path through the body from one electrode to the other. Another pair of pads is usually applied to the corresponding muscles on the other side of the body (see figure 7.26).

In *split padding*, one pad is placed on the motor-point of a muscle and the other of the pair is placed on the equivalent muscle on the other side of the body. The current must pass through the full 'thickness' of the body from one pad to the other. This method is not recommended (see figure 7.27).

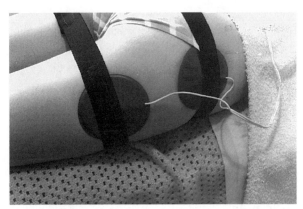

Figure 7.26 Duplicate motor padding

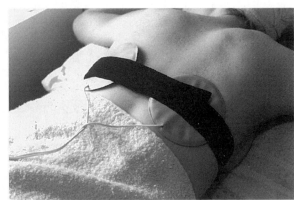

Figure 7.27 Split padding

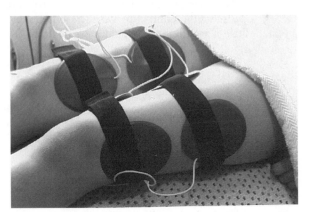

Figure 7.28 Longitudinal padding

Longitudinal padding is useful where the motor-point of a muscle is not easy to locate. One pad is placed near the origin and the other near the insertion of the *same* muscle. The current *has* to pass the motor-point. The padding is usually repeated on the other side of the body (see figure 7.28).

On the face where a number of motor-points are close together, normal padding-up is not possible. An electrode mask is available which has a number of electrodes set in it to treat the whole face at once (see figures 7.29 and 7.30).

The extra facilities on faradic units

Almost all faradic machines available offer a host of optional extras. There are few if any basic machines on the market. Most are *multi-outlet* machines capable of operating up to 12 pairs of electrodes simultaneously.

The outlet to each pair is completely independent of the others. It is *isolated* electrically by the special faradic transformer and its intensity can be controlled by its own potentiometer (see figure 7.29). To do this, the transformer has several separate secondary windings – one for the outlet to each pair of electrodes. These transformers are specially made for faradic units and as a result are quite expensive.

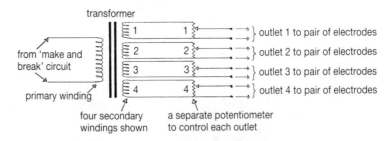

Figure 7.29 The special transformer of a multi-outlet faradic machine

To demonstrate some of the other features of faradic units, connect the output from one of the outlets to an *oscilloscope*. The effects of operating the various controls may then be displayed on the screen.

Duration of the faradic pulse

Normally, each of the short, sharp faradic pulses lasts about 0.3 of a millisecond (about 3/10000 of a second). A few machines have a *'duration'* or *'pulse width'* control to vary the time each pulse lasts. There is, however, little if anything to be gained by doing so (see figure 7.32).

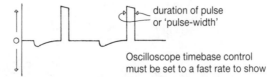

Figure 7.30 Duration or pulse-width of faradic pulses

Frequency of faradic pulses

Many machines have a *'frequency'* control labelled between, say, 40 and 120. Alternatively there may be a switch labelled *'smooth'* and *'vibro'*. Adjusting this control does have an effect which can be felt by the client. The numbers refer to the *frequency* of pulses per second. A pulse frequency of 40–60 pulses per second produces a *vibrating* contraction of the muscle. This is known as *incomplete tetany* of the muscle or the *'vibro'* effect. The muscle vibrates because it has time to *relax* a little after each pulse before the next contracts it again (see figure 7.31a)

Turning up the frequency to around 90 pulses per second produces a steady contraction, a *complete tetany* or the *'smooth'* effect. The muscle does not have time to relax between one pulse and the next (see figure 7.31b).

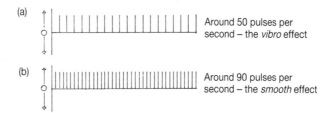

Figure 7.31 Smooth and vibro faradic frequencies as displayed on an oscilloscope

For some time physiotherapists have considered faradic not to be fully effective in their treatment of muscles. Recent research has shown the structure and the motor nerve control of a muscle to be much more complex than was thought. Within a muscle are fibres of *three* main types. (For muscle structure see chapter 16, page 188). The motor nerves which control each type of fibre communicate with different frequencies of pulses.

slow oxidative – non-fatiguing 'stamina' fibres – constitute up to 50 per cent of a muscle and are stimulated by frequencies of 6 to 15 pulses per second.

fast oxidative-glycolytic – the main 'strength' fibres with a tendency to fatigue also constitute up to 50 per cent of a muscle and are stimulated by frequencies of 20 to 45 pulses per second.

fast glycolytic – the 'explosive power' fibres for sprinting, jumping and throwing are very quickly fatigued and are stimulated by frequencies of 50 to 70 pulses per second.

Obviously, this means that machines offering a range of 40 to 120 pulses per second cannot fully stimulate all the fibres of a muscle. Some of the new generation of faradic machines have extended the low frequency range to as little as *one* pulse per second. This, plus the computer technology of easily available microprocessor 'chips', means they can deliver programmes of different pulse frequencies to work *all* the fibres of a muscle.

At the maximum 120 pulses per second, the stimulation of muscles is much less effective. The motor nerves cannot transmit pulses much faster than this. However, because higher frequencies pass through the skin more easily and with less discomfort, some manufacturers are producing electronic muscle stimulation machines employing much higher frequencies of 400, 600 and even 800 pulses per second. At these frequencies they have found that the faradic type pulses have no effect. Instead they employ a *square wave alternating current* which has been shown by experiment to be effective (see figure 7.32).

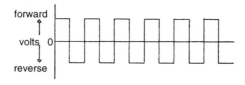

Figure 7.32 Square wave alternating current

Timing the surges and intervals

Most machines have controls to adjust the length of the *stimulation period* and *interval*. Typically, each is adjustable between 0.5 seconds and 2 seconds.

Adjust the timebase control of the oscilloscope to show the stimulation periods and intervals as in figure 7.33. Then adjust the stimulation period and interval controls and see what effect they have.

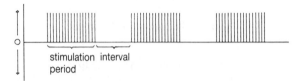

Figure 7.33 Stimulation periods and intervals as shown on an oscilloscope

In use, the stimulation period control is set just long enough to give a good contraction, and the interval control to allow the muscle to just fully relax; any longer is really wasting treatment time.

On most multi-outlet machines all the muscles are made to contract and relax in unison. Some machines are now available which offer 'split' stimulation. Whilst half the outlets are on 'contract' the other half are on 'relax', then vice-versa. This makes it possible to 'pad-up' pairs of antagonistic muscles in a way that causes the flexor and extensor (see page 189) to contract *alternately* and so can produce *active* exercise of the muscles *and joints*.

Programme or mode control

Some clients are consciously or unconsciously apprehensive and tend to fight against the contractions, thus preventing its full effect. The 'programme' or 'mode' control switches in a 'random' pattern of varied lengths of *intervals*, making it difficult for such clients to anticipate when the next contraction is coming.

The surge envelope

The succession of pulses which makes up one surge or stimulation period is known as a *surge envelope*. The nature of the contraction can be varied according to the strength of the individual pulses making up the surge.

A straightforward on and off surging with all pulses of the same strength tends to produce a rather uncomfortable *snatch* contraction. This is because the first few pulses of each surge pass more easily through the skin before its *resistance* builds up, and are thus more effective at causing a contraction.

In most machines, therefore, the first few pulses of each surge are of a lower intensity gradually building up to full strength. Your machine may show this on the oscilloscope (see figure 7.34).

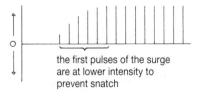

the first pulses of the surge
are at lower intensity to
prevent snatch

Figure 7.34 The start of a faradic surge

Some machines may produce a surge of gradually increasing pulses, causing the muscle to contract harder and harder – then suddenly let go as the surge ends (see figure 7.35).

Others truly surge, the pulses gradually increasing in strength then subsiding gently, contracting and relaxing the muscle, just as the old-fashioned modified faradic did by sliding the iron core in and out (see figure 7.36).

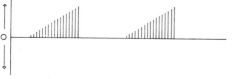

Figure 7.35 The triangular surge envelope as shown on an oscilloscope

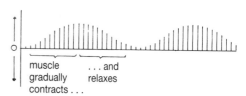

Figure 7.36 A truly surged faradic current

The polarity control

As already stated several times, the major obstacle to the passage of an electric current through the body is the *resistance* of the skin. It is this resistance which produces the *sensation* in the skin as the current flows through it. For some clients the sensation in the skin is unpleasant, even unbearable, when sufficient current is flowing to give satisfactory contractions.

Many faradic units have a *polarity* control labelled 'single' and 'dual' or 'monophasic' and 'biphasic'. In 'single' or 'monophasic' position the normal faradic current flows (see figure 7.37a). Switch to 'dual' or 'biphasic' and the direction of each alternate pulse is *reversed* (see figure 7.37b).

Normal faradic pulses flow all in one direction. The movement of *ions*, which *is* the current, is therefore all in one direction. The *first* pulse of a surge moves the ions easily, the next finds it a bit harder, and so on as the resistance builds up. Switched to 'dual' or 'biphasic', each alternate pulse is *reversed* and the ions just vibrate easily back and forth. The resistance is less and so the sensation is *reduced*.

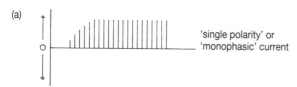

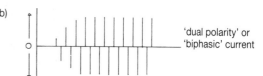

Figure 7.37 Single and dual polarity faradic currents

The physical and physiological effects of faradic treatment

Very simply, the purpose of faradic and similar therapies is to cause muscles alternately to *contract* and *relax* – to *exercise* them with *no* physical effort on the part of the client. Hence the exercise is often called *passive* exercise. Because no movement of the joints and limbs occurs, it is *isometric* exercise.

Its purpose is *figure-control* by improving the *tone* of muscles. The lifestyle of most people makes little use of many of the muscles of the body, particularly those of the upper arms and shoulders, the abdomen and the buttocks and thighs. The underutilised muscles gradually stretch and when relaxed hang slack, resulting in a deterioration of the figure and adding extra centimetres to the measurements. This together with a lack of responsiveness due to a reduced rate of metabolism within the muscles is *lack of tone*. An exercised muscle will remain under a certain amount of tension even when relaxed and is said to have improved *muscle tone*.

By toning up the slack muscles in this way it is possible to reduce the measurements of the waist, the hips, the thighs and the upper arms and generally firm and trim the figure.

Similarly, by toning up the muscles of the face and neck the facial features may be improved. Many clients find it difficult to exercise their facial muscles for themselves.

Because any reduction in measurements is solely the result of improved muscle tone and does *not* involve any loss of *weight*, it is illegal to call faradic therapy a *slimming* treatment.

The effect of deliberately exercising a muscle whether by voluntary contraction or by faradism is to improve its metabolism and its responsiveness. This creates a demand for extra oxygen and energy foods and an increased output of waste materials which causes the dilation of the capillaries within the muscle and increases the blood supply to it. The alternate contraction and relaxation of the muscle increases the movement of waste from it through the pumping action on the veins and lymphatic vessels.

Using certain modern machines with microprocessors, the venous and lymphatic drainage of a leg may be further enhanced by special padding techniques and *sequential contraction* of the muscles from foot to thigh (see figure 7.38).

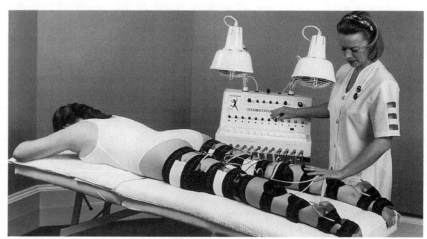

Figure 7.38 Client receiving lymphatic drainage treatment by sequential contraction from an electronic muscle stimulator. (courtesy – Carlton Professional)

Faradic in combination with other treatments

Often faradic therapy is used as part of a programme of treatments for the client. Maybe more than one type of electrotherapy will be included in the programme. For instance, *through-body galvanism* might be used as a preliminary to *faradic* therapy. By stimulating the metabolism, galvanism improves the response to the faradic current. Machines are available which feed both galvanic and faradic currents to the same pair or a separate pair of electrodes. After a period of galvanism, the faradic is switched on and will continue after the galvanism is switched off.

Timing the treatment

The duration of a faradic treatment is not really critical. For the padding-up method, the treatment could last 20 minutes or so. The manual method using the mushroom-stick should produce at least 12 contractions in each muscle treated to be of any real value.

Contra-indications and precautions

The contra-indications to faradic treatment are those to treatment in general. One additional precaution is to avoid using the treatment close to the *heart*. The current could act rather like a pacemaker and affect the heartbeat.

Care should be taken when padding-up the client and starting the treatment. Always make sure all the intensity controls are set to zero before switching on the machine. Then turn up each control until the client feels a tingle under its pair of pads. Then turn each up further until a good contraction is obtained with each pair. Some of the latest machines will not turn on until all the intensity controls have been set to zero.

Things to do

1 Collect manufacturers' information literature on the many different makes and models of electronic muscle stimulation machines.

2 Learn how to use as many different makes of E.M.S. equipment as possible. There are many 'extra' features on equipment with which you should become familiar.

Self-assessment questions

1 Distinguish between a variable resistance and a potentiometer as intensity controllers.

2 Draw a sinusoidal current as it would be displayed on an oscilloscope.

3 Describe briefly how a faradic current brings about the contraction of a chosen muscle.

4 What is meant by electromagnetic induction?

5 Draw a diagram to show how a single faradic pulse might be displayed on an oscilloscope.

6 What is a modified faradic current?

7 What is the 'vibro' effect in faradic therapy? What frequency setting on the machine brings about the vibro effect?

8 What is the advantage of 'dual polarity' or 'biphasic' faradic current?

9 What is the advantage of the first few pulses or a faradic surge being of lower intensity?

10 What is the purpose of the 'programme' of random intervals between surges available on some machines?

11 Name the three types of fibres within a muscle. State the most effective pulse frequency for stimulating each type of fibre.

8 Interferential Therapy

Introducing interferential therapy; resistance and impedance; skin impedance; the principle of interferential therapy; physical and physiological effects; the electrodes; interferential currents; a demonstration of interference

Introducing interferential therapy

Despite all its modifications and extra features, the *faradic* type of muscle stimulator still causes some skin sensation beneath the electrodes, and in a number of clients this is sufficient to be unpleasantly uncomfortable.

Interferential therapy is an alternative form of muscle stimulation which creates virtually *no* sensation in the skin. The reason is that it employs electric currents to which the skin offers virtually negligible resistance. Figure 8.1 shows interferential therapy in progress on a client.

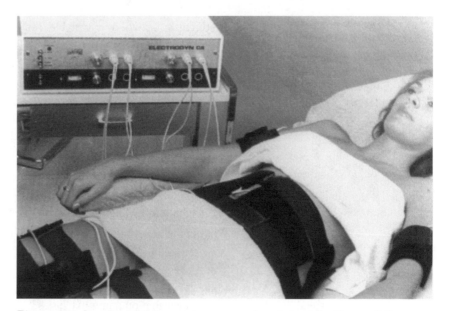

Figure 8.1 Interferential therapy in progress (courtesy of the George Solly Organisation)

Resistance and impedance

Strictly speaking, the term *resistance* should be used *only* with reference to a smoothly flowing *direct current*. The value of *resistance* of a substance to the passage of direct current through it is relatively constant.

However the resistance to *alternating current* can differ widely from that to direct current. Usually it is *very* much less. This 'resistance' to alternating current is called *impedance*. The value of *impedance* depends not only on the substance but also on the *frequency* of the alternating current.

Impedance reduces as the *frequency* is *increased*

To confuse matters, impedance is also measured in the same units as resistance, *ohms*.

The resistance and impedance of skin

How much the skin resists the passage of electricity through it depends on a number of factors:

1 *The moisture content.* The more moist the skin, the better it conducts electricity.
2 *Its greasiness.* Grease on the skin serves as an insulator and so increases its resistance.
3 *The area of electrode* in contact with the skin. The larger the area, the less the resistance.

If we consider an electrode in contact with 1 cm^2 of skin, to a smooth *direct current*, the *resistance* is about 100 000 ohms. To an *alternating current* at 'mains' frequency of 50 hertz, the *impedance* is a mere 3000 ohms. While for an alternating current of 4000 hertz it has fallen to an almost negligible 40 ohms (see table 8.1).

Table 8.1   The resistance and impedance of 1 cm^2 of skin

Direct current	– smooth	– Resistance	100 000 Ω
Alternating current	– 50 hertz	– Impedance	3000 Ω
Alternating current	– 4000 hertz	– Impedance	40 Ω

Explanation of skin resistance and impedance

As has been explained previously, an electric current flows through the body as the *movement of ions*. It can flow easily *only* if the ions can migrate *freely*.

However, in the body this migration will most likely involve the ions passing from cell to cell through the cell membranes, and this is difficult. In the *Stratum corneum* of the epidermis there are the added difficulties of a low water content and a substantial fatty content. The *resistance* of skin to *direct current* is therefore *high*.

When a current first starts to flow, the ions will not encounter such barriers as cell membranes immediately, so initially the resistance is quite low but soon rises to its high level.

The *impedance* to *alternating current* is less because the ions are made to vibrate back and forth and *not* flow continuously in the same direction. They do not have to pass through cell membranes.

The higher the frequency the less will be the physical movement of the ions in each direction, and so the lower the impedance. At very high frequencies, it will be only the *electrons* in the ions which will vibrate and not the ions themselves. The impedance is even lower.

The principle of interferential therapy

Having established that higher-frequency alternating currents can pass through the skin with very little impedance and so create very little sensation, there is a major obstacle to their use for muscle stimulation. Only frequencies up to a little over 100 hertz can be accepted by the motor nerves to bring about the contraction of muscles.

The solution is to employ *two* of these higher-frequency currents. They are actually called *medium frequencies* to distinguish them from the real high frequencies used in high-frequency therapy.

The *interferential therapy unit* produces *two* medium-frequency currents. Each is fed through the treatment area on the client by a separate circuit:

Circuit I – carries an alternating current at a *fixed* frequency of, say, 4000 hertz

Circuit II – carries a second alternating current at a frequency which can be *varied*, either manually by a control or automatically, from 4000 hertz down to 3900 hertz. The difference of up to 100 Hz is the important factor

Each outlet on the machine feeds the two currents to a group of *four* electrodes set at the corners of an imaginary square. The two frequencies are fed to the electrodes as shown in figure 8.2.

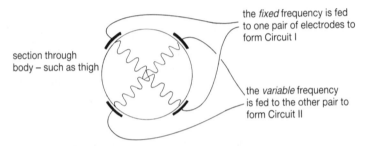

Figure 8.2 Applying interferential currents to the body

Where the two currents cross a *third* frequency is generated. Its value is equal to the *difference* between the other two frequencies. This third frequency is known as the *beat frequency*. It is produced by the two original frequencies *interfering* with each other – hence *interferential therapy*.

If the two original frequencies are different, there are times when they *reinforce* each other and times when they *cancel* each other out. This is shown in figure 8.3.

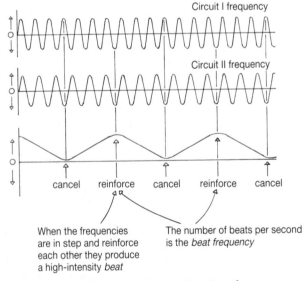

Figure 8.3 Producing an interferential or beat frequency

The *beat frequency* is equal to the *difference* between the two original frequencies. For instance, if *circuit I* is fixed at 4000 hertz and *circuit II* is adjusted to, say, 3990 hertz, the beat frequency will be 10 hertz. That is, 4000 minus 3990.

So, by passing two medium-frequency currents through the body, the *low-frequency* necessary to bring about muscle contraction can be generated *in the tissues*. It does not have to penetrate the skin, so it causes no painful skin sensation.

Physiological effects of interferential therapy

The interferential therapy machine can perform a number of tasks, depending on the mode in which it is set.

A constant 100 hertz beat frequency will produce a soothing, analgesic effect useful for alleviating pain.

A variable beat frequency cycling every few seconds between 0 and 10 hertz will produce *motor stimulation* of a group of muscles.

A variable beat frequency cycling between 0 and 100 hertz will also generally improve the tone of the tissues in the area, increasing blood and lymph flow and the rate of metabolism.

Motor stimulation

The motor stimulation produced in interferential therapy differs from faradic stimulation and may feel not unpleasantly strange, particularly to those who have undergone faradic therapy. The current is not 'surged', so there are no definite contractions and relaxation intervals. Instead the muscles in the area contract and *vibrate* gently *in turn* as the beat frequency 'drifts' between 0 and 10 hertz. To see why, we must consider how impulses from the *brain* travel along motor nerves.

A motor nerve is a bundle of nerve fibres each supplying a particular muscle, and these fibres are not well insulated from each other. Each fibre carries its signal from the brain as a series of pulses. So they do not get mixed up and cause the wrong muscles to contract; they are each 'tuned' to carry pulses at a *different* frequency.

The best frequency is generated within the motor nerves in the area of treatment. As the varying beat frequency *coincides* with the 'tuned' frequency of a particular nerve fibre, it will accept the signal, take it to the muscle and that muscle will contract. As the beat frequency changes it will no longer be accepted by *that* fibre and the muscle relaxes, but it may be accepted by another nerve and its muscle contracts instead.

The electrodes

As already stated, because two separate electric currents are being passed through the treatment area simultaneously, the electrodes must be in *groups of four*. Different sized electrodes are available, but they are always connected in their fours to a multipin socket on the machine.

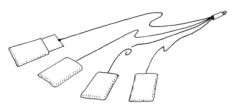

Figure 8.4 Electrodes for interferential therapy on larger areas of the body

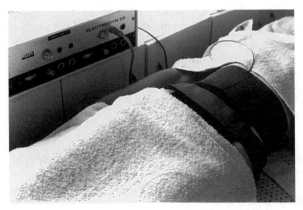
Figure 8.5 Interferential electrodes on the abdomen

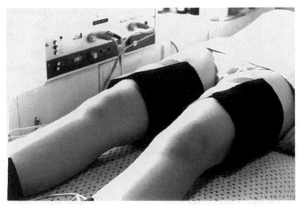
Figure 8.6 Interferential electrodes on the thighs

For larger areas, such as the abdomen and thighs, rectangular carbon plastic electrodes or metal plate electrodes in *viscose covers* are used (see figure 8.4, 8.5 and 8.6).

For smaller areas, such as the shoulders, the four electrodes are incorporated in a single viscose pad. For the face, a 'pen' electrode is available with the four metal 'buttons' at its tip (see figure 8.7, 8.8 and 8.9).

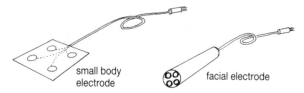

small body electrode

facial electrode

Figure 8.7 Electrodes for smaller areas of the body and the face

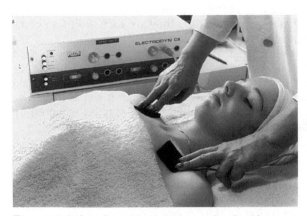
Figure 8.8 Interferential electrodes on the shoulder area

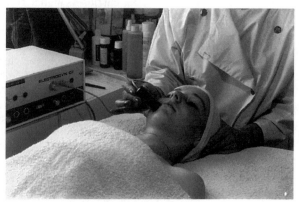
Figure 8.9 Interferential therapy on the face

A demonstration of interference

The principle of the production of a beat frequency is quite difficult to comprehend. However, it can quite easily be demonstrated if suitable apparatus is available.

If an interferential therapy unit is available, it can be connected through an *oscilloscope*. Both circuits of the unit should be fed to the same input terminals of the 'scope as shown in figure 8.10.

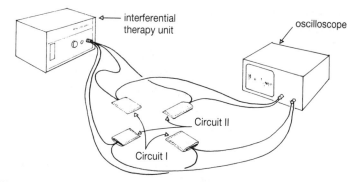

Figure 8.10 How to display interferential currents on an oscilloscope

On the screen, the combined outputs of the two circuits as they interfere with each other should show as in figure 8.11. Some adjustment of the oscilloscope controls will be necessary to achieve this result.

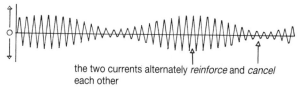

the two currents alternately *reinforce* and *cancel* each other

Figure 8.11 Interferential current as shown on an oscilloscope screen

An alternative demonstration of interference and beat frequency may be done using two *audio-signal generators* connected to the *same* input of the oscilloscope. By connecting each generator to a *loudspeaker,* a very audible and rather painful-to-the-ear demonstration is possible (see figure 8.12).

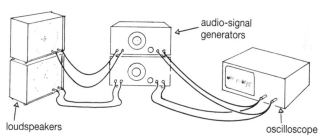

audio-signal generators

loudspeakers

oscilloscope

Figure 8.12 A laboratory demonstration of interferential currents and beat frequencies

Switch on one signal generator. Set it to *sine-wave* at a frequency of 4000 hertz. You will hear a high whistle from the loudspeaker. Adjust the oscilloscope to show close packed sine-waves across the screen.

Turn down the first generator and switch on the second, and set it to produce the same 4000 hertz whistle. Now turn up the first one again. If the generators are not quite set identically, the sound will now alternately boom out loudly and die away, and the sine-waves on the screen will alternately increase and decrease in height.

Now gently adjust one of the generators slowly up or down from 4000 hertz. Note how the increases and decreases in sound, the *beats*, become more frequent eventually becoming a 'twitter' or warble. This is the beat frequency.

1   What is the main advantage of interferential therapy over faradic therapy?

2   What is meant by impedance?

3   How does the impedance of skin vary with the frequency of an alternating current passing through it?

4   How does interferential therapy differ from faradic therapy in the way it contracts the muscles?

5   What is the distinctive feature about the electrodes in interferential therapy?

6   What is the frequency of the alternating currents used in interferential therapy?

7   What is an interferential current?

9 High Frequency

What is high frequency?; high frequency in therapy; production of high frequency; more about capacitors; inductances; high-frequency therapy unit; high-frequency electrodes; intensifier electrodes; direct and indirect high frequency; physiological effects; precautions and contra-indications

What is high frequency?

High frequency is a beauty treatment which both therapists and clients either love or hate, because without reasonable care it is quite easy to give both yourself and the client rather frightening but quite harmless electric shocks.

So why use it? Depending on how it is used it can be warming and soothing, or stimulating, or astringent, or mildly antiseptic.

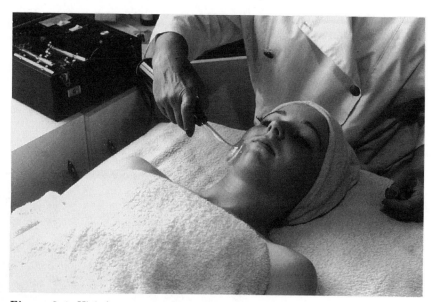

Figure 9.1 High-frequency treatment

A high-frequency current is basically a *very* rapidly alternating current.

An alternating current alternating relatively few times each second is a *low-frequency* current – for instance the 'mains' which alternates with a frequency of 50 hertz.

Alternating current alternating at a few thousand hertz is *medium frequency*. The 4000 hertz currents used in interferential therapy are an example.

An alternating current alternating at 100 000 or more hertz (even millions of hertz) is *high frequency*. At these frequencies the current has some unusual properties which are utilised in the therapeutic treatments.

Properties of high frequency

High frequency passes through the body very easily; remember high frequency means *low impedance*. This also means that it passes easily through all kinds of other substances which are normally electrical insulators, and at high voltages the current is *very* difficult to contain. Hence the ease with which it can stray and give those little electric shocks.

The tissues of the body have a high *water* content. Concentrated through the area being treated the *energy* of the high-frequency current is absorbed by the *water molecules*, 'exciting' or vibrating them and making them *warm*. High frequency *warms* the tissues.

A most unusual but very useful effect of a high-frequency current is that it will pass along a conductor such as a wire or a metal rod right to its end. Then its energy passes clean off the end of the conductor to be *transmitted* as *radio waves*. All radio, television and radar broadcasting depends on this effect. The frequencies used in therapy equipment must be such that they do not cause undue interference to radio and TV reception!

Placed close to, but *not* touching, another conductor such as a piece of metal or the body, the high frequency will jump the gap as a *spark*. It is this sparking which produces the stimulating and antiseptic effects in therapy. It is also the sparks which, if unexpected, cause those minor electric shocks!

High frequency in therapy

Two basic types of high-frequency currents are used for therapeutic purposes.

One is a lower-frequency high frequency at *high voltage* – not really a contradiction! This is the current produced by the beauty therapist's high-frequency machine, and by the physiotherapist's *diathermy* equipment. The frequency is in the region of 100 000–250 000 hertz, and if it is transmitted from the electrodes it is radiated as *longwave band* radio waves.

The other is a higher-frequency, lower-voltage current used for *epilation*, the permanent removal of unwanted hair. Its frequency is typically 27 120 000

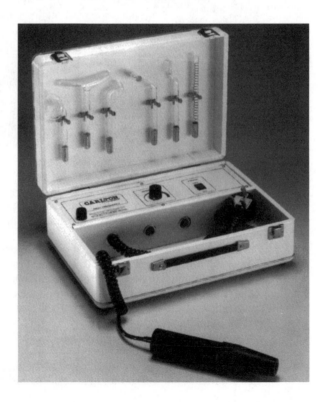

Figure 9.2 Beauty therapist's high-frequency unit (courtesy Taylor Reeson Laboratories Ltd)

Figure 9.3 Physiotherapist's diathermy unit

Figure 9.4 Shortwave epilation unit (courtesy of Depilex Ltd)

hertz (or 27.12 megahertz). This, if transmitted from the epilation needle, is radiated as *shortwave band* radio waves. This hair removal method is called *'shortwave epilation'*.

Producing a high-frequency current

The major electronic components involved in the production of high-frequency currents are the *capacitor* and the *inductance*.

The *capacitor* we have already encountered briefly in chapter 6 in its role of *smoothing* a direct current. We will now look at it in more detail. The inductance will then be considered.

The capacitor

A capacitor is in many respects an electrical version of a spring. In its *smoothing* role, it smooths the 'bumps' in an electric current just like a car's springs smooth the ride over the bumps in the road.

A bow is a spring which stores *energy* as one pulls back the string, to be released suddenly to fire the arrow. A camera flashgun has a capacitor which is charged with electricity to fire the flash when you take the photograph.

Wind up your alarm clock and you give it energy to drive it for the next 30 hours or so. A capacitor can release its charge over a long period too.

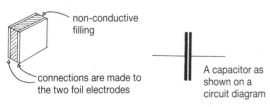

non-conductive filling

connections are made to the two foil electrodes

A capacitor as shown on a circuit diagram

Figure 9.5 The construction of a capacitor

Figure 9.6 Capacitors come in a wide variety of shapes and sizes

Hang a load from a spring. Pull it down and let go. The load will bounce up and down, gradually coming to a halt. Connect a suitable electrical 'load' in the form of an *inductance* to a capacitor. Give it a pulse of electricity and it will produce a current which 'bounces' back and forth in the circuit, gradually coming to 'rest'. It produces an *alternating* current.

A capacitor is constructed rather like a sandwich. The 'bread' is a pair of metal foil electrodes. The 'filling' is a layer of a non-conductor such as paper, a mineral called mica, or a plastic (see figure 9.5).

Larger capacitors are rolled up like a swiss roll and so are cylindrical. The capacity of a capacitor is measured in *farads* or more commonly *microfarads* named after Michael Faraday, the famous scientist. One microfarad is one-millionth of a farad.

Finding out about capacitors

The best way to find out about capacitors is to try some experiments with them. Often in science laboratories they have some really big capacitors for experimental and demonstration purposes. *Beware*, a fully charged capacitor of this size can hold quite a 'handful' of electricity and can give a very sharp shock if you touch the two connections.

To show charging and discharging the capacitor

Connect a voltmeter and, if you wish, an oscilloscope to the capacitor as shown in figure 9.7. Set the oscilloscope so the 'spot' tracks slowly across the centre of the screen in about 2 seconds. To the battery connect a pair of leads each ending in an insulated probe. Have on hand another lead with a probe on each end.

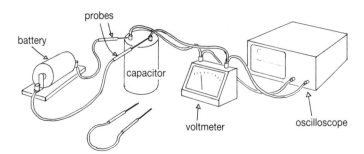

Figure 9.7 To show the charging and discharging of a capacitor

Touch the battery leads on the capacitor terminals. This will charge the capacitor. The voltmeter will show battery voltage and the oscilloscope light-spot will move up the screen. They will also show that the capacitor *retains* this charge. Make sure that the battery connections are the right way round for the voltmeter, or its pointer will try to move the wrong way!

Now take the other lead and touch its probes on the capacitor terminals. This will *discharge* it, and the voltmeter and oscilloscope will show this.

You can discharge the capacitor more slowly by connecting a suitable *resistor* to its terminals. A low-value resistor of a few tens of ohms should do, such as one of those slide rheostats often found in laboratories. This time the voltmeter pointer will return slowly to zero and the oscilloscope will show a trace like that in figure 9.8.

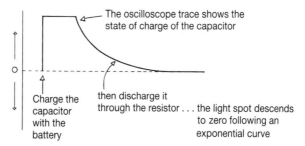

Figure 9.8 The charging and discharge of a capacitor as shown on an oscilloscope

The inductance

Now is the time to introduce the *inductance*, sometimes known as a *choke*. This is a bit like 'half-a-transformer', an iron core with just a single coil of wire wound round it. The size or value of an inductance is measured in units called *henries* named after the eighteenth century American scientist, Joseph Henry.

In the next experiment we are going to charge the capacitor then discharge it through an *inductance*. To obtain the required effect, the value of the inductance must be matched to the value of the capacitor. Laboratory suppliers usually offer a suitable inductance to match their demonstration capacitor. Set up the experiment as shown in figure 9.9.

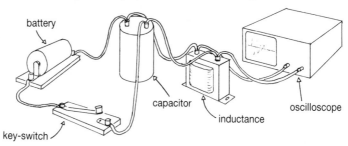

Figure 9.9 Demonstration of the discharge of a capacitor through an inductance

Press down the key-switch to *charge* the capacitor. Then watch the oscilloscope screen as you release the key to let the capacitor *discharge* through the inductance. You should see a trace like that in figure 9.10.

Notice how the capacitor literally 'bounces' the current back and forth round the circuit until it gradually fades away. It is a diminishing or '*damped*' *alternating current*.

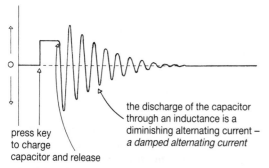

Figure 9.10 Oscilloscope trace of the discharge of a capacitor through an inductance

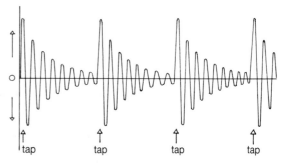

Figure 9.11 Repeated pulses recharge the capacitor to sustain the alternating current

If you keep tapping the key to '*make and break*' the battery supply, it will repeatedly recharge the capacitor so it produces a more sustained alternating current output as shown in Figure 9.11.

The high-frequency treatment unit

Figure 9.12 'Black-box' high-frequency unit

Now let us relate this to the high-frequency machine. The *frequency* of the damped alternating current depends on the values of the capacitor and inductance. If *small* values are chosen, a *high-frequency* alternating current will be produced. The frequency produced by the high-frequency machine is between 100 000 and 250 000 hertz.

If some kind of *transformer* is used instead of the inductance, the output voltage can be stepped to a *high* value. The output of a high-frequency machine is at several hundred thousand volts. Do not worry, the current flow is too small to be dangerous!

This 'special transformer' in the high-frequency machine is an *induction coil* called an *Oudin coil*. The high-voltage, high-frequency current is not easy to confine with the insulation of a wire, so the Oudin coil is inside the handpiece which holds the electrode. This is why the electrode holder is so fat!

The cabinet of the machine contains the capacitor and the '*make and break*' vibrator to recharge it repeatedly. In the old original 'black-box' high frequency, the vibrator was a mechanical device worked by an electromagnet, like the works of an electric bell. This is what makes the buzzing noise when the machine is working. In modern machines an *electronic* 'make and break' is used instead.

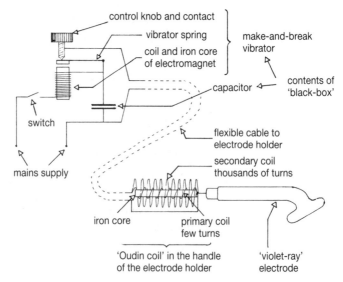

Figure 9.13 The circuit of a 'black-box' high-frequency unit

The high-frequency current

The high-frequency output from these machines is therefore an *alternating current* at *high frequency* (100 000–250 000 hertz), very high voltage (100 000s volts) but quite low power, so the actual current flow is very small.

This current is sometimes called a *Tesla* current after the almost forgotten pioneer of alternating current and high frequency, *Nikola Tesla*. He was an

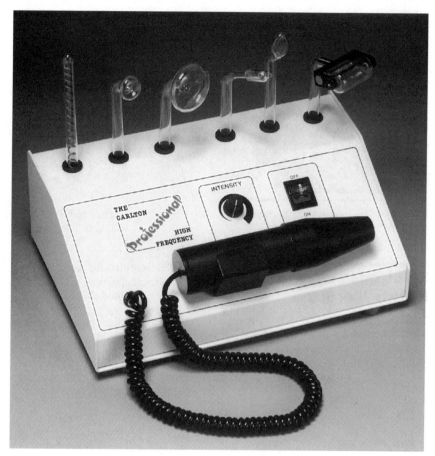

Figure 9.14 A modern high-frequency unit (courtesy of Taylor Reeson Laboratories Ltd)

East European immigrant to the USA who eventually persuaded the US power companies that they should generate *alternating* current so they could use transformers to transmit it at high voltage over long distances. His contributions to our electrical knowledge though were rather 'swamped' by the '*invention factories*' of Thomas Alva Edison and Alexander Graham Bell.

Applying high frequency to the client

The beauty therapist's high-frequency unit transmits the high-frequency energy to the client via a *single* electrode. Rather unusually for an electric current, it does *not* need two connections to complete a circuit. The high-frequency energy is 'earthed' or dispersed into the client's body. The effects of the current are concentrated around the point of contact of the electrode and so they can be only *superficial*. The rather special electrodes required are described below.

Physiotherapists often require a much *deeper* warming effect from their high-frequency '*diathermy*' machines. They often have *two* electrodes which are on 'angle-poise' arms. These are positioned either side of the treatment area and the high-frequency energy is 'beamed' as *radio waves* through the body between them. Alternatively, there may be a very flexible 'rope' cable electrode which is loosely wound round the treatment area.

Figure 9.15 A diathermy machine with angle-poise electrodes

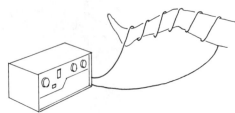

Figure 9.16 Diathermy machine with rope electrode wound on a leg

Electrodes used in beauty therapy

A variety of *glass* electrodes is used for beauty therapy high-frequency treatments. For most purposes a metal electrode would rather painfully shower the client with *sparks*!

The glass electrodes are glass 'envelopes' shaped to suit each treatment. Inside is almost a *vacuum*. The high frequency is introduced through the metal cap which is a *push fit* into the electrode holder. Modern ones are square-ended so they cannot turn in the holder during use. A selection is shown in figure 9.17.

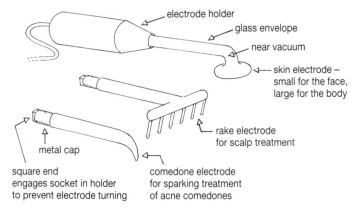

Figure 9.17 Glass high-frequency electrodes

The high-frequency energy causes *ionisation* of some of the atoms of the small amount of air inside the electrode. In the ionisation, electrons are 'knocked off' the atoms turning them into charged *ions*. The current then flows easily through the tube to its point of contact with the skin, by causing these ions to vibrate. The ions, however, soon regain their electrons and give out energy in the form of *light* and *ultra-violet* rays. Electrodes containing *air* produce a *violet* glow. They are called MacIntyre *violet-ray tubes*.

Some electrodes contain a little *mercury vapour* and glow *blue* instead. Some contain *neon* and glow *orange*! Being made of glass, the ultra-violet produced cannot escape. But beware, there are tubes made of *quartz* and these do let out quite high doses of ultra-violet rays. These are indistinguishable from glass electrodes but are *not* available from beauty therapy suppliers and should not be used for beauty treatments.

Intensifier electrode

To improve its efficiency in transferring the high-frequency energy to the skin, an *intensifier electrode* has an internal wire connecting the contact cap to a metal disc just inside the glass where the electrode contacts the skin. This means more of the energy finds its way to the skin (see figure 9.18).

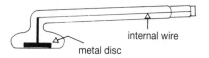

Figure 9.18 An intensifier electrode

Saturator electrode

In the *indirect* method of applying high frequency, the client is *charged* with high-frequency energy by holding a *saturator* electrode while the therapist massages the treatment area by hand. Several types of saturator are available. The simplest is a length of *metal tube* which fits into the electrode holder. This can give uncomfortable handfuls of sparks if not held firmly! A cylindrical glass electrode is far more comfortable to use. It may be of the *intensifier* type with an internal metal coil (see figure 9.19).

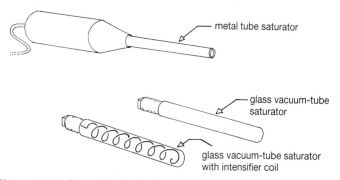

Figure 9.19 Saturator electrodes

Direct and indirect application of high frequency

High-frequency treatment may be used on the client in *two* ways – the *direct method* of application and the *indirect method*.

In the *direct method*, the therapist holds the electrode in contact with the treatment area and gently moves it over the skin. The electrode *discharges* its high-frequency energy into the skin at the point of contact. Apart from the *warming effect*, there will be the *stimulating effects* of the *sparking* which occurs between the electrode and the skin. The overall effect of *direct high frequency* is of a *stimulating warmth* (see figure 9.20).

In the *indirect method*, the client is given the *saturator* electrode to hold. To prevent unnecessary strain on the electrode, the client should grasp the electrode holder with one hand and the electrode with the other. The client then becomes *charged* with high-frequency energy. The therapist then massages gently the client's skin and the high frequency *discharges* from the client to the therapist's fingers at the point of contact, concentrating its energy – its *warmth* – in this area. There is little sparking so little *stimulation*.

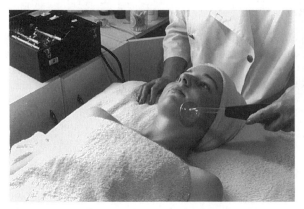

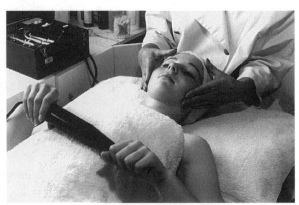

Figure 9.20 Direct high-frequency treatment   **Figure 9.21** Indirect high-frequency treatment

In brief:

> *Direct high frequency* is *warming* and *stimulating*
> *Indirect high frequency* is *warming* and *soothing*

Physiological effects of high frequency

The physiological reactions of the body to high-frequency treatment are the responses to the *warming* and, in the case of direct application, the responses to the *sparking*. In a sense, the two sets of responses are in *conflict*.

Physiological effects of the warming

Warming decreases nervous responses. It is *soothing*. Warming causes dilation of blood vessels, increasing fluid flow through the area, in effect to disperse the heat. This in turn will lead to increased metabolism and an increased rate of healing in damaged tissues. In 'fat depot' areas of the body such as the bust, it might encourage fat deposition; however, those using the treatment to 'add inches' in this area are often sadly disappointed with the results, or lack of them!

Warming does, however, increase perspiration and sebum secretion which contribute to the deep cleansing of the area and might be beneficial to a dry skin.

Physical and physiological effects of sparking

Now to consider the conflicting effects brought about by the *sparking* which accompanies the *direct method*. These effects are twofold – the first is due to the *stimulation* and the second is due to the *antiseptic* effect.

A tingling sensation is felt as the sparks trigger the nerve endings in the skin. This *stimulates* skin sensations. It also has an *astringent* effect, tightening the skin and closing the pores to reduce *sebum* output. Direct high frequency is drying to a greasy skin.

The *antiseptic action* of sparking is threefold, so in theory should be most effective. The sparks themselves might burn and kill bacteria on the skin. Sparks produce ultra-violet rays which kill bacteria. Sparks ionise oxygen of the air forming *ozone* which also kills bacteria.

Oxygen [O_2] becomes Ozone [O_3]

Ozone is unstable and soon breaks down:

Ozone [O₃] → Oxygen [O₂] and *oxygen atoms* [O]

The oxygen atoms, called *nascent oxygen* or *'active'* oxygen, are a strong *oxidiser* and are lethal to micro-organisms.

Now the reality. Despite the strong sickly smell of ozone which accompanies high-frequency treatment, the amount produced is *tiny*, far less than one part in a million, so its antiseptic action is not fantastic. A good chemical skin bactericide lotion could probably do just as well.

Skins which might benefit from high frequency

Direct high-frequency treatment is of value on *oily skins* where its astringent action reduces sebum secretion and its antiseptic action lessens the likelihood of spots. It is said to be of value on *aging skins* where the astringent stimulant action tightens, but very temporarily. It is useful on *acne-prone skins* for its antiseptic action and for its ability to 'burn out' the blackheads or comedones.

The burning-out can be done by lifting and angling the facial electrode to shower sparks on the blackhead, or by using the special narrow *acne electrode* in the same way (see figure 9.17 on page 106).

Precautions and contra-indications

Contra-indications to high frequency are virtually non-existent. From that point of view the treatment is perfectly *harmless*. *But*, it is all too easy to cause those accidental little *shocks* which so easily disturb even the least apprehensive client.

First you must fully explain what the client will *feel* and particularly explain the *sparking*. The treatment can frighten a client who does not know what to expect.

Then make sure your client cannot touch any metal objects nearby. Be particularly careful that the hands are not near the metal frame of the beauty chair or couch, otherwise the current will 'earth' from them to the metal. It is also a good idea, for a similar reason, to remove any items of metal jewellery, particularly those which hang loosely over clothing. Tight-fitting items like wedding rings need not be removed.

When commencing the treatment either do not turn on the machine until the electrode is placed on the skin, or 'short-out' the electrode with a finger until it is in contact. Similarly, at the end of the treatment, turn off the machine or short-out again before lifting the electrode. This is to avoid sparks jumping the gap between the electrode and the skin. The latest electrode holders incorporate a press button switch so current is produced only when button is pressed.

You may also read that high frequency should not be used on the skin following the use of alcohol-based or sulphur-containing lotions, the fear being that you might set fire to the skin – a most unlikely occurrence!

Therapists often complain that they are getting lots of electric shocks from their high-frequency machines and wonder what has gone wrong. The simple answer is that the machine has become contaminated with skin cream or talc and the current is 'tracking' through this across the machine. One can easily appreciate that a film of moisture cream could conduct high frequency, but it is not easy to believe that *talc* does too. The cure is to wipe over the machine and the electrode holder with a cloth moistened in alcohol, not forgetting to clean out the socket into which the electrodes fit.

Collect manufacturers' information literature on available high-frequency machines.

Self-assessment questions

1 Describe briefly the construction of a capacitor.

2 Describe two functions of a capacitor in an electrical circuit.

3 Draw a diagram of the current produced by the interaction of a capacitor and an inductance as it would appear on an oscilloscope.

4 What is the frequency and the voltage of the high-frequency current?

5 Explain briefly how the high-frequency current brings about a warming of the tissues being treated.

6 What is (a) a saturator electrode, (b) an intensifier electrode?

7 State three ways in which the sparking of direct high-frequency treatment can have a germicidal effect.

8 Explain why the direct method of application has a stimulant effect yet the indirect method has a soothing effect.

10 Epilation by Shortwave Diathermy

Unwanted hair; epilation and depilation; galvanic versus shortwave; the hair follicle – the target for epilation; the shortwave current; the epilation unit; how shortwave epilation works; reasons for regrowth; hair-growth cycle; the tweezer method; blend; needle hygiene

Unwanted hair

Since the dawn of mankind, people have been troubled by *hair* – too little where more is wanted and too much where they want none. Among the earliest archaeological finds have been flint tools with extremely sharp blades which it is believed were used as razors.

While for a man, body and facial hair is a sign of his masculinity, a woman with an excessive hair growth, particularly on the face, is considered most unfeminine. Should a man not wish to sport a moustache or beard he is quite prepared to perform the daily ritual of shaving, keeping his options open should he wish at some time to let it grow. Those women who have a noticeable growth of facial hair often find it most embarrassing and would be only too delighted if it could be banished – for ever!

Epilation and depilation

First let us sort out the words. Both *epilation* and *depilation* mean the removal of unwanted hair. Why, then, two words? What is the distinction?

Depilation refers to a temporary removal of hair. Sooner or later there will be a regrowth.

> Plucking
> Waxing
> Shaving
> Depilatory creams

are means of depilation (see volume 1).

Epilation is the *permanent* removal of hair. Since it involves the destruction of the hair follicle, done properly there should be no regrowth. It must be done by one of the available *electrical* methods:

> Galvanic
> Shortwave
> Blend

Galvanic epilation

Galvanic epilation has already been fully described in chapter 6. Briefly it involves the use of a *direct current* of electricity to destroy the growing part of the hair follicle by *chemical* action. It is a lengthy, tedious and *very exact* technique which is safe only in very skilled hands and has largely been superseded by the shortwave method.

Shortwave epilation

Shortwave epilation uses a *high-frequency alternating current* to destroy the hair follicle by its *heating effect*. It too is an exact technique which is perfected only by skilled training and lots of practice, but it is much quicker than the galvanic method and in skilled hands is much less likely to disfigure the skin.

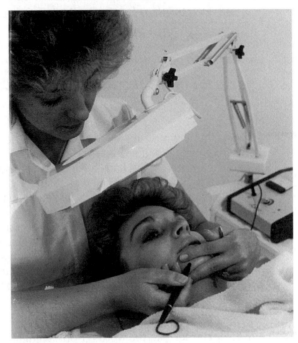

Figure 10.1 Shortwave epilation treatment in progress (courtesy of Westlands Health and Beauty Clinic)

Structure of the hair follicle

Let us now consider the structure of a hair follicle so we may pinpoint our 'target' (see figure 10.2).

If there is to be *no regrowth* in the follicle, it is essential that the means of regrowth is destroyed. At the base of the follicle is a cluster of blood capillaries, the *dermal papilla* covered by a dome of *dividing cells* which are actually part of the germinative layer of the epidermis. It is from this layer of dividing cells that the hair grows, its nourishment being supplied through the capillaries of the *dermal papilla*. If further hair growth is to be prevented, it is these structures which must be destroyed (see figure 10.3).

Normally in electrical epilation, the current is introduced into the follicle through a fine *needle electrode*. Much of the skill is in inserting the needle into the follicle so the destructive effects of the current will 'hit the target'.

The shortwave current

The current used in the shortwave method is a *high-frequency alternating current*. When a current of this type is fed to the needle electrode, it is quite possible for the needle to act as an *aerial* and *transmit* the energy as *radio waves*. The current is often referred to as *radio frequency* or 'RF'.

To minimise the possibility of causing *interference* to radio and TV broadcasts, the epilation machine must have been carefully tuned at the factory to its *allocated frequency* of

27 120 000 hertz – or 27.12 megahertz

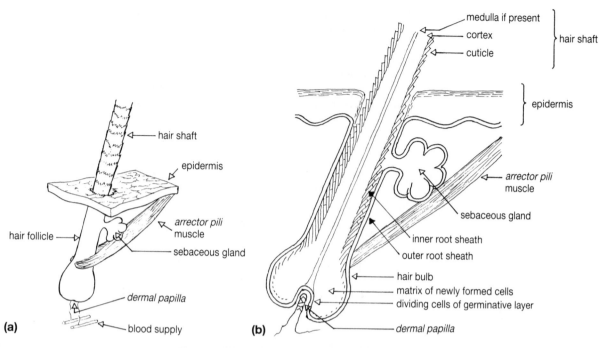

Figure 10.2 (a) The hair follicle. (b) Vertical section diagram of a hair follicle

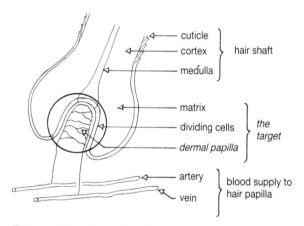

Figure 10.3 The hair bulb – the target for epilation

This frequency is on the *shortwave radio band*, actually on that part of the waveband called Citizen's Band or 'CB'. Hence the treatment is called *shortwave epilation*.

The shortwave epilation unit

The high-frequency current for epilation differs from that of the high-frequency therapy machine in several ways. Its frequency is much higher. Its voltage is considerably lower so it is much easier to 'contain' within a cable. It is a constant or *sustained* alternating current and not a 'damped' one.

It is however generated in a similar way by a combination of a *capacitor* and an *inductance*, but this time a transistorised *oscillator* circuit gives an electrical 'push' to each cycle of alternation of the current to maintain it at a constant level.

The inductance used is usually an 'open' type with no iron core. It consists of just a few turns of very thick wire. It is called a *shortwave coil*.

The capacitor is a *variable capacitor* or 'tuning' capacitor. Should the epilation unit ever need to be repaired, it must be done by a service engineer who has the necessary test equipment to retune it to the *correct* frequency.

You can if you wish display the output current of the epilation unit on the *oscilloscope* screen. How to do it is shown in figure 10.4.

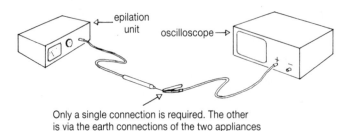

Only a single connection is required. The other is via the earth connections of the two appliances

Figure 10.4 Connecting a shortwave epilation unit to an oscilloscope

Fit an *old* needle in the needle holder and connect a single wire from it to the *positive* or 'signal' terminal of the oscilloscope. Use a small crocodile clip to connect to the needle.

Turn the timebase control of the oscilloscope to its highest value. Then when you press the start button of the epilation unit, the current will be displayed on the screen as shown in figure 10.5.

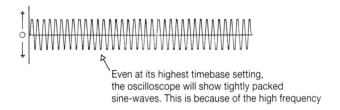

Even at its highest timebase setting, the oscilloscope will show tightly packed sine-waves. This is because of the high frequency

Figure 10.5 The shortwave current as shown on an oscilloscope

Timing the epilation current

The current is not passed until the needle has been inserted in the hair follicle. Then it is passed for only a few seconds. The intensity and duration of the current are found by experience and by trial and error on the first few hairs. This information is then noted on the client's record card. A *milliammeter* on the epilation unit shows the current intensity.

On most machines there is an automatic timer set by a control on the front panel. The current is started either by a push button on the electrode holder or by touching a foot switch. It then stops automatically (see figure 10.6).

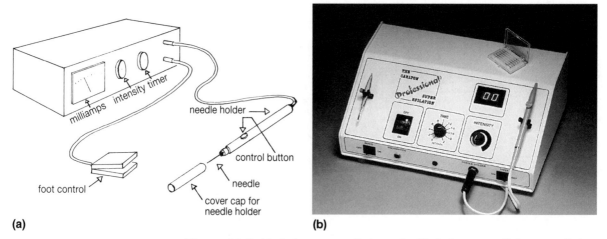

(a)
(b)

Figure 10.6 (a) A shortwave epilation unit. (b) A shortwave diathermy epilation unit (photograph courtesy of Taylor Reeson Laboratories Ltd)

How shortwave epilation works

The needle is inserted in the follicle so that its tip is close to the *dermal papilla*. The current is started. The high-frequency signal is carried by the needle to its tip. Its *energy* is absorbed by the water molecules in the cells at the base of the follicle and *heats* them. This is *inductive heating* or *diathermy*. The heat *kills* and destroys the cells in an area around the needle tip by *coagulating* the cell proteins.

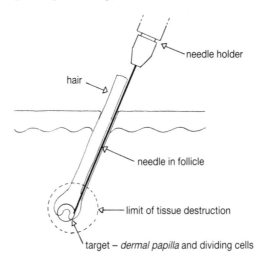

Figure 10.7 An epilation needle inserted into the hair follicle

Percentage kill and reasons for regrowth

To clear *all* the hairs from an area of skin in one treatment would be too painful and damaging to the skin. To clear completely *part* of the area might look rather odd. Normally in each treatment the hairs are taken at random, gradually thinning the growth so that by the end of the series of treatments the hair is all gone.

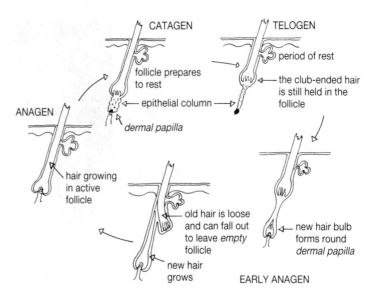

Figure 10.8 Hair growth cycle

However, it is quite likely that there will be some regrowth. A good operator can expect a 70 per cent '*kill*' of the hair follicles. There are a number of reasons for this *regrowth*.

Some follicles may be '*empty*'. Body hairs are of two types: the slowly and continuously growing, downy *vellus* hairs, and the more rapidly growing and strong *terminal* hairs. Terminal hairs go through a *growth cycle* (see figure 10.8). The hair grows actively for a certain period, then after a period of 'rest', it falls out as a new one grows to take its place. At this stage the follicle appears to be empty, so during epilation it will be passed over.

Some follicles are *curved*. Even by stretching the skin it might not be possible to straighten the follicle sufficiently for the needle to reach the correct target, so the *papilla* may not be destroyed (see figure 10.9).

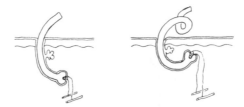

Figure 10.9 Curved follicles grow wavy and curly hairs

Some follicles are *multiple* and may contain a small tuft of hairs, usually a main one which *is* destroyed by the treatment and several smaller ones. Often one of these then enlarges to take over as the main hair in the follicle (see figures 10.10 and 10.11).

Then of course, there is always the possibility of *poor technique*. Incorrect insertion of the needle, insufficient current intensity, too short a time for the current, will all result in the *papilla* not being destroyed. This is why the professional societies of *electrolysists* insist on proper training and a long period of supervised practice before accepting new members for registration.

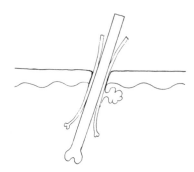

Figure 10.10 A multiple hair follicle (photo – Hugh Rushton, courtesy of the Philip Kingsley Trichology Clinic)

Figure 10.11 Section through a multiple hair follicle

The tweezer method

In recent years a new variant of shortwave electrical epilation has hit the headlines. This is the *tweezer method*. 'Much easier' . . . 'no needle to insert' . . . 'no needle hygiene problems' . . . 'no special training needed' . . . 'anyone can do it' . . . were the claims. But how effective is it? And how safe? How does it work? . . . indeed *does* it work? In the USA it took a court case to establish that it could and did work.

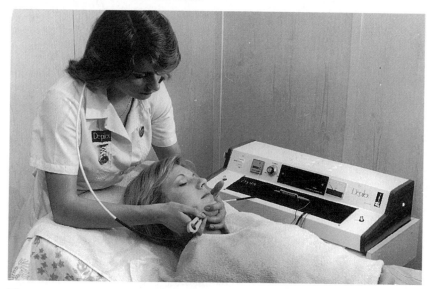

Figure 10.12 Tweezer epilation in progress (courtesy of Depilex Ltd)

How the tweezer method works

The tweezer epilation unit is essentially the same as the needle type but because there is more opportunity for the current to be lost, it has to be much more powerful. A tweezer machine can be used with a needle for the needle method, but a needle machine is not powerful enough to be used for the tweezer method.

Instead of a needle in a needle holder, the current is delivered to a special screened and insulated *tweezer*. The offending hair is gripped with the tweezer tips and the current is passed until the hair is loose and comes away. It can work because in effect the hair is made to act *as its own needle*!

The method

First the hairs are *cut* if necessary so they are no more than 6 mm (a quarter of an inch) long. This is so that the epilation current is not lost by travelling *up* the hair to be transmitted as *radio waves* from its tip. A long hair can act as a transmitting aerial.

The hairs are then *moistened* with a moisturising lotion to make them *more conductive* to the epilation current.

Each hair is then gripped with the tweezer and the current is started. It travels *down* the hair on the moisture film into the follicle (see figure 10.13).

Deep in the follicle, the *energy* of the high-frequency epilation current is absorbed by the *high water content* of the *living* tissues of the hair bulb and the follicle, heating them by *diathermy*, coagulating their proteins and killing the cells. The hair is gently 'waggled' to loosen it, and out it comes. Treating each hair does take rather longer than the needle method.

With luck, the tissue destruction will include the *papilla* and the germinative cells, and there will be *no regrowth* from that follicle.

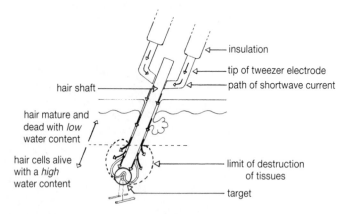

Figure 10.13 How the tweezer method destroys the hair *papilla*

Percentage kill and reasons for regrowth

The tweezer method is by no means as effective in the short term as the needle method. Only about 30 per cent *'kill'* is claimed compared with 70 per cent. The main reason is that the destruction has *not* reached the 'target' and the *papilla* and germinative cells remain intact. As you can see from figure 10.13, they are right on the edge of the area of destruction. Several attempts might be required to reach them. This is particularly likely to occur if the 'waggling' is too vigorous and the hair comes away too soon before the current has had a chance to do its job properly.

As with the needle method, incorrect current intensity and timing can lead to failure, and the problems of *empty* and *multiple* follicles still apply. A real advantage is that the method *can* deal with *curved* follicles.

Blend

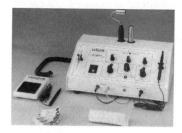

Figure 10.14 Blend
epilation unit (courtesy
of Carlton Professional)

Prior to the 1960's, galvanic 'electrolysis' was *the* method of epilation (see pp 68–9). Shortwave or RF was introduced in Europe in the 1960's, and due to its much shorter treatment time for each follicle, it soon displaced the much slower galvanic method.

In the USA, too, RF had been introduced but stayed very expensive so galvanic remained prominent for much longer. Indeed, in Europe, many operators preferred galvanic for those 'difficult' curved and multiple follicles.

Research in the USA showed that a *blend* of both galvanic and RF could combine the advantages of both –

galvanic – the sodium hydroxide or 'lye' produced is very effective at coagulating cell proteins and destroying the hair papilla (see page 69).

RF or shortwave – because chemical reaction proceeds faster in warm conditions, the heat generated by the RF speeds up the coagulation process.

In the late 1980's, blend machines from the USA were brought into Britain but were *very* costly. However, British companies soon introduced simplified and much less expensive machines and since then the blend method has become very popular. For blend, these simpler machines produce the two currents simultaneously. They can also be used for the galvanic and RF methods individually.

There are, however, further advantages to be gained by staggering or sequencing the currents –

a) If the hair follicles tend to be dry, they are not very conductive. The warmth generated by using RF straight away will dehydrate them further and reduce their conductivity even more. In such cases one could use galvanic first to generate the lye, then add the RF to warm and speed its reaction.

b) If the follicles are already moist and conductive, one could use RF first to pre-warm the follicle, then add the galvanic to provide the lye which will then act quickly.

These machines employ computer technology to sequence the currents automatically. They may also have a test mode to check the conductivity of the client's follicles.

There are, however, no hard and fast rules for blend. The mix and sequencing of the currents will depend in part on the nature of the follicles and in part on the preferences of the experienced operator.

Needle hygiene

Hygiene is of the utmost importance in electrical epilation, in particular *needle hygiene*. *Stringent* precautions must be adhered to if *cross-infection* from client to client is to be prevented. Cross-infection is most likely when clients share the same needle. As a result of unhygienic practice, electrical epilation might be responsible for the transmission of *blood-borne* diseases; *infectious hepatitis* and more recently Acquired Immune Deficiency Syndrome or AIDS. Ideally, a *new sterile needle* should be used for each treatment.

But needles are expensive. At worst, all clients should have their *own* needle, kept in a file between treatments and effectively *sterilised* before and after each treatment.

It is now recommended that needles **MUST NOT BE SHARED** by clients.

Most methods of sterilising needles have been proven to be woefully inadequate. These include dipping into surgical spirit, dipping into a solution of cationic surfactant – such as cetrimide – or running the machine in the hope that the current will kill the bacteria. These methods are *not* fully effective.

Figure 10.15 Glass bead furnace needle steriliser (courtesy of Taylor Reeson Laboratories Ltd)

The *only* acceptable method for needle sterilisation is the *electric glass bead furnace*. Before and after a treatment, the needle is dipped into the furnace for a few seconds to be heated to white heat and be *thoroughly* sterilised. Even this method is still the subject of intense argument as to its effectiveness (see figure 10.15).

THE ONLY REALLY SAFE PROCEDURE IS TO USE A NEW NEEDLE FOR EACH CLIENT TREATMENT

After use, the needle should be sterilised before being placed in a 'sharps box'.

Sharps boxes containing used needles must not be disposed of through normal waste collections. Many hospitals are prepared to accept them for disposal.

Things to do

Collect and study manufacturers' information literature on the different makes of epilation equipment.

Self-assessment questions

1 Distinguish between epilation and depilation.

2 Distinguish between the way in which the hair follicle is destroyed by galvanic epilation and by shortwave diathermy.

3 What is the *dermal papilla* of the hair follicle and what is its importance in the growth of the hair?

4 What is the allocated frequency of the shortwave epilation current?

5 What is a co-axial cable and why is this type of cable necessary to carry the shortwave current to the epilation needle?

6 List reasons why there may be a regrowth of hair after treatment by shortwave epilation.

7 Briefly describe the growth cycle of a terminal hair.

8 Explain briefly how the tweezer method of shortwave epilation works.

9 Why is it important that a new sterilised needle should be used for each epilation treatment?

10 Show on a diagram an epilation needle correctly inserted into the hair follicle.

11   **Rays, Light and Colour**

Electromagnetic radiations; rays travel in straight lines; rays as waves; light; reflection and mirrors; transparency, refraction and lenses; colour; wavelengths and the electromagnetic spectrum; inverse square law; cosine law

Electromagnetic radiations

The beauty therapist will frequently use a *heat lamp* for pre-warming the clients, or some kind of *ultra-violet lamp* for enhancing their suntan. The heat rays and ultra-violet rays produced are just two types of *electromagnetic radiations*.

The full range of radiations in the *electromagnetic spectrum* is

> Radio waves – radio, TV and radar
> Infra-red rays – heat rays
> Light
> Ultra-violet rays
> X-rays
> Gamma-rays – from radioactive substances
> Cosmic rays – in outer space

All these types of rays are in the output of the *sun*. Luckily the atmosphere prevents most of the harmful ones reaching us down on the Earth.

The speed or velocity of rays

The speed or *velocity* at which rays travel through space has been accurately measured. They travel at

> 300 000 000 metres per second
>   or
> 186 000 miles per second

Even at this amazing speed, it takes rays 8 minutes and 20 seconds to cover the 93 000 000 miles from the Sun to the Earth. The light from the stars takes many *years* to reach us.

Rays travel in straight lines

Rays leave their source travelling in *all* directions (see figure 11.1).

Unless they are diverted by some means, rays travel in *straight lines* – or so it would appear. This is why a lamp can cast *shadows* (see figure 11.2).

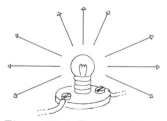

Figure 11.1 Rays travel from their source in all directions

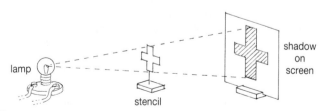

Figure 11.2 Rays travel in straight lines

Rays travel as waves

Although the general path of a ray is a straight line, it actually travels as side-to-side ripples known as *transverse waves*.

To explain transverse waves, we need to imagine that the path of the ray consists of '*energy particles*'. The *energy* from the source makes the energy particles *vibrate* from side to side and the vibration is passed on from one particle to the next (see figure 11.3). The effect can be shown by making ripples run along a rope as in figure 11.4.

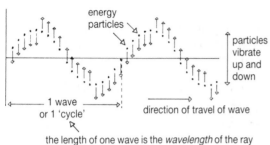

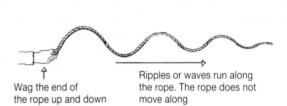

Figure 11.3 The energy particle theory of waves

Figure 11.4 Waves along a rope

Do not worry unduly if you cannot imagine the energy particles. The explanation is a theory. As yet, no-one has found proof that energy particles exist. You will see later, though, that it does help us understand some of the properties and features of rays.

Light

Because we can *see* it, we can demonstrate many of the properties of rays with *light*. To do the experiments a *ray lamp* will be needed. This is a low-voltage lamp enclosed in a box open at one end. Figure 11.5 shows a typical one.

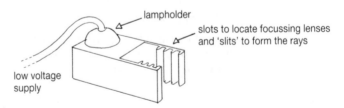

Figure 11.5 A ray lamp for experiments with light

Also needed will be suitable flat or plane mirrors, curved mirrors, 'slits' to fit the ray lamp, 'cylindrical' lenses and glass or Perspex blocks and prisms.

To show the paths of the rays, it is useful to work on a flat white surface and to be able to darken the room.

You will also need a variety of mirrors and lenses to look into or look through.

For the *ray lamp experiments* you will need to make the ray lamp give out a narrow parallel beam, or better still *three* parallel beams. To do this, fit a suitable 'slit' and a suitable cylindrical lens in slots in the ray lamp (see figure 11.6).

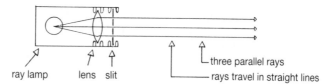

Figure 11.6 Producing parallel rays from a ray lamp

Reflection of rays

Rays are *reflected* by shiny polished surfaces such as that of a *mirror* or a lamp *reflector* (see figure 11.7). Infra-red and ultra-violet rays are reflected in the same way as visible light.

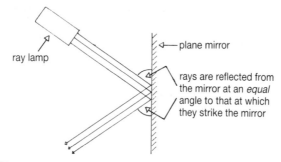

Figure 11.7 Reflection at a mirror surface

Mirrors

When doing *make-up*, a mirror is needed to show the client what has been achieved. In a hairdressing salon, the stylist works largely from behind the client, relying on the mirror to see the front of the style. The mirror used is a flat or *plane mirror*.

Look at yourself in a plane mirror. After the initial shock! study the *image* of yourself in the mirror. The *image* in a *plane mirror* is

---

Life size
Upright
As far behind mirror as object is in front
Laterally inverted

'Laterally inverted' means the lefts and rights are reversed. For the reason why, look again at the ray box experiment (see figure 11.8).

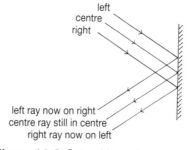

Figure 11.8 Lateral inversion at a plane mirror

This means of course that when you look at yourself in a mirror, you do *not* see yourself as others see you. However, when in the hairdresser's the stylist holds up a second mirror to show you the back of your hairstyle, you see the back as others see it. Lateral inversion has occurred *twice* – once in each mirror.

Curved mirrors

It is quite possible that on your dressing table or in the bathroom you have a double-sided mirror. One side is plane, the other side is dished inwards in the centre. It is a *concave mirror*.

Look at yourself in a *concave mirror*. You will have to be fairly *close*. Note how it *magnifies*. The *image* of a *close object* in a *concave mirror* is

> Upright
> *Magnified*

The ray lamp will show why the mirror magnifies (see figure 11.9).

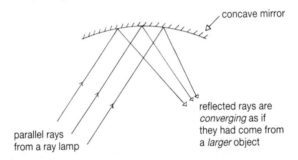

Figure 11.9 Reflection by a concave mirror

The concave mirror is useful for attending to the details of your make-up. Some men like a magnifying mirror for shaving.

Now use the concave mirror to look over your shoulder at a *distant* object. The *image* of a *distant object* in a *concave mirror* is

> Inverted – upside down
> Diminished – made smaller

The ray lamp will show why in figure 11.10.

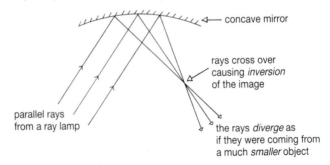

Figure 11.10 Rays from a concave mirror cross over to produce an inverted image

When visiting the supermarket you may have caught sight of yourself in the security mirrors. You will have noticed how much *smaller* everything looks, but also what a wide field of view you can see in a relatively small mirror. This mirror is dished outwards in its centre; it is a *convex* mirror (see figure 11.11). The *image* in a *convex mirror* is

Upright
Diminished

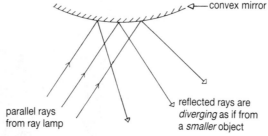

Figure 11.11 Reflection by a convex mirror

Transparency

If light rays will pass through a substance, the substance is *transparent*. If they will not pass through, the substance is *opaque*.

Being transparent to *visible light* does not mean a substance is transparent to other types of rays such as infra-red or ultra-violet.

Window glass – is transparent to light and *infra-red* but is *opaque* to *ultra-violet*

Water – is transparent to light and *ultra-violet* but is *opaque* to *infra-red*

It is no use trying to sunbathe indoors by the window; you will never get a tan behind a closed window! On the other hand, it is equally no use going into the sea to escape the sun if you feel that you have overdone your sunbathing on the beach!

Refraction

If rays strike the surface of a transparent substance at an angle, they will be bent off course or *refracted* as they pass into the substance.

The ray lamp will show this happening through a rectangular glass block (see figure 11.12).

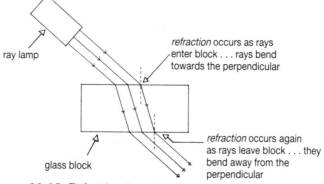

Figure 11.12 Refraction through a glass block

Lenses

Lenses work by *refraction*. Just as a concave mirror magnifies, so does a *convex lens*. A convex lens is one which is fatter in the middle.

Use a convex lens to look at a fairly *close* object. The *image* of a *close* object seen through a *convex lens* is

> Upright
> *Magnified*

The ray lamp shows why (see figure 11.13).

The *magnifier lamp* used when doing electrical epilation incorporates a convex lens (see figure 11.14).

Figure 11.14 Illuminated magnifier on equipment trolley (courtesy of Taylor Reeson Laboratories Ltd)

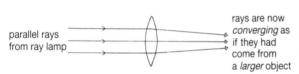

Figure 11.13 Refraction through a convex lens

If you hold up a convex lens to look at a *distant* object, the image will be inverted and diminished (see figure 11.15).

The other type of lens is a *concave lens*. This type is thin in the middle and thick at the edges. The *image* through it is upright and *diminished* (see figure 11.16).

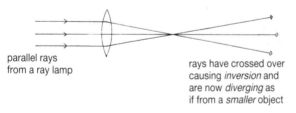

Figure 11.15 A distant object viewed through a convex lens is inverted and diminished

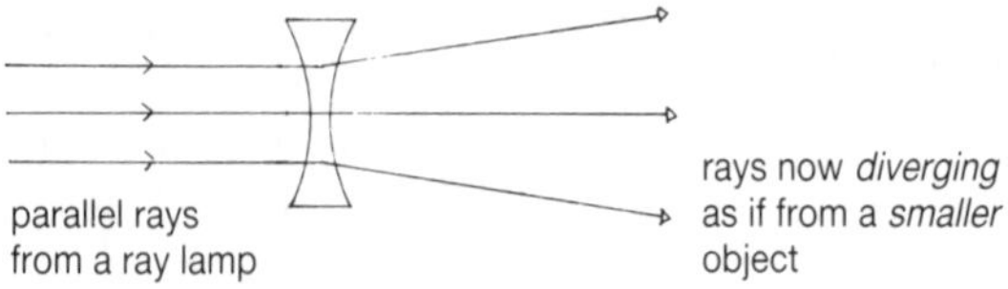

Figure 11.16 Refraction through a concave lens

Colour

Very important in our appreciation of our surroundings and of ourselves is the ability to see in *colour*. But how does colour work?

A classic experiment by Sir Isaac Newton, a pioneer of science, shows that the white light from the Sun or from a lamp actually consists of light of a variety of colours (see figure 11.17).

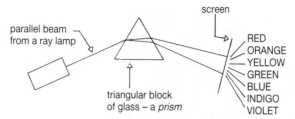

Figure 11.17 Dispersion of a beam of white light to produce a spectrum

On the screen appears a spread of the *seven* colours of the *visible spectrum*. The colours are red, orange, yellow, green, blue, indigo and violet, the colours of the rainbow.

You will notice that when light is *refracted* through the prism, the different colours are refracted different amounts. As will be seen later, the rays of different colours have different *wavelengths*.

The *longer wavelength* red is refracted *least* by the prism
The *shorter wavelength* violet is refracted *most*

Seeing colour

It has long been known, however, that with just *three* colours of light it is possible to *mix* any colour. These are the three *primary colours*:

Red – Long wavelength
Green – Middle wavelength
Blue – Short wavelength

Mixing these primary colours of light in various proportions will produce any shade of any colour.

This is what happens in *stage lighting*. With *red*, *green* and *blue* lamps any colour effect may be produced.

A *colour television* picture is made up of just tiny red, blue and green dots on the screen.

We see the *colour* of something because the *retina*, the 'film' of nerve cells at the back of the *eye*, is sensitive to the

---

'*redness*' – Long wavelengths
'*greenness*' – Middle wavelengths
'*blueness*' – Short wavelengths

The *brain* then compares the redness, greenness and blueness of the light from the object, 'mixes' its colour, and 'paints' it in on the image of that object.

Colour triangle

The mixing of any colour from the three primary colours can be demonstrated with a *colour triangle* apparatus (see figure 11.18). This is a triangular white screen with a coloured lamp at each corner: red, green and blue, the *primary* colours.

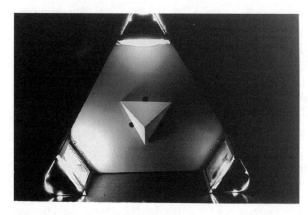

Figure 11.18 Apparatus to demonstrate the colour triangle

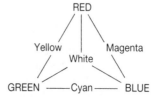

Figure 11.19 The colour triangle

The triangle shows a full spectrum of colours round its sides, pastel shades towards the centre and white in the middle (see figure 11.19).

The three 'midway' colours, *yellow*, *magenta* and *cyan*, are the *complementary* or secondary colours.

You will note that

	red and *green*	makes	*yellow*
	green and *blue*	makes	*cyan*
	blue and *red*	makes	*magenta*
and	*red*, *blue* and *green*	makes	*white*

This kind of colour mixing works only with coloured lights. It is called *additive colour mixing*.

Mixing dyes, pigments and paints

With dyes and pigments it is possible to mix colours too. In fact with just three colours it is possible to mix any colour. These three colours are *complementary colours*:

	yellow
	magenta – a deep cherry red
	cyan – a greenish blue
Yellow	contains 'redness' and 'greenness'
Magenta	contains 'redness' and 'blueness'
Cyan	contains 'greenness' and 'blueness'

Mix together *yellow* and *magenta*. The 'redness' predominates, giving scarlets and oranges.

Mix together *cyan* and *yellow*. The 'greenness' predominates, giving the greens.

Mix together *cyan* and *magenta*. The 'blueness' predominates, giving a range of blues, mauves and purples.

Mixing all three should cancel out all the colours and give black. In practice it gives the browns. This type of colour mixing is known as *subtractive colour mixing*.

The wavelengths of electromagnetic rays

As explained already, rays travel as waves. The range of *wavelengths* of the various kinds of radiations is enormous, varying from thousands of metres for longwave *radio* to minute fractions of a millimetre for *cosmic rays*. For the very tiny measurements, we need to extend our table of units of measurement.

Units of measure of length

1 metre (m)	= 1000 millimetres (mm)
1 millimetre (mm)	= 1000 micrometres (μm)
1 micrometre (μm)	= 1000 nanometres (nm)

μ is the Greek letter 'mu', the Greek m.

A *nanometre* is therefore a very short measure indeed, just one-millionth of a millimetre, yet it is the most frequently encountered unit of measurement of the *wavelength* of rays.

In older books, wavelengths are measured in Ångstrom units. An *Ångstrom* is an even smaller unit than a nanometre:

1 nanometre (nm) = 10 Ångstroms (Å)

We can now show the *wavelengths* of the various radiations of the full *electromagnetic spectrum* (see figure 11.20).

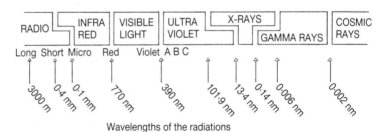

Wavelengths of the radiations

Figure 11.20 The electromagnetic spectrum

Radiations used in beauty therapy

In beauty therapy, use is made of a number of types of radiations:

Ultra-violet sunray treatment uses that part of the ultra-violet band adjacent to visible light

Heat ray treatments use two bands of infra-red rays –
'*infra-red*' uses infra-red of around 4000 nm
'*radiant heat*' uses infra-red adjacent to the red end of the visible light band

In recent years, there has been much interest in the cosmetic use of *lasers*. No-one has yet been able to demonstrate that they have any beneficial effect. The ones used produce an intense yellow beam of around 500 nm wavelength.

While not used in the form of rays in beauty therapy, *high frequency* and *electrical epilators* can both give out *radio waves*. High-frequency machines produce longwave radio waves. Epilation units work on the shortwave band on 11 metres wavelength.

Wavelength and frequency

With some types of radiations, it is customary to use the term *frequency* rather than wavelength. For instance, *radio waves* are usually distinguished by *frequency*.

Frequency

The frequency of a radiation is the number of waves passing a point each second. The units of measurement are *hertz, kilohertz* and *megahertz*.

A frequency of one wave past a point per second is 1 hertz (Hz)

1000 Hz = 1 kilohertz (kHz)
1000 kHz = 1 megahertz (MHz)

You may recognise the abbreviations from your radio dial.
To compare *wavelength* and *frequency*:

$$\text{Frequency} = \frac{\text{Velocity of rays}}{\text{Wavelength}}$$

Example
If a ray has a wavelength of 1200 metres and the velocity of rays is 300 000 000 metres per second:

$$\text{Frequency} = \frac{300\,000\,000}{1200}$$

$$= 250\,000 \text{ Hz or } 250 \text{ kHz}$$

250 kHz is the sort of frequency at which a *high-frequency machine* operates.

Rules governing the intensity of radiation

When treating a client with either a *heat lamp* or an *ultra-violet lamp*, the *intensity* of rays received by the skin is governed by *two* factors other than the output of the lamp. These are:

The distance between lamp and skin
The angle at which the rays strike the skin

The inverse square law for radiation

With a *heat lamp*, it is quite obvious that the *closer* you get to the lamp, the *higher* will be the intensity of the rays reaching the skin. You can feel the rays, and if you get too close you will feel the scorching and move away.

The same is true of an *ultra-violet lamp*: the closer your skin, the higher the intensity. But there is a *serious problem*. You *cannot feel ultra-violet rays*, so you cannot tell if you are overdosing the skin – until your *sunburn* appears.

The relationship between the *distance* from the lamp and the *intensity* is the *inverse square law for radiation:*

> The *intensity* falls in proportion to the distance from the lamp *squared* or
>
> $$\text{Intensity} = \frac{1}{(\text{Distance})^2}$$

This means that if you *double* the distance from lamp to skin, the *intensity* falls to a *quarter*. If you *halve* the distance, the intensity is up *four* times (see figure 11.21).

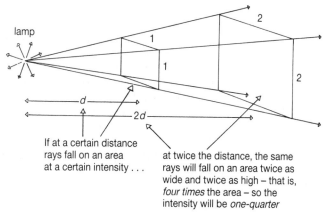

lamp

1

1

2

2

d

2*d*

If at a certain distance rays fall on an area at a certain intensity . . .

at twice the distance, the same rays will fall on an area twice as wide and twice as high – that is, *four times* the area – so the intensity will be *one-quarter*

Figure 11.21 The inverse square law for radiation

An experiment may be done to show this using a lamp, a small *solar* cell and a sensitive *milliammeter*. Do the experiment in a darkened room (see figure 11.22).

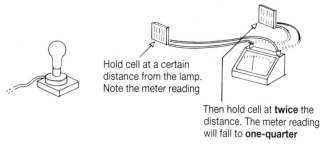

Hold cell at a certain distance from the lamp. Note the meter reading

Then hold cell at **twice** the distance. The meter reading will fall to **one-quarter**

Figure 11.22 Using a solar cell to demonstrate the inverse square law

This demonstrates how important it is when using an *ultra-violet lamp* to set it at the *correct distance* from the client: too far away and the dose will be too low and the treatment ineffective, too *close* and the client will receive an *overdose* and will be burned.

The cosine law for radiation

To get the correct dose from a *heat lamp* or an *ultra-violet lamp*, it is important that as far as possible the rays strike *at right angles* to the skin.

The *cosine law* shows how the intensity falls if the rays do not strike perpendicularly (see figure 11.23).

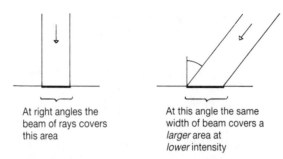

At right angles the
beam of rays covers
this area

At this angle the same
width of beam covers a
larger area at
lower intensity

Figure 11.23 The cosine law compares the intensity with the angle at which rays strike

How much the intensity is lower can be found by measuring the angle from the perpendicular and looking up its *cosine* in mathematical tables. The cosine gives the reduction in intensity. For example, in figure 11.23 the angle shown is about 35°. Its cosine is 0.819. The intensity is therefore down to about 0.8 of what it would be if the rays fell perpendicular to the skin.

The cosine of 60° is 0.5. If rays fall at 60° from the perpendicular, the intensity is down to *half*.

The problem is that the average body is far from *flat*. Even so, you must try to position a ray lamp so the rays fall as near perpendicular as possible on as much of the skin as possible.

Self-assessment questions

1   Why is the light from a lamp able to cast sharp shadows?

2   Distinguish between the reflection and refraction of light.

3   What is lateral inversion and how does it affect the view of oneself one sees in a mirror?

4   In what way might a concave mirror be useful when doing one's make-up?

5   Distinguish between transparent, translucent and opaque.

6   What type of lens gives a magnified image?

7   List the seven colours of the visible spectrum in order of decreasing wavelength.

8   Name the three primary colours of light.

9   In mixing colour pigments, what colour results from mixing (a) yellow and cyan, (b) magenta and cyan?

10   What fraction of a millimetre is (a) a micrometre, (b) a nanometre, (c) an Ångstrom unit?

11   What is measured in hertz?

12   What is the inverse square law for radiation?

13   Explain the importance of the inverse square law when doing ultra-violet treatment with a combined health lamp.

14   What is the cosine law for radiation?

15   How does the cosine law affect the way a ray lamp is positioned with respect to the client?

12

Heat Radiation Treatments

Infra-red and radiant heat; physical and physiological effects of heat lamps; types of heat lamps; precautions and dangers with heat lamps; safety checks on heat lamps; contra-indications to heat radiation treatments

Infra-red and radiant heat

To the therapist there are two distinct heat radiation treatments:

> *Infra red* and *Radiant heat*

Tell this to a physicist, and he will either look in amazement or laugh. To him, infra-red, radiant heat and heat rays all mean exactly the same thing.

In beauty therapy and physiotherapy, the terms are used to distinguish two bands of heat rays:

> *Infra-red* refers to the *longer wavelength* heat rays
> *Radiant heat* refers to the *shorter wavelength* heat rays

An *infra-red lamp* or *non-luminous generator* gives out a gentle warmth with little or no visible glow. The lamp runs at a relatively low temperature so the intensity of its output is comparatively low and consists almost entirely of infra-red rays with a peak output at 4000 nm wavelength.

A *radiant heat lamp* or *luminous generator* gives out a bright visible glow and an intensely 'feelable' heat. To do this, the lamp runs at a much higher temperature. Its output is a mixture of heat rays and visible light rays with a peak at around 1000 nm wavelength.

The graphs in figure 12.1 compare the outputs of the two kinds of lamps.

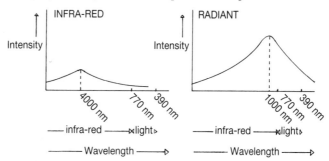

Figure 12.1 Comparison of the outputs of infra-red and radiant heat lamps

The physical and physiological effects of heat lamps

Both infra-red and radiant heat lamps are used for *heat* treatments. The difference between them is the *way* in which they induce the warmth in the part of the body being treated.

The first difference is in the *penetration* of the rays into the skin. From the feeling of *'deep warmth'* which heat lamps induce, one gets the impression of *deeply* penetrating rays. This is not so.

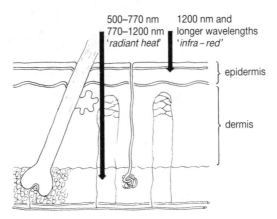

500–770 nm
770–1200 nm
'radiant heat'

1200 nm and
longer wavelengths
'infra-red'

epidermis

dermis

Figure 12.2 Penetration of heat rays into the skin

As figure 12.2 shows, *radiant heat* penetrates only into the dermis and *infra-red* reaches no further than the living layers of the epidermis. That is the extent of the *physical* warming effect of heat rays.

Why then can they warm one so *deeply*? The answer is in the *physiology* of the process.

How radiant heat warms the tissues

The more intense rays of *radiant heat* penetrating deep into the dermis heat the skin *directly*. The natural response of a skin which becomes too hot is to cool itself by the *two* means available to it:

1　The heat causes the *dilation* of the blood vessels and lymph vessels in the skin. The extra fluid flow is intended to carry the heat away from the skin *down* into the underlying tissues. Hence the sensation of *deep warmth*.
2　The extra fluid delivered to the skin supplies the sweat glands which secrete sweat profusely, the *evaporation* of which is intended to *cool* the skin.

The *reddening* effect on the skin caused by radiant heat is due to the actual heating of skin. It is termed *hyperaemia*.

Because the heat rays penetrate to the dermis, the pain nerve endings send a *stimulating tingling* sensation which tends to 'jam' the pain sensation from any injury in the treatment area. This is a *counter-irritant* effect.

How infra-red warms the tissues

Because infra-red rays are of low intensity and because they penetrate only into the epidermis, there is *very little direct heating* of the skin.

It seems though that the rays cause an *irritation* response in the live epidermal cells which, possibly through the release of histamine, causes the blood vessels in the dermis beneath to dilate.

The extra blood flow then brings the *body's own heat* to the area to create the *deep heating effect*.

The *reddening* this time is due to an *irritant* reaction and is called *erythema*. There is little stimulation of the pain nerve endings in the skin so the warming effect is *soothing* rather than stimulating.

The beneficial effects of warming the tissues

The higher temperature *increases the rate of metabolism*. Repairs to damaged tissues are speeded up. Muscles are made more ready to respond and more able to stretch. Remember when one muscle contracts, the other muscle of the *antagonistic pair* must be able to stretch.

The *increased rate of circulation* means that waste products are removed and swelling is reduced, thereby *easing pain*. The dilation of blood vessels leads to *lower blood pressure*, useful for relieving *hypertension*. But take care, lowered blood pressure can lead to *fainting*, particularly when the client stands up after the treatment.

The warmth increases secretion of both *sweat* and *sebum*, so deep cleansing the skin.

Heat lamps

As already stated, heat lamps are of *two* main types:

> *Infra-red* or *non-luminous*
> *radiant* or *luminous*

In practice, most types of lamp can be either *non-luminous* or *luminous* depending on the voltage at which they operate and therefore the *temperature* they reach.

Fireclay heat lamps

The older heat lamps consisted of a fireclay support with a *Nichrome* heating element wound round it. They may be the short type in a bowl-shaped reflector or the long type in a half-cylindrical reflector like an electric fire (see figure 12.3).

The reflectors of heat lamps must be carefully designed so the output is beamed *evenly* on to the client without any 'hotspots' which could burn the client.

(a) **(b)**

Figure 12.3 (a) Fireclay heat lamps: left – short type; right – long type. (b) Fireclay heat radiation generator

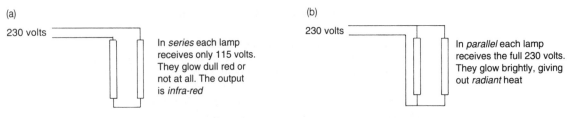

(a)

230 volts

In *series* each lamp receives only 115 volts. They glow dull red or not at all. The output is *infra-red*

(b)

230 volts

In *parallel* each lamp receives the full 230 volts. They glow brightly, giving out *radiant* heat

Figure 12.4 Heat lamps in series and parallel

The short type usually glows brightly, its output is mostly *radiant*. The long type is often used in pairs, as shown in figure 12.3. They can then be switched to operate with very little glow as infra-red or brightly as radiant.

As *infra-red*, the two lamps are connected in *series* as in figure 12.4a. For *radiant*, the lamps are switched into *parallel* as in figure 12.4b.

In another kind of fireclay lamp, the heating element is completely embedded in the clay. This type produces no visible glow at all; its output is entirely *infra-red* (see figure 12.5).

Figure 12.5 Fireclay infra-red generator

Steel tube lamp

This type of lamp consists of a steel tube about 1 cm in diameter. The Nichrome heating element is inside the tube. The space between the element and the tube is packed with magnesium oxide powder. This construction is exactly the same as a cooker radiant hotplate, a kettle element or an immersion heater.

Usually the elements are mounted in a half-cylindrical reflector. Again it is possible to switch them in *series* so they do not glow giving *infra-red*, or in *parallel* so they glow brightly producing *radiant heat* (see figure 12.6).

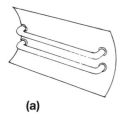

(a)

(b)

Figure 12.6 (a) and (b) Steel-tube-type heat lamp. Note the guards required by law

Quartz heat lamp

A quartz heat lamp consists of a translucent rod of quartz with the heating element embedded inside it. Long heaters of this type are used as radiant space heaters in bathrooms. Shorter ones are often fitted into *combined health lamps* and *solarium units* where they serve a dual function. Apart from using them as *heat lamps* in their own right, they are used to supply supplementary heat during ultra-violet treatments (see figure 12.7).

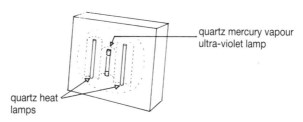

Figure 12.7 Quartz heat lamps in a combined health lamp

All the lamps so far, particularly the steel and fireclay types, require a considerable *warming-up time* before they are ready to use. They should be switched on at least 15 minutes before they are required. They usually have a power consumption of 500–1000 watts.

Filament lamps

The filament or *incandescent* lamp is like a large lighting lamp but with a built-in reflector. Because they are much more powerful than the average lighting lamp, they would be uncomfortably bright were it not for being made of *red* tinted glass. This cuts down the light output but lets the heat rays out (see figure 12.8).

These lamps can have power outputs up to 1000 watts, but normally 300 watt are the largest used. The bigger lamps tend to explode!

The filament type lamp is essentially a *radiant lamp*. Many modern units are, however, fitted with *dimmers* so the lamp can be turned down to give more of an *infra-red* output.

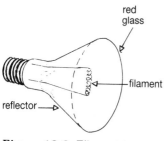

Figure 12.8 Filament-type radiant heat lamp

These lamps are relatively fragile and demand careful handling. Should it be necessary to replace a lamp, it is essential that a *good-quality* replacement be fitted. There are cheaper versions but there is no guarantee that the glass is of even thickness. If it is not, the output will be *uneven* and there may be dangerous 'hotspots'. To test a lamp, shine it on a white wall. A good lamp will give an even red illumination. A poor-quality lamp might give bright and dark patches.

Placing the lamp

Normally the lamp is placed 45–60 cm from the skin and arranged so the rays fall perpendicular to as much of the skin in the area as possible. This distance should not be too close for comfort and should be set with a fully warmed-up lamp.

Treatment times

Heat ray treatments usually occupy 10–30 minutes. The time depends on the relative 'bulk' of the treatment area.

Dangers with heat lamps

The most obvious danger with heat lamps is *burns* to the client. Radiant heat can be felt as a burning sensation, so it is easy for the client to report a too-high intensity. Infra-red though is not so 'feelable', so it is quite possible to overdose.

Overdosing with heat rays can cause an over-dilation of the capillaries in the skin, resulting in a mottled or 'corned-beef' effect which can be *permanent*.

Headaches can result from too great a flow of blood to the brain. Shining a heat lamp in the eyes can scorch the retina of the eye. Shield the head and the eyes when using heat lamps to treat the face.

When treating the whole body, remember that the lowering of the blood pressure could cause the client to *faint* when he or she gets up. Clients should be asked to sit on the side of the couch until they feel ready to stand.

Too great a loss of water from the body could lead to *constipation*. The increased perspiration continues long after the treatment has finished. Care should be taken to ensure that the client does not become *chilled*.

Safety checks on heat lamps

Before each use, the lamp must be checked to see if it is in *safe* working order. These checks are particularly important with a heat lamp because of the possibility of inflicting *burns* on the client. They do, however, apply to any equipment on an angle-poise type stand.

1   Check the lamp for *electrical safety* – the plug, the flex and the switches.
2   Make sure the lamp is properly *guarded*. It is now a legal requirement that heat lamps have guards over them.
3   Check the tightness of the angle-poise joints. They must hold the lamp in position and not allow it to droop on to the client. Tighten if necessary.
4   Make sure, when buying a new lamp, that it is *stable* and will not topple even when its angle-poise is fully extended.

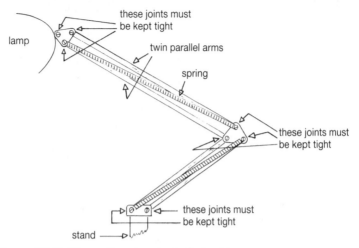

Figure 12.9 The angle-poise stand of a heat lamp

Contra-indications to heat treatments

By dilating the blood vessels in the treatment area, heat ray treatments will *lower* the blood pressure and induce a greater rate of blood circulation. *Do not treat* clients who already have low blood pressure. It could cause fainting. Do not treat clients with *artery* disease. It may 'overtax' the heart.

Heat ray treatment relies on the client reporting the feel of the rays to the therapist. Do not use on areas with defective skin sensation. The client could be unknowingly burnt.

Things to do

1 Collect manufacturers' information literature on heat lamps.

2 Study various types of heat lamps, particularly with respect to safety features.

Self-assessment questions

1 What is the peak wavelength of (a) infra-red and (b) radiant heat radiations?

2 How far does (a) infra-red and (b) radiant heat penetrate into the skin?

3 Briefly explain how (a) infra-red and (b) radiant heat warm the tissues in the treatment area.

4 What effect does the warmth resulting from a heat lamp treatment have on (a) blood pressure and (b) metabolism in the tissues.

5 Why is it not advisable to use filament heat lamps of greater than 300 watts for therapeutic purposes?

6 Why is it important to ensure a heat lamp is fully warmed up before the start of a treatment?

7 Why after a heat radiation therapy to the whole body might a client feel faint after rising from the treatment couch?

8 Why is it important to protect the eyes during heat radiation treatment to the face?

9 What are the effects on the skin of an overdose of heat radiation?

10 State two precautions which should be taken to ensure client safety when using a therapeutic lamp mounted on an angle-poise floor stand.

13

Ultra-violet

Sunshine; UV-A, UV-B and UV-C; ultra-violet lamps; the filament lamp; the arc lamp; quartz mercury vapour lamps; fluorescent ultra-violet lamps; penetration of ultra-violet into the skin; ultra-violet and vitamin D; the tanning response and melanin formation; sunburn; premature aging; safety with ultra-violet treatments

Is sunbathing good for you

What better on a hot sunny day, than to strip off to one's bare essentials and lay back for a good sunbathe to develop that healthy, rich golden tan.

Figure 13.1 Sunbathing (courtesy of Camera Press Ltd, London)

That is the dream. What about the reality? Is sunshine so good for us? How healthy is that rich golden tan? . . . and what if *real* sunshine is not available?

The truth is that a little sunshine is good for you, but too much of a good thing can definitely be bad, leading to sunburn, premature aging, even skin cancer.

If real sunshine is not available, many sun-worshippers resort to the *artificial* sunshine of the *ultra-violet lamp* – the *solarium* or the *sunbed*.

Sunshine

Before dealing with the ultra-violet lamps, let us consider real sunshine. The sun emits at *very* high intensity, the full range of electromagnetic radiations:

> Radio waves
> Infra-red
> Visible light
> Ultra-violet
> X-rays
> Gamma-rays
> Cosmic rays

The rays spread out through space, reducing in intensity as they do so. Remember the inverse square law. Having travelled the 93 000 000 miles to the Earth, the rays meet their most formidable hurdle – the atmosphere.

Of the rays which reach the atmosphere, only about 7 per cent will come through to the Earth's surface. The other 93 per cent will be absorbed by the atmosphere.

The *actual* amount of rays passing through the atmosphere depends on the *latitude* and the *season*. The nearer the sun is to being overhead, the less 'thickness' of atmosphere the rays must pass through and so the less the absorption. This means that the sunshine in *tropical* and *equatorial* regions is much stronger than in more temperate latitudes.

Thankfully, the 93 per cent of rays absorbed by the atmosphere include all the dangerous X-rays, gamma-rays and cosmic rays, and *most of the ultra-violet* too.

Visible light is absorbed somewhat by the air. The blue part of the spectrum tends to be scattered by the air, making the sky *blue* and the sun *golden yellow*.

Heat rays are partially absorbed by water vapour in the air and, as we all know on a dull day, better still by *cloud* (see figure 13.2).

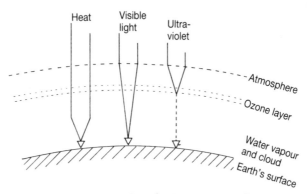

Figure 13.2 Absorption of the Sun's rays by the Earth's atmosphere

By the time the sunshine reaches us on Earth, its make-up is

Infra-red – 80 per cent
Visible light – 13 per cent
Ultra-violet – 7 per cent

All rays of wavelengths less than 295 nm are absorbed completely by the atmosphere. When we consider the various types of ultra-violet lamps, we will use this composition of sunlight for comparison.

A smoky atmosphere is an excellent *ultra-violet filter* and a beneficial effect of ultra-violet is its ability to form vitamin D, the bones and teeth vitamin, in our bodies. During the last century, in the then new towns of the Industrial Revolution, many of the children suffered from *rickets*, the vitamin D deficiency disease in which the bones become weak and bendy. They had to be taken on occasional outings into the countryside so *real* sunshine could shine on them!

Reflection of sunshine by the Earth's surface

The nature of the Earth's surface where the rays strike has an effect on the overall intensity:

Grass reflects only	2.5	per cent of radiation
Sand reflects	17	per cent of radiation
Water reflects only	5	per cent of radiation
Snow reflects	85	per cent of radiation

You may think 'How will this affect me?' . . . . Here's how.

Sunbathing on the beach will be more effective than on the lawn at home because of the reflection from the sand. But when you feel yourself starting to burn, it is no use thinking you will escape by going into the sea. Water absorbs infra-red so you will feel cooler, but it is transparent to ultra-violet. You can still sunburn *under water*.

On your winter sports holiday you may well get quite a tan or even sunburn. The reflection off the snow *almost doubles* the effective intensity of the sunshine. And much of it is *shining upwards*, so beware of sunburn under the chin! Do not forget to remind your winter sports clients about these skin care problems. Tell them to make sure to use their sunscreens and to apply them under the chin and the nose.

UV-A, UV-B, UV-C

For therapeutic purposes it is usual to refer to three bands of ultra-violet rays designated UV-A, UV-B and UV-C. Frequent reference will be made to them in the following pages. They are *artificial* subdivisions of the ultra-violet waveband according to the *physiological* effects of the rays on the body:

UV-A.   Wavelength 400–315 nm with a peak effect at 340 nm
These rays produce a rapid *direct tan* in only those people who do tan easily. The tan is however not very long lasting.

UV-B.   Wavelength 315–280 nm with a peak effect at 297.6 nm
The effect of these rays is twofold. They cause *sunburn*, but at the same time they initiate a much longer lasting tan which may last weeks or months after exposure to the rays.

UV-C.   Wavelength 280 nm and less
These rays in particular are lethal to living cells. Do not worry about them too much. Sunlight 'cuts off' at 295 nm so does not contain UV-C. The output of many ultra-violet lamps contains UV-C but it is absorbed by the air between lamp and skin. So long as you maintain the *correct distance* from the lamp, it will not reach the skin. Even if it did, most UV-C does *not* penetrate the *Stratum corneum* of the skin.

Ultra-violet lamps

Anything which glows really *white hot* will give out *ultra-violet* in addition to heat and light. An ordinary electric lamp filament produces ultra-violet, but do not try tanning under an electric light. The ultra-violet cannot escape through the *glass* of the bulb. Ordinary glass is *opaque* to ultra-violet.

Ultra-violet filament lamp

For a filament lamp to give out ultra-violet, it must be made of a special glass called *Vitaglass*. This glass is transparent to ultra-violet down to 280 nm wavelength, so it lets through UV-A and UV-B.

Such a lamp is the 'Ultraphil' by Philips. These may be used singly in a simple *health lamp* or in multiple in some makes of *solaria* (see figures 13.3 and 13.4).

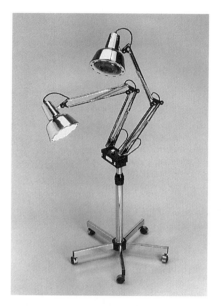

Figure 13.3 Filament-type ultra-violet and radiant heat treatment lamps (courtesy of Taylor Reeson Laboratories Ltd)

Figure 13.4 Solarium with filament ultra-violet lamps (courtesy of Norpe Saunas of Finland (UK) Ltd)

How a lamp filament produces rays

To understand what happens when a substance is made to give out *radiation*, we must first remind ourselves of the *structure of the atom* (see chapter 5), and in particular the layers or shells of electrons which surround its nucleus.

When an electric current is forced through a high-resistance lamp filament, its *energy* is absorbed by the *tungsten* atoms of the filament. In absorbing the energy, electrons in the atom are forced to move from an inner shell to one further out. However they almost immediately fall back again and the energy must be given out in the form of *rays*, a mixture of *heat*, *light* and *ultra-violet*.

The arc lamp

The electric arc ultra-violet lamp is essentially a very simple device but it is *not* so simple to operate. The lamp has to be 'driven'. When you switch on, nothing happens. To start the lamp you must 'strike' the arc. Then the lamp needs constant attention to keep it working. Figures 13.5 and 13.6 show an electric arc 'sun ray' lamp.

An *electric arc* is in effect a continuously sustained spark. In the *arc lamp*, the arc is sustained between two electrodes made of either *carbon* or *iron*.

The distance between the tips of the electrodes may be adjusted by screw knobs behind the reflector. To operate the lamp, plug in and switch on.

Figure 13.5 Carbon arc sunray lamp

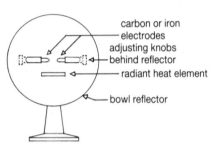

Figure 13.6 Arc ultra-violet lamp

Nothing will happen! To *strike the arc*, gently screw the electrodes together until they just touch. The continuous spark of the arc will then start. Now screw the electrodes *apart* until the arc is at its brightest.

As the lamp operates, the electrodes gradually burn away and the gap gets wider. From time to time you will have screw them together a little or else the lamp will go out. Do not forget to *wear protective goggles* when using an ultra-violet lamp. Ultra-violet rays damage the eyes.

How the arc lamp works

When the arc is struck, a momentary short-circuit generates sufficient heat to *evaporate* and *ionise* some atoms of *carbon* or *iron* from the tips of the electrodes. It is these ions which carry the electric current across the gap.

The *ionisation* is not the same as that which occurs in a salt solution. It is rather like what happens to the *tungsten* atoms of the lamp filament. The electrical energy forces electrons to move outwards from the atom and one or more may be driven away altogether. If the atom loses electrons which are *negatively charged*, it becomes a *positive* charged *ion*.

However the highly energised ions soon attract back the 'lost' electrons and revert to being ordinary atoms again, but in doing so release the energy as *rays*.

The 'mix' of rays from an *arc lamp* is

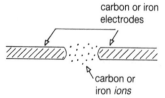

Figure 13.7 The electric arc

Infra-red – heat – 85 per cent		Compare with sunshine	80 per cent
Visible light – 10 per cent			13 per cent
Ultra-violet – 5 per cent			7 per cent

The ultra-violet is down to 290 nm, which embraces UV-A and UV-B.

The difficulty in operating the lamp results from the arc being *open* rather than enclosed. The ions can easily escape, so they must be replaced by evaporating more from the electrodes. Also if there was *no air* between the electrodes – just ions – the arc could be started without having to touch the electrodes together. Arc lamps today are *museum pieces*. Modern lamps are *enclosed*.

The quartz mercury vapour lamp

The quartz mercury vapour lamp is such an enclosed lamp. The enclosure or 'envelope' is made of *quartz* which is transparent to ultra-violet. Inside is almost a vacuum; the air has been removed and replaced with a little *argon* gas and a few drops of *mercury* which evaporates. There is an electrode each end (see figure 13.8).

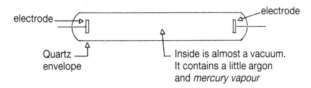

Figure 13.8 Quartz mercury vapour lamp

The lamp operates on about 125 volts. Mains is cut down to this voltage by a *resistor* wired *in series*. To start the lamp needs a 'kick' of higher voltage. This is necessary to *ionise* the *argon* atoms so the *arc* can strike. A special starter circuit is used to do this. Once the argon starts to ionise, the current flows easily between the electrodes producing the *arc* or *discharge*. Closed lamps are often referred to as discharge lamps. As the lamp heats up, the *mercury* evaporates and ionises and the light changes from greenish-blue to intense bluish white.

The mercury atoms then continually ionise and revert back to being atoms. As a result, they give out their rays. The *output* of the lamp is

Infra-red – heat	– 52 per cent	}	Compare with sunshine	{	80 per cent
Visible light	– 20 per cent				13 per cent
Ultra-violet	– 28 per cent				7 per cent

The ultra violet is down to 189 nm. This means that it includes UV-A, UV-B and UV-C.

You will notice that the heat output is way down compared with sunshine. To make it *feel* like sunshine, the heat is made up by supplementary *infra-red* or *radiant lamps*.

There are *two* types of quartz mercury vapour lamps – the '*low-pressure*' lamp and the '*high-pressure*' lamp. Both actually operate at the *low pressure* of a near-vacuum, but the 'high-pressure' type operates at a slightly '*higher* low pressure' than the 'low-pressure' type!

The low-pressure quartz mercury vapour lamp

The low-pressure lamp is a *straight* tubular lamp, usually between two and four inches long (see figure 13.9). This type is used in most *combined health lamps* and in many *solarium units*.

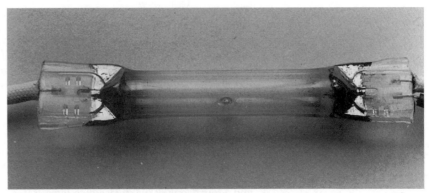

Figure 13.9 Low-pressure quartz mercury vapour ultra-violet lamp

A typical combined health lamp uses a single 'low-pressure' ultra-violet lamp together with usually a pair of *infra-red* or *radiant* lamps (see figures 13.10 and 13.11). The ultra-violet lamp is usually about 250–500 watts power and the heat lamps usually total about 1000 watts.

Figure 13.10 Combined health lamp (courtesy of Norpe Saunas of Finland (UK) Ltd)

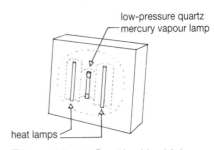

Figure 13.11 Combined health lamp

A *solarium* consists of a bank of *two*, *three* or *four* combined units, so the whole body may be treated (see figure 13.12).

High-pressure quartz mercury vapour lamps

The 'high-pressure' lamp may be in either a straight or 'U'-shaped quartz tube. These lamps can be made with power ratings of several kilowatts.

These lamps have gained much popularity in suntanning treatments in recent years. They can be filtered to produce an almost pure UV-A output at very *high intensity* which for suitable clients can result in a very rapid tan indeed. The client though must be the type who tans easily anyway.

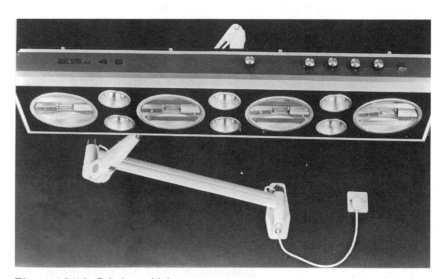

Figure 13.12 Solarium with low-pressure quartz mercury vapour lamps (courtesy of Nordic Saunas Ltd)

A small 'high-pressure' unit for face or part-body treatment may have a power of three kilowatts while a 'high-pressure' solarium might require up to 12 kilowatts and of course will need special electrical installation and maybe even a three-phase 415 volt supply. Because of the amount of *ozone* produced a forced ventilation system is essential too.

Figure 13.13 High-pressure facial solarium (courtesy of Helionova Ltd)

Figure 13.14 High-pressure solarium (courtesy of Helionova Ltd)

The Kromeyer or cold quartz lamp

Unfiltered, the quartz mercury vapour lamp gives off an appreciable output of UV-C, the tissue destructive rays. These rays are absorbed by the air and do not travel far from the lamp. In medical use, UV-C is valuable to kill infection

147

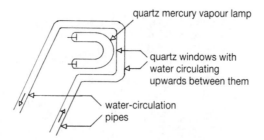

Figure 13.15 Water-cooled Kromeyer ultra-violet lamp

in open septic wounds or to treat growths on the skin. To use UV-C the lamp must be brought *very close* to the area being treated, so it has a water-cooled window to absorb the heat output (see figure 13.15).

Deterioration of a quartz lamp

After a long period of use the quartz of the lamp will be changed by the ultra-violet and become less transparent to ultra-violet rays. To compensate for this, the output of the lamp is uprated by reducing the value of the *series resistor*. Eventually the lamp must be replaced, even though it may still be in 'working' order. For this reason, it is important to keep a *record* of the *time* for which the lamp is operated. The usual working life is around 500 hours.

Fluorescent tube ultra-violet lamps

In *sunbeds*, the source of ultra-violet is a bank of *fluorescent tube* lamps. These are similar in appearance and operation to the familiar fluorescent lighting tubes except that they emit a blue visible light and *ultra-violet* rays.

The lamps are usually five or six feet long, though shorter ones are sometimes used. The lamp consists of a long tube of special glass called *Vitaglass* which is transparent to ultra-violet down to 280 nm wavelength.

At each end is a filament electrode. Inside the tube is almost a vacuum except for a little *argon* and *mercury vapour*. Inside the glass is a coating of a *phosphor* (see figure 13.16).

A fluorescent lamp requires a special operating circuit. When switched on, the *starter* allows current to flow through the *filament-electrodes* to heat them.

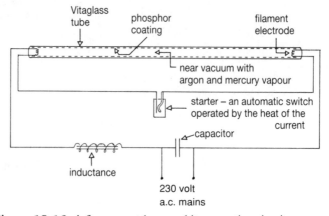

Figure 13.16 A fluorescent lamp and its operating circuit

It then switches off the heating circuit, causing a strong 'kick' of electricity to strike the arc by *ionising* the *argon* and then *mercury vapour* atoms. The *capacitor* and *inductance* then amplify the 230 volt mains to an effective 600 volts or more in order to maintain the arc between electrodes which are several *feet* apart. The starter circuit may require several attempts to establish the arc, resulting in those flashes before the lamp settles into continuous operation.

Some of the highly energised ions and electrons rushing around inside the tube *collide* with the *phosphor* coating. Their energy is transferred to the atoms of the phosphor, *ionising* them. They then produce the final output of the lamp as they revert to being atoms. The output of a *fluorescent ultra-violet* lamp consists of

> Very little *heat*
> Blue-violet *visible light*
> *Ultra-violet*

By careful selection of the *phosphor*, it is possible to tailor the output of the lamp exactly to requirements. Originally, *sunbeds* produced *pure UV-A* with *no UV-B* and of course *no UV-C*, the idea being *tan without burn*.

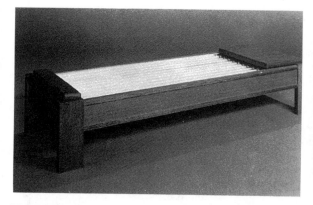

Figure 13.17 A basic fluorescent sunbed (courtesy of Sun Health Anglia)

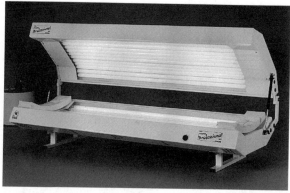

Figure 13.18 A sunbed with overhead unit (courtesy of Taylor Reeson Laboratories Ltd)

Figure 13.19 The fluorescent tubes and operating circuits (courtesy of Sun Health Anglia)

However, a large proportion of the population do not tan at all with pure UV-A. More recent sunbeds use lamps which also produce a *tiny* amount of UV-B – just enough to initiate the tanning reaction in these people, but not enough to cause sunburn.

Individually, fluorescent lamps produce little heat but when ten or twelve plus their 'works' are in close proximity in a sunbed, a *cooling fan* is essential to keep them and the *acrylic* bed surface cool.

There are over *fifty* types of fluorescent ultra-violet tubes. Always replace any faulty or 'time-expired' tubes with the *same* type, unless you wish to tan in stripes! These lamps too have a limited working life of usually about 1500–2000 hours. When time-expired, they should all be replaced together.

R-UVA sunbeds

The intensity of ultra-violet from the original sunbeds is limited by how close together the tubes may be fitted. To use as much of its output as possible, each tube is backed by a reflector and space has to be left between the tubes for the reflected rays to come through. This limits the sunbed to about eight tubes (see figure 13.20).

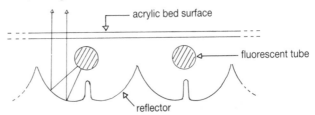

Figure 13.20 The reflectors of a sunbed

To develop a tan, a number of sessions will be required on a sunbed, which means it cannot compete with the high-speed tanning of the high-pressure solarium.

A recent development is the R-UVA tube by Philips. This is a tube with a *built-in reflector*. Since no separate reflector is required, neither is the gap between the tubes, so they can be packed much closer together. Fifteen or more can be fitted across a sunbed, and the same too across its overhead unit.

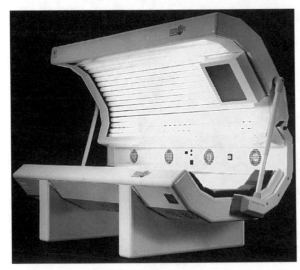

Figure 13.21 An R-UVA sunbed with closely packed fluorescent tubes (courtesy of Helionova Ltd)

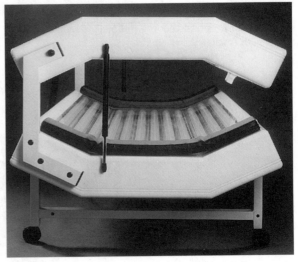

Figure 13.22 The closely packed tubes of an R-UVA sunbed (courtesy of Helionova Ltd)

The intensity of ultra-violet produced by these modern beds is now up to almost half that of a high-pressure solarium and four or five times that of the original sunbeds. One of these sunbeds with an overhead unit doing 'both sides at once' can tan almost as fast as a high-pressure unit and at a fraction of the cost.

Ultra-violet and the skin

Sunbathing and the effects of ultra-violet is a case of 'a little of what you fancy does you good', but an excess is bad. The effects of ultra-violet on the skin are a very 'mixed blessing'. Some are beneficial; some are harmful. Much of what happens is the result of the skin trying to *protect* itself and the body inside from the harmful effects of an excess of the rays. The skin is quite effective at preventing the rays penetrating deeply into the body.

Penetration of ultra-violet into the skin

The major factor in preventing the penetration of excess rays is the *Stratum corneum*, the horny layer of the *epidermis*. This consists of layer upon layer of flat transparent scales, the *squames*. As the rays pass into and out of each layer, some are reflected back or scattered at each surface until under normal circumstances very little remains to pass into the living cell layers beneath (see figure 13.23).

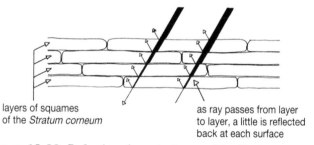

layers of squames
of the *Stratum corneum*

as ray passes from layer
to layer, a little is reflected
back at each surface

Figure 13.23 Reflection of rays by layers of the *Stratum corneum*

If you have some microscope slides, try stacking more and more together and looking through them. Notice how the more there are, the less light gets through. This demonstrates the screening effect of the *Stratum corneum*.

In the case of the skin, more UV-A than UV-B gets through the *Stratum corneum* but *no* UV-C (see figure 13.24).

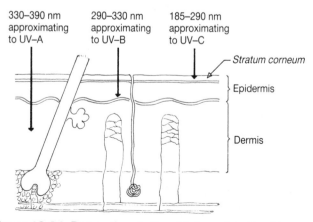

330–390 nm
approximating
to UV–A

290–330 nm
approximating
to UV–B

185–290 nm
approximating
to UV–C

Stratum corneum

Epidermis

Dermis

Figure 13.24 Penetration of ultra-violet rays into the skin

The *Stratum corneum* is maintained at such a thickness that with the 'usual' intensity of ultra-violet falling on it, very little passes through and no damage is caused to the live cells beneath. The *Stratum corneum* of exposed skin such as the face, neck and hands will be thicker than that of those parts normally covered by clothing.

Exposure to *higher than normal* intensities of ultra-violet will though allow sufficient rays to pass through the epidermis possibly to cause damage to the living cells beneath.

In a skin which has *active melanocytes* producing melanin pigment granules, the extra ultra-violet will develop the colour of this melanin, resulting in a *tan*. The tan is the skin's second line of defence against ultra-violet.

However not everyone's skin is in such a state of readiness. Their melanocytes are inactive. In this case *damage* will be caused to the live cells, resulting in the reddening, the discomfort and maybe the blistering and peeling of *sunburn*.

In either case, more UV-B will penetrate to the *Stratum germinativum* to stimulate its dividing cells into greater activity. They will produce new epidermal cells at a more rapid rate which will eventually *thicken* the *Stratum corneum* and thereby *reduce* the entry of ultra-violet to its original level.

The general increase in metabolism in the skin is reflected throughout the body as a *tonic invigorating effect* – the feeling of *'well-being'* that sunshine causes.

The physical, physiological and psychological effects of ultra-violet

The effects of ultra-violet rays are a mixture of the beneficial, the protective and the harmful.

Beneficial effects:
    Vitamin D production
    Stimulation of metabolism
    Tonic effect

Screening responses against excess:
    Suntanning
    The irritant effect of sunburn
    The thickening of the *Stratum corneum*

Damaging effects:
    Short-term – sunburn
    Long-term – premature aging
                 skin cancer

Vitamin D – the sunshine vitamin

A regular supply of *vitamin D* is required by the body to assist the incorporation of *calcium* to strengthen the bones and teeth. The vitamin may be obtained in *two* ways:

1   In *food* – A normal varied diet including dairy produce will supply all the vitamin D required, even though some people might care to make sure by taking a vitamin supplement.
2   Through *sunshine* – The vitamin may be made in the body with the help of *ultra-violet*.

In the body are two substances which can be converted into vitamin D. These *precursor* substances are *7-dehydrocholesterol* and *ergosterol*. When vitamin D is required these are moved to exposed skin where, using *ultra-violet* energy:

7-dehydrocholesterol becomes *cholecalciferol* or vitamin D_3
Ergosterol   becomes *ergocalciferol* or vitamin D_2

Both vitamin D_2 and D_3 are identical in their function in the body. The actual chemical changes performed by *ultra-violet* are quite small but they are the essential 'finishing touch' required to make the working vitamin.

The diagrams of the molecules in figure 13.25 will help to explain. In these diagrams each of the angles represents the position of a carbon atom.

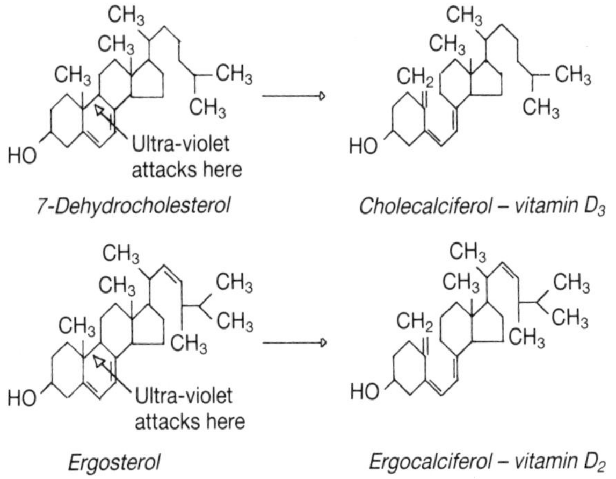

Figure 13.25 The formation of vitamin D

The potential for making vitamin D in the skin is so enormous that merely exposing the *face* for less than an hour on an *overcast December day* will make all that is required for the day. The body is, though, able to regulate what it makes in the skin so a long day's sunbathing will not cause over-production.

On the other hand, it *is* possible to overdose with vitamin D in the diet and excesses cannot be disposed of. *Gross* excesses in the diets of some 'vitamin addicts' can result in *calcium* being laid down in all kinds of strange places in the body – a condition called *hypervitaminosis-D*. It could prove *fatal*.

The tanning response

The development of a *tan* involves *three* mechanisms in the skin:

1 *Immediate response.*
   Uncoloured granules of *leucomelanin* in the *Stratum corneum* are converted into the coloured *melanin*. In this process the amino acid *tyrosine* in the granules is converted into melanin by the action of UV-A. Actually, wavelengths between 660 and 300 nm will do this. They include part of the visible spectrum, but 360–340 nm of the UV-A band is most effective. The process will be described later. Many people's skins do not have leucomelanin granules under 'normal' circumstances, so they are *not* able to tan quickly.

153

2   *Delayed response.*
    As UV-B stimulates more rapid production of new skin cells, so deeper granules are brought more quickly to the *Stratum corneum* to develop their colour. This stage of the tan develops in 1–2 days. It is brought about by wavelengths 320–290 nm, approximating to UV-B. Without the third stage, the tan will fade after about a week.

3   *Melanogenesis – the true tan.*
    A more prolonged exposure to UV-B will stimulate the *melanocytes* to produce ready-coloured melanin granules (see figure 13.26). Once started, they will continue to be active for many weeks or even months with *no* further exposure to ultra-violet – thus producing a *lasting tan*.

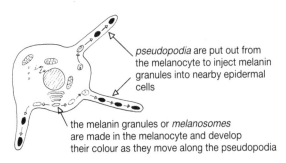

pseudopodia are put out from the melanocyte to inject melanin granules into nearby epidermal cells

the melanin granules or *melanosomes* are made in the melanocyte and develop their colour as they move along the pseudopodia

Figure 13.26 Production of melanin granules in a melanocyte

The formation of melanin

There are two forms of melanin. True melanin or *eumelanin* is a deep brown or black. *Pheomelanin* is a reddish, yellow colour. The colour of the *tan* is a combination of these.

Both are formed from an *amino acid* called *tyrosine* which once *oxidised* with the help of *ultra-violet energy*, will pass through a selection of intermediate substances to form the melanins. For those whose chemistry will 'stand the strain', figure 13.27 shows what happens. Again the angles are the positions of carbon atoms.

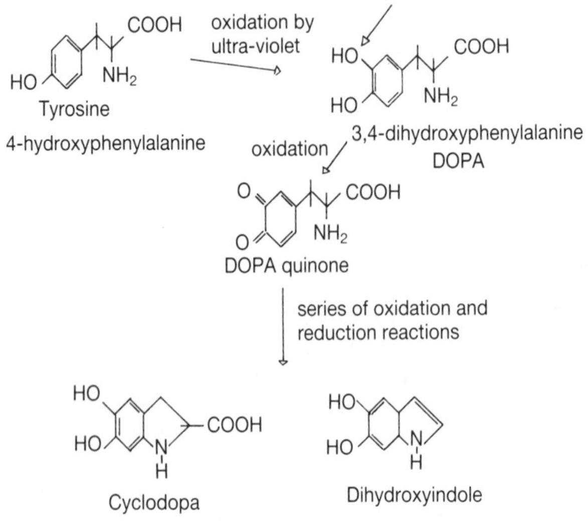

Tyrosine
4-hydroxyphenylalanine

oxidation by ultra-violet

3,4-dihydroxyphenylalanine
DOPA

oxidation

DOPA quinone

series of oxidation and reduction reactions

Cyclodopa

Dihydroxyindole

Figure 13.27 Stages in the formation of melanin pigments

To form eumelanin

Probably cyclodopa and dihydroxyindole then *polymerise*. That is, molecules of them link together in large numbers to form the dark brown or black pigment granules. How they join is shown in figure 13.28.

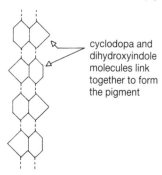

cyclodopa and dihydroxyindole molecules link together to form the pigment

Figure 13.28 The eumelanin polymer

To form pheomelanin

Cyclodopa combines with *cystein*, another amino acid, to form *cysteinyl dopa*. This then turns into *dihydroxybenzothiazine* which *polymerises* to form the much smaller *pheomelanin* granules which, depending on their size, are yellowish or reddish in colour.

The rapidly produced tans from a quick tan sunbed include more *pheomelanin* than normal, resulting in a rather yellowish effect!

Sunburn

For many unfortunate people, sunbathing means one thing – *sunburn*. People vary considerably in the way in which their skin reacts to the sun. The white population may be divided into *four* groups depending on how easily they tan – or burn:

Group 1. *Quick tan – no burn*
Such people's skin contains leucomelanin. It will *tan* quite quickly and rarely burns.
Safe time in the Sun – 40 minutes plus.

Group 2. *Tan easily – burn a little at first*
The melanocytes are active but melanin production has to be stepped up.
Safe time in the Sun – 20–30 minutes.

Group 3. *Burn easily – tan eventually*
Melanocytes have to be activated by exposure to UV-B.
Safe time in the Sun – 10–20 minutes.

Group 4. *Very sensitive*
Burn very easily with little chance of developing a tan.
Safe time in the Sun – 5–10 minutes.

The safe times quoted are for the first exposure of unprotected skin. However easily you tan (or burn!) you will be able to spend longer in the sun if you use an appropriate *sunscreen* cream or lotion. These are detailed in Volume 1 – Chapter 15.

> **ON NO ACCOUNT SHOULD YOU USE A SUNSCREEN TO EXTEND THE TIME YOU SPEND UNDER AN ULTRA-VIOLET LAMP.**

The mechanism of sunburn

When the skin is exposed to more ultra-violet than usual, the excess of UV-B has to be 'stopped' by the living layers of the *epidermis*. This sets off an *irritant action* very like that caused by a chemical irritant or a minor burn or scald.

The UV-B damages the cells. Some will die and 'self-destruct'. This releases from them their chemical 'cry for help' – *histamine*, which passes into the dermis. Here it triggers the pain nerve endings, resulting in *itch* or *pain* depending on the amount of damage. Histamine also causes dilation of the dermal blood vessels, the greater blood flow causing the *redness* or *erythema*.

If the damage to the epidermis is severe, fluid from the blood will fill the spaces left by the destroyed cells, causing *swelling* or *oedema*. This will separate layers of cells and as they migrate nearer the surface, the outer layers will *peel*.

The four degrees of sunburn

Sunburn does not necessarily follow the complete sequence. How far it goes depends on the severity of the initial burn. There are four recognised degrees of sunburn:

First degree   – a slight reddening which fades within 24 hours
Second degree – a definite redness and slight itch which lasts 2–3 days
Third degree   – an intense reddening, hot and sore with swelling; lasts about a week
Fourth degree – an intense reddening, hot and sore; the swelling leads to blistering and peeling

---

Assessing the sensitivity of a skin

A useful guide to deciding the recommended dose for ultra-violet treatment is the time it takes to cause the first signs of sunburn – the *minimum perceptible erythema*. The dose required to produce this is the *minimum erythemal dose*.

Tan without burn

Makers of sunbeds and 'high-pressure' solaria claim that you can tan without sunburn. This is done by employing an output which is almost entirely UV-A with just a little UV-B to initiate the tan.

However, the lack of UV-B means that the thickening process for the epidermis does not occur so excesses of UV-A can still penetrate to the dermis. Abusing the skin in this way for long periods can cause *premature aging*.

Premature aging

The excess of UV-A reaching the dermis causes severe disruption of its elastic fibre network. The result is a loss of *elasticity* which allows the skin to wrinkle.

Those holiday-makers who can manage only an annual fortnight in the Sun need not worry unduly. It is the long-term sunworshippers whose skin is really at risk . . . and those who regularly spend hours and hours on sunbeds.

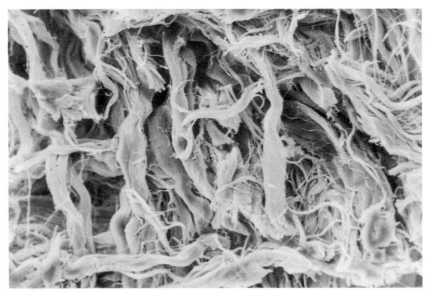

Figure 13.29 Collagen fibre network of the dermis (photo – Hugh Rushton, courtesy of the Philip Kingsley Trichology Clinic)

Even then all is not lost. If the skin is protected from the Sun or the use of sunbeds is stopped, the elastic fibres will gradually be restored and the skin will regain its elasticity, but it means abstaining from sunbathing for a long time.

Safety in the use of ultra-violet

It happens to almost everyone: a beautiful sunny day, on the beach sunbathing. You stay that little bit longer – *sunburn*!

Brand new sunlamp! You use it for the recommended time and you have nothing to show for it. So you give it a bit longer – *burn*! Those goggles are a bind so you leave them off. A bit later on your eyes feel as if they are full of grit.

The effects of ultra-violet are not immediate so it is not possible to know there and then that you have received a harmful excess. This is all the more reason for setting *strict safety standards* and *following them* meticulously.

Ultra-violet and the law

There *is* legislation controlling the use of ultra-violet lamps for therapeutic purposes.

It requires salons and clinics offering ultra-violet therapy to register with the local authority. However most authorities now no longer keep such a register; a few still do. Check with your local authority before installing ultra-violet equipment in your salon.

For private use at home, lamps could at one time be bought *only* on production of a doctor's prescription. This has now been discontinued.

Safety in the construction of ultra-violet lamps

Apart from the usual considerations of electrical safety, it is essential to ensure that lamps are of sound *mechanical* construction. Units are available for both commercial and home use, and one might be tempted to purchase the much cheaper home-type rather than one specifically designed for commercial use. This can prove a false economy. The amount of use of a professional unit is at least *ten* times that of private use, and this is taken into account in the design of the equipment.

Even so, it is as well to check that sunbeds are not likely to collapse and that the angle-poise or counterbalance systems of overhead units are not likely to let them droop or drop suddenly on to the client. Do not forget to check the condition of these systems from time to time (see figures 13.30 and 13.31).

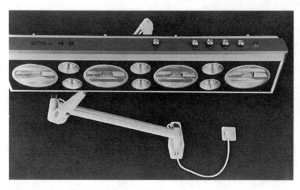

Figure 13.30 Solarium on an angle-poise wall mounting (courtesy of Nordic Saunas Ltd)

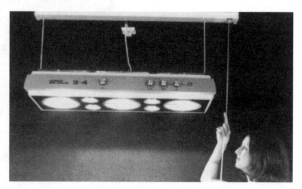

Figure 13.31 Solarium supported by cables and weights (courtesy of Nordic Saunas Ltd)

Ultra-violet treatment cubicles

It is not for modesty reasons that each ultra-violet treatment unit must be in its own 'ray-proof' booth or cubicle. It is so that the treatment is confined to the client and there is no 'casual dosing' of others nearby. It could otherwise be quite likely that the therapist would be overdosed with 'stray' rays from other people's treatments (see figure 13.32).

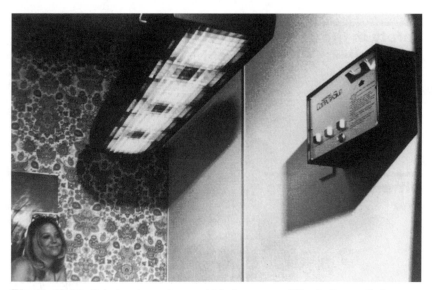

Figure 13.32 Solarium in a private cubicle (courtesy of Nordic Saunas Ltd)

For the same reason, only the client should be in the cubicle during the treatment.

Good ventilation of the cubicles is essential. Ultra-violet produces *ozone*. Ozone in the air can be nauseating and in excess can cause respiratory problems. Suppliers of 'high-pressure' solaria insist that a forced ventilation system is part of the deal.

Safety and the ultra-violet client

There is a temptation for clients, particularly first-timers, left alone in the cubicle to abuse the rules by extending the dose time or shortening the distance between themselves and the solarium unit.

In the pre-treatment briefing before using a solarium, it is essential to stress the dangers of overdosing and to reassure them that, with most equipment, they will have nothing to show for the treatment until sometime afterwards.

Some manufacturers offer devices to make sure the equipment, particularly quartz mercury vapour solaria, is as 'idiot-proof' as possible. These include *key-operated* master switches, *remote controls* out of reach of the client and in one case dose-coded *tokens*. Coin-operated units are *not* a good idea. It is so easy for a client in a busy health centre to buy more time unnoticed by the attendant (see figures 13.33, 13.34 and 13.35).

Figure 13.33 Key-operated master switch on a solarium (courtesy of Nordic Saunas Ltd)

Figure 13.34 Remote controls for a solarium (courtesy of Nordic Saunas Ltd)

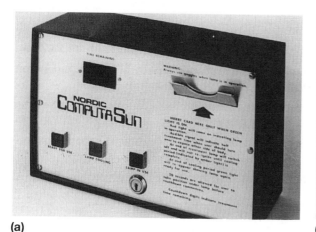

(a)

(b)

Figure 13.35 (a) Token control unit and (b) token for a solarium (courtesy of Nordic Saunas Ltd)

The consultation

Most important to ensure that clients do not suffer discomfort is the pre-treatment consultation and instruction by the therapist. During this, the client should be made fully aware of the consequences of overdosing, particularly from quartz mercury vapour lamps. A check should be made for contra-indications, in particular whether the client has been taking medicinal drugs.

Most are *photosensitisers* and make one extra sensitive to sunshine. The client should be asked to *wash* or *shower*. This is to remove *grease*, which can screen against ultra-violet, and *perfume*, of which some ingredients are photosensitisers.

If the client is to use a *quartz mercury vapour* health lamp or solarium, a check must be made for sensitivity. A card stencil with hinged flaps is placed over an area of skin. The rest of the body is covered. The lamp is switched on and the flaps are opened one at a time at short intervals. This will show how long it takes to produce the first signs of erythema. From this, the dose for treatment may then be prescribed.

This dose may be as little as *one* minute 'per side' – the client turns at 'half time' to treat the other side – up to eight minutes per side maximum. This is at 90 cm (36 inches) distance from the lamp. It is quite in order to use a measuring tape to check the distance.

Sunbed hygiene

Unlike a treatment couch which is prepared with fresh towels and tissue for each client, a *sunbed* must involve direct body contact with the uncovered bed. This means there is the possibility of *cross-infection* from one client to the next. The sunbed must therefore be cleaned with a suitable *detergent steriliser* between clients.

Things to do

1 Collect manufacturers' information literature on the many makes of ultra-violet therapy equipment.

2 Compare the cost-effectiveness of ultra-violet suntanning treatment with the various types of ultra-violet equipment: quartz mercury vapour solaria; fluorescent sunbeds with and without overhead units; fluorescent sunbeds with R-UVA tubes; and high-pressure mercury vapour solaria.

Self-assessment questions

1 List seven types of electromagnetic radiations emitted from the Sun.

2 What part of the atmosphere absorbs (a) much of the heat radiation from the Sun, (b) most of the ultra-violet radiation from the Sun?

3 What is the shortest wavelength of the Sun's radiations which reaches us on the surface of the Earth?

4 Why should a person on a winter sports holiday take special precautions against sunburn?

5 What are the wavelengths of ultra-violet radiations known as (a) UV-A, (b) UV-B and (c) UV-C?

6 With an old-fashioned electric arc lamp, how did one 'strike the arc'?

7 What type of ultra-violet lamp is used in a combined health lamp?

8 What is a 'cold quartz' ultra-violet lamp and for what purpose is it used?

9 What is the difference between R-UVA and 'ordinary' fluorescent ultra-violet lamps? What is the advantage of the R-UVA type?

10 How does the *Stratum corneum* of the skin prevent much of the harmful radiation of the sun reaching the live tissues beneath?

11 What is the difference in the role of UV-A and UV-B in producing a suntan?

12 What effect does an excess of ultra-violet radiation have on the collagen fibres of the dermis? Which ultra-violet rays are mostly responsible for this effect?

13 Which vitamin can be produced in the body with the aid of ultra-violet radiation? What is its purpose in the body?

14 What is (a) a melanocyte, (b) eumelanin and (c) pheomelanin?

15 What are the four groups into which the white population can be divided on the basis of their sensitivity to sunshine? State the 'safe time' each group can spend in the sun without burning.

16 Which ultra-violet rays are mainly responsible for sunburn? Briefly describe the symptoms of sunburn.

17 What is the 'minimum erythemal dose'?

18 What precautions should be taken by the therapist to ensure clients using solaria are not overdosed with ultra-violet?

19 Why should ultra-violet equipment be in individual cubicles and away from the rest of the salon?

20 Why is good ventilation essential in ultra-violet treatment cubicles, particularly when powerful 'high-pressure' units are in use?

14

Hydrotherapy

*What is hydrotherapy; physiological effects of water;
hydrothermal treatments; skin surface temperature;
temperature tolerance; hot, cold and contrast baths;
steam baths; saunas; sauna equipment; humidity and
relative humidity; hygrometer; hygiene with steam baths
and saunas; mud baths, wax baths and foam baths*

Introducing hydrotherapy

The literal meaning of hydrotherapy is 'treatment with water'. It encompasses a wide variety of treatments which use *water* in all its forms – liquid, ice and vapour, both still and moving:

Hot baths	Cold baths	Contrast baths
Hot showers	Cold showers	Impulse showers
Steam baths	Saunas	Plunge pools
Whirlpool baths	Aerated baths	Foam baths
Spa baths	Mud baths	Wax baths

Hydrotherapy is not new. Most cultures on all the continents have made use of the therapeutic effects of water since pre-historic times: sea bathing, mineral springs, hot springs, hot volcanic mud . . . .

The Romans had developed considerable technology in their famous bath complexes. Communal bathing was the norm in Roman society and they built swimming bath sized hot and cold pools, steam rooms and hot rooms. When they came to Britain 2000 years ago they built baths here too. Famous among them and still in a remarkable state of preservation are the Roman baths at Bath (see figure 14.1).

Figure 14.1 Therapy pool in the Roman baths at Bath

Figure 14.2 Hot air channels beneath the floor of the hot room – Roman baths at Cheltenham

The physiological effects of hydrotherapy

Hydrotherapy treatments are of two main types:

1 *Hydrothermal therapy* is the use of water to warm or cool the body.

2 *Hydrokinetic therapy* is the use of the *mechanical* properties of water:

> Buoyancy   – the flotation effect of water
> Hydrostatic pressure – the resistance to movement in water
> Mechanical impact   – of water on the move

Table 14.1 lists some of the useful effects of hydrotherapy and the treatments which produce them. Some of these effects are not within the scope of the health and beauty therapist. The diuretic effect and the inducing or reducing of fever are medicinal applications of hydrotherapy.

Table 14.1 Effects of hydrotherapy and the treatments to produce them

Therapeutic effect	*Hydrotherapy treatments*
Relief of pain	Hot bath, Cold bath, Whirlpool bath
Sedative, relaxation	Warm baths
Local anaesthetic	Cold baths, Ice packs
Stimulant, tonic	Cold baths, Contrast baths, Whirlpool baths
Perspirant, cleansing	Hot baths, Steam baths, Sauna
Diuretic – increased urine	Cold baths
Inducing fever	Hot baths
Reducing fever	Tepid baths

Hydrothermal treatments

Depending on the temperature of the water relative to the temperature of the surface of the skin, water can be used either to *deliver heat* to the body or to *remove heat* from the body.

Skin surface temperature

The temperature of the surface of the skin is somewhat less than the 37°C of internal body temperature.

> Skin surface temperature is 33°C or less

Hand and foot temperatures can be well down in the 20s°C. You can measure those temperatures with a thermometer. An ordinary thermometer is not very satisfactory for this. An *electronic thermometer* fitted with a *surface* probe will give more accurate measurements (see figure 14.3).

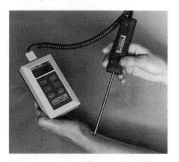

Figure 14.3 Measuring skin surface temperature with an electronic thermometer

Water at 33°C	neither delivers heat to the body nor takes it away. It is *neutral*. This is a suitable temperature for *hydrokinetic* baths and pools
Water above 33°C	delivers heat to the body, a *hyper*thermal effect
Water below 33°C	takes heat from the body, a *hypo*thermal effect

Temperature tolerance of the body to water

You will need a bowl of *hot* water. Adjust its temperature by adding more hot or cold water until you can just bear to keep your hand, or better still, your *elbow* in it continuously. Measure its temperature. You will find:

> the *maximum temperature* tolerable is 45°C or not much more

Next you will need a bowl of very cold water. Ice will probably be needed to make it cold enough, again so that you can just keep your elbow in it continuously:

the *minimum temperature* tolerable is 4–5°C

Contact with water at much above 45°C will *scald*. Scalding water does not have to be near boiling. Prolonged immersion in water below 4°C may cause *frostbite* as living tissues start to be killed.

Temperature tolerance to air

The body can withstand exposure to *air* at much higher and much lower temperatures than those of water, so long as the air is *still*.

Skin can remain in contact with *hot* air at up to 140°C before it causes a *burn*. The temperature in a *sauna* can range from 70°C up to 110°C. The greater tolerance to air temperatures is because air holds *less* heat than water, and air in contact with the skin is soon cooled to near skin temperature. A further *cooling effect* comes from the *evaporation* of sweat by the heat of the air.

Skin can also withstand prolonged contact with *cold* air at temperatures way below freezing point. *Minus* 30 or 40°C is quite 'tolerable' so long as the air is fairly still.

The stillness of the air is critical. A blast of hot air *will* burn and an icy blast will freeze the skin.

Immersion baths

For whole body immersion baths, a conventional bathroom bath tub is quite suitable. It is filled with sufficient water at the required temperature to cover the client's body. Its temperature is checked with a thermometer.

Hot bath

A hot bath at 37 to 42°C will cause the following physiological effects:

> Increased blood circulation in the skin as the body disperses the heat
> The pulse initially drops, then increases to increase the circulation
> The blood pressure initially rises, then falls as the blood vessels dilate
> The breathing rate increases but the breaths are shallow
> The metabolic rate increases
> There is profuse production of sweat

The overall effect is initially *stimulating*, then *relaxing*. Any pain is relieved and the bather gets a feeling of lassitude or laziness.

A hot bath should last 20–30 minutes and should be topped up to maintain its temperature. After the bath a *cold* shower or 'plunge' will act as an *astringent* to stop the sweating, constrict the skin's blood vessels and so removes the risk of contracting a *chill*.

Cold bath

The water in a cold therapeutic bath is at 10–27°C. The *shock* of immersing oneself in the cold water initially causes the breath to be held and the pulse to quicken. Once settled in the water, breathing resumes, albeit slowly and the pulse drops perhaps to below normal.

Soon follows a *reaction* in the form of a feeling of *warmth* and well-being. While in the bath the skin capillaries constrict and the skin looks bluish. On getting out, the capillaries dilate and the skin reddens.

The overall effect is *stimulating* and *invigorating*. The appetite is improved, the metabolic rate is increased and the blood pressure is slightly up.

A cold bath is a short, sharp treatment. It will last from as little as 4 seconds to 3 minutes. The 'plunge pool' which often accompanies a sauna is a *cold* pool. Come out before you start to *shiver*. Too long in a cold bath will *slow* the metabolism – the start of *hypothermia*.

Contrast baths

Contrast baths are not often convenient to arrange. You need *two* bath tubs side by side so the bather may quickly transfer from one to the other.

> The *hot* bath contains water at 38–46°C
> The *cold* bath contains water at 10–18°C

The treatment cycle consists of immersion alternately in the *hot* bath for 1–4 minutes and the *cold* bath for 20–60 seconds. The sequence may start with either hot or cold. The client should make up to *nine* changes but always finish with *cold*. The whole treatment should last for 10–30 minutes. The alternate constriction and dilation of the superficial blood vessels is beneficial to the circulation and the responsiveness of the nervous system.

The impulse shower

The impulse shower cubicle is fitted with a normal shower head for a *hot* shower and spray bars for *cold* sprays. The unit has an electronic control system to alternate the hot and cold sprays. The cold spray may even be supplied by a special pump which *pulses* the cold jets producing a percussive, massaging effect (see figure 14.4).

Figure 14.4 An electrically controlled impulse shower (courtesy of Nordic Saunas Ltd)

Partial immersion baths

Physiotherapists often make use of smaller immersion baths which are to treat a single arm or the legs. In beauty therapy you do of course use a *foot bath*.

Steam baths and saunas

People are often confused by the terms 'steam bath' and 'sauna'.

> A *steam bath* employs the *wet heat* of hot water vapour
> A *sauna* uses the *dry heat* of hot air

Both are very effective treatments for the whole body. The physiological effects are essentially the same as those of a hot bath.

The *sweating* caused is very profuse and results in a refreshing *deep cleansing* of the skin. The consequent loss of *water* can produce a dramatic *weight loss* of perhaps several pounds, but sadly it is only temporary. Quenching the thirst soon puts it all back!

Actually, one should be very wary of the water loss. It can lead to *dehydration*. Do not go alone into a steam bath or sauna and lie down. The water loss could make you feel tired and you could fall asleep. In a not-well-supervised sauna, it could prove fatal.

Steam baths

A steam bath may be a *cabinet* in which one person may sit for treatment with the head out in fresh air, or it may be a *room* in which several people may take the treatment together (see figures 14.5 and 14.6).

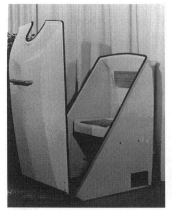

Figure 14.5 A steam cabinet (courtesy of Taylor Reeson Laboratories Ltd)

(a)

(b)

(c)

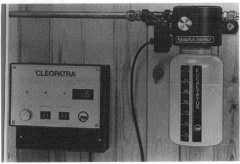

(d)

Figure 14.6 A steam room [inset – steam generator and aromatic essence injector] ((a) and (c) courtesy of Dale Saunas Ltd; (b) and (d) courtesy of Nordic Saunas Ltd)

166

The room or cabinet is supplied with steam from a suitable boiler. Initially this is *wet steam* at 100°C but on mixing with the air it cools and condenses to become *water vapour* at well below 100°C. The *maximum* tolerable temperature in a *steam bath* is around 45°C.

The body is heated by the *water vapour*. This is tiny droplets of liquid hot water. This has the high heat capacity of liquid hot water so the heating is very effective. Because the air in a steam bath is *saturated*, the sweat cannot evaporate so it has no cooling effect. It just runs off the skin.

Whether a client prefers to use a steam *cabinet* or steam *room* depends on a number of factors which are detailed in table 14.2.

Table 14.2 The steam cabinet and steam room compared

Steam cabinet	Steam room
Individual treatment Privacy Can adjust for individual clients	Group treatment Social Cannot adjust for each client
Head is out of steam Hair may be kept dry Client breathes *fresh air*	Head is in steamy atmosphere Hair gets wet Client breathes *saturated hot air*
Some clients do not like the restriction of a cabinet	Some clients equally feel shut-in in a steam room
Capital cost is low	Capital cost is high – several £1000s
Space requirement is small – many models fold away	Space requirement is large
Running costs are lower Boiler is typically around 2 kW using 2 units per hour and the cabinet soon warms up for use	Running costs are high Room must operate for the whole working day plus a considerable warm-up time Boiler is typically 5–7 kW. If electric it would use 5–7 units per hour

Sanitisation

Because they operate under warm moist conditions which are ideal for the breeding of germs, it is important that steam cabinets and steam rooms and their furnishings are regularly cleaned and disinfected. A 1 per cent lysol solution is effective.

Contra-indications

Because of the water loss from the body, clients with already low blood pressure may feel *faint* and, because the lost water is made up for by extra absorption from the intestine, sufferers from *constipation* may find their condition aggravated.

Breathing *hot saturated air* in a steam room may cause breathing difficulties. The air is *cooled* as it enters the lungs and water condenses from it to 'waterlog' the lungs. In theory one could *drown*. Clients with lung damage or with asthma should avoid steam rooms.

Sauna

The traditional idea of a Finnish sauna is of a pine log cabin on the banks of a lake. In the cabin you swelter in the heat of a powerful stove. Then it is outside for a plunge in the lake, or in winter, a roll in the snow!

Figure 14.7 A sauna cabin by a lake in Finland (courtesy of the Finnish Tourist Board)

Sauna temperature

The temperature in a sauna can range from 70°C to as high as 110°C. Yes, that is higher than the boiling point of water!

> 70°C – mild sauna
> 90°C – strong sauna
> 110°C – very strong sauna for hot countries

The air does not *feel* as hot as it is, firstly because *hot air* does not have as high a *heat capacity* as water and is soon cooled on contacting the skin, and secondly because the *sweat* it causes quickly *evaporates* resulting in a *cooling effect* on the skin.

The effects of a sauna

The main effect of heating the skin is to cause *profuse sweat loss* which deep cleanses and refreshes the skin. To bring water to the skin and dissipate the heat the *circulation* is stimulated. The considerable loss of sweat causes a dramatic weight loss – albeit temporary. Because the sweat *evaporates* rather than running off the skin, the extent of the water loss from the body is not always appreciated and can possibly lead to *dehydration*.

The shower or plunge

After a sauna, a cold shower or a plunge in a pool *cools* the skin. Its *astringent* action closes the pores, stops the sweating and its cooling effect prevents *chills*. The temperature of the pool or shower is 15–21°C. You should stay in for from 5 seconds to at most 2 minutes.

The sauna cabin

Most saunas are designed around the idea of the log cabin. The pine log construction enables the walls to 'breathe' so they absorb any condensation rather than letting it run down. Figures 14.8 and 14.9 show pine log sauna cabins for indoor and outdoor installation. The interior view in figure 14.10 shows that the internal flooring and furnishings are in pine too. Metal fittings and furnishings would become too hot to the touch and could possibly burn clients.

Figure 14.8 Indoor sauna cabin (courtesy of Elite Saunas)

Figure 14.9 Outdoor sauna cabin by the pool (courtesy of Nordic Saunas Ltd)

Figure 14.10 Interior of a sauna (courtesy of Elite Saunas)

Figure 14.11 A sauna stove

The sauna stove

The heat is provided by a powerful electric stove. On top is a tray of stones or '*coals*' on to which clients may pour water which boils to increase the humidity in the sauna. A typical sauna stove is shown in figure 14.11.

Because of their power ratings, sauna stoves cannot be run from a socket.

Table 14.3 The stove must be powerful enough for the sauna

Capacity of sauna (persons)	Power of stove (kW) Indoor	Outdoor
1–2	3	
2–5	5	10
5–7	7.5	12.5
7–10	10	
10–15	12.5	
15–20	15	20

They must be wired direct from the consumer unit. Some of the more powerful stoves may require a *three-phase* supply. Table 14.3 shows how the power of the stove is matched to the capacity of the sauna.

Humidity in a sauna

The rapid evaporation of sweat which occurs in a sauna is because the *relative humidity* of the air in there is *very low*.

Humidity is the water vapour content of the air
Relative humidity (RH) is the *measure* of humidity

$$\text{Relative humidity (per cent)} = \frac{\text{Actual water vapour content of air}}{\text{Maximum it } can \text{ hold at that temperature}} \times 100$$

For *comfort* the air should have a *relative humidity* of 60–70 per cent. If the air is *too moist*, one feels hot and sticky because the sweat cannot evaporate to cool the body.

If the air is *too dry*, one feels tired and the throat tends to be dry. These are signs of dehydration.

Air with a relative humidity of 100 per cent is holding the maximum water vapour it can at that temperature. It is *saturated*. The air in a *steam bath* is saturated.

Relative humidity in a sauna

As air is *heated* so its capacity to hold water vapour *increases* (see figure 14.12). If water is not available to fill this capacity, the *relative humidity decreases*. In a sauna the relative humidity might be as low as 10 per cent.

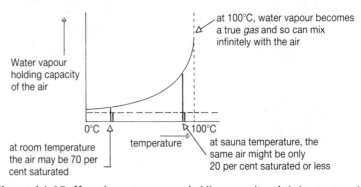

Figure 14.12 How the water vapour holding capacity of air increases with temperature

At the *low humidity* in a sauna, *sweat evaporates rapidly*, so the *cooling* effect of evaporation is great. A sauna does not *feel* as hot as it really is.

The rapid water loss is not very noticeable so the danger of *dehydration* is high. The greater water loss through the *lungs* may cause breathing difficulties. If the sauna is too hot, the lungs may be scorched.

Measuring humidity

Relative humidity is measured with a *hygrometer*. Do not confuse it with a *hydrometer* which measures relative density! There are *two* types of *hygrometer*.

The *dial* type is usually a *hair hygrometer*. A bundle of human hairs expands when it is moist and contracts when it dries. The expansion and contraction is used to turn the pointer on the dial (see figures 14.13 and 14.14).

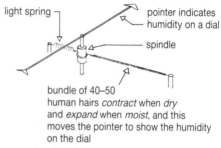

Figure 14.13 Dial-type hygrometer and thermometer in a sauna (courtesy of Elite Saunas)

Figure 14.14 A hair hygrometer

The *wet and dry bulb hygrometer* consists of two thermometers mounted side by side (see figures 14.15, 14.16 and 14.17). A wick round the bulb of one dips into a reservoir of water. In dry air conditions, water evaporates from the wick causing a cooling effect so the thermometer reads 'lower' than it might. The drier the air the lower the reading. The readings are compared with a set of tables or a graph to give the relative humidity percentage.

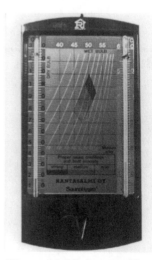

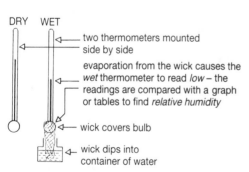

Figure 14.15 Wet and dry bulb hygrometer

Figure 14.16 A wet and dry bulb hygrometer for weather use

Figure 14.17 A wet and dry bulb hygrometer for a sauna (courtesy of Rantasalmi)

Pouring water on the coals

The users of a sauna are provided with a bucket of water and a ladle. They ladle water on to the coals in a tray on top of the stove.

The water *boils* and the sauna *feels hotter*! – Why?

The steam increases the humidity. This reduces the rate of evaporation of sweat, so lessening the cooling effect: the sauna *feels* hotter. This lessens the water loss from the body and the risk of dehydration. It also lessens the likelihood of scorching the lungs.

Sauna hygiene

If care is not taken to cleanse and disinfect a sauna regularly, it could become a source of infection. Although the *air* in a sauna is too hot for the active growth of bacteria, the walls and furnishings are not.

Regular scrubbing out with a suitable disinfectant will reduce the build-up of infection.

With clients barefoot using the sauna, there is a risk of spreading foot infections – verrucas and athlete's foot. It is possible to obtain special disposable sauna slippers made of reinforced paper (see figure 14.19).

Figure 14.18 Pouring water on the stones produces a 'heat wave' (courtesy of Nordic Saunas Ltd)

Figure 14.19 Sauna slipper

Mud baths

A mud bath is rather like having a face pack all over the body. A variety of clays and similar materials may be used to make the 'mud'. A few 'specials' are:

> Mineral-laden volcanic muds – for example, Parafango from Italy. This contains sulphur, iron, assorted silicates – and it is slightly radioactive!
> Ooze is mud from the deep ocean bed – and is made up of the remains of millions of minute marine organisms
> Peat is the remains of plants which once grew on boggy ground

The mud is made by mixing with water at 36–42°C to a buttery consistency. It can then be applied to the whole or part of the body.

Mud is a good way of conveying *heat* to the body. It has a high heat capacity but because it is a poor conductor of heat, it is delivered gradually over a long period. The mud bath will last for about 20 minutes. Then the mud is washed off with a *warm* water spray.

Wax baths

Molten wax, too, is a very effective way of delivering *heat* to the body. The treatment may be applied to a limb or to the whole body. So that the wax does not trap the hairs on the skin, the treatment area is covered first with grease-proof paper or polythene sheet.

The wax is melted and heated to 52–55°C in a suitable thermostatically controlled wax heater.

To treat a limb, the limb is dipped in the molten wax, then withdrawn to let the wax set to form a glove. It is then immersed in the molten wax for the duration of the treatment – 20–30 minutes. The limb is then withdrawn to let the wax set so it may be peeled off (see figure 14.20).

To treat the whole body, cover it with greaseproof paper or polythene. Paint on the molten wax liberally. Allow it to set and leave it on for 20–30 minutes. Peel it off. Figure 14.21 shows a wax bath being applied.

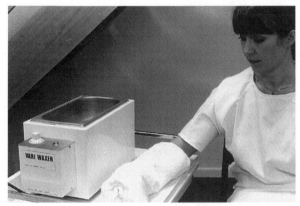

Figure 14.20 Wax bath on a limb (courtesy of E.A. Ellison and Co Ltd)

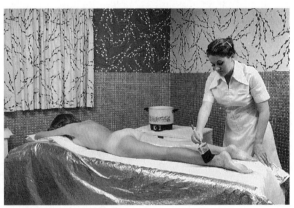

Figure 14.21 A wax bath body treatment (courtesy of Champneys at Tring Health Resort)

Foam baths

A detergent foam is an excellent heat insulator. When in a foam bath the body heat is retained, allowing it to heat up. The physiological effects are those of heating the body.

A foam bath may be prepared in an ordinary bath tub. A special perforated 'duckboard' fits in the bottom of the bath. Four to six inches (15 cm) of water at 38–43°C is run into the bath and the detergent foam agent is added.

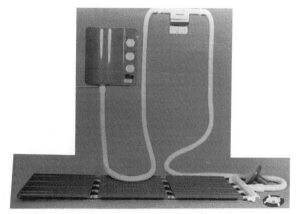

Figure 14.22 Duckboard and pump for foam or aerated baths (courtesy of Health Spa, Peterborough)

Figure 14.23 A foam bath in progress. The foam additive contains seaweed extract (courtesy of Champneys at Tring Health Resort)

An electric pump then pumps air through a hose under the duckboard. Air bubbles emerge through the perforations to create the foam which is 90 per cent air and 10 per cent water.

When the foam is about 6 inches (15 cm) from the top of the bath, the client gets in to be *warmed* and gently *stimulated* by the exploding bubbles (see figures 14.22 and 14.23).

Things to do

1 Collect manufacturer's information literature on hydrotherapy equipment.

2 Visit a Roman bath complex such as at Bath.

Self-assessment questions

1 What is the difference between (a) hydrothermal and (b) hydrokinetic therapy?

2 What is (a) normal human body temperature, (b) the typical temperature of the skin surface?

3 What is the maximum bearable temperature of (a) water and (b) still air in contact with the skin?

4 List the physiological effects of immersion in a hot bath.

5 Why is a cold shower or plunge desirable after a steam bath or sauna?

6 Why is a steam cabinet preferable to a steam room for clients with respiratory problems?

7 What is (a) humidity, (b) relative humidity?

8 Why does pouring water on the coals make a sauna feel hotter?

9 Briefly describe the working of a wet and dry bulb hygrometer.

10 Why is wax valuable as a heat treatment for the body?

15 | **Hydrokinetic Therapy**

Mechanical properties of water; buoyancy and flotation; Archimedes' principle; density; hydrometer; movement in water; hydrogymnastics – exercise in water; exercise pools; whirlpool and aerated baths; Water hygiene

What is hydrokinetic therapy?

How about taking the weight off your legs after a tiring day by relaxing in a warm bath, or getting some real exercise with a good long swim, or toning up in a stimulating Jacuzzi?

This is *hydrokinetic therapy* at work: making use of the *mechanical properties* of water. These properties are threefold:

1 *Buoyancy or flotation*
   As you lie in the water you can feel yourself trying to float.
2 *Hydrostatic pressure*
   When you swim, the water resists your movements and makes it a really valuable exercise.
3 *Mechanical impact*
   In the Jacuzzi whirlpool bath you are stimulated by the jets of aerated water impinging on your skin.

Buoyancy and flotation

Buoyancy is the tendency of an object immersed in water to attempt to *float*. When any object is put in a liquid there is an upward force, an *upthrust* upon it, which causes an *apparent* loss of weight. If the object *does* float, the apparent loss of weight is complete; in water it weighs *nothing*.

The apparent loss of weight can be demonstrated by hanging an object such as a stone or a piece of metal, by a thread from a spring balance. Take note of the weight of the object then slowly lower it into a beaker of water. Notice how its 'weight' reduces as it enters the water (see figure 15.1).

If, instead of a stone or metal object, you use a piece of wood, before it is fully immersed it will be afloat. The thread will slacken and the balance will indicate zero weight (see figure 15.1).

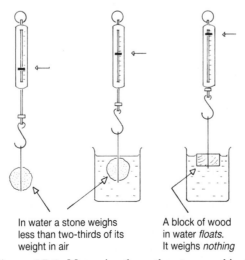

In water a stone weighs
less than two-thirds of its
weight in air

A block of wood
in water *floats*.
It weighs *nothing*

Figure 15.1 Measuring the upthrust on an object in water

In water you too can *float* – just! Not much of you will protrude from the water. The knack is to make sure it is your nose and mouth that protrude so your lungs fill with *air*! Fill your lungs with water and you will *sink* – and drown!

It is the *weightlessness* while in water that is so relaxing. It is also very valuable to the *physiotherapist* trying to restore some strength into muscles severely weakened by injury or disease.

While it might be impossible for such a damaged muscle to lift the weight of its limb in air, it is quite possible that it could move the limb immersed in water in the physiotherapy pool. Then as the muscle regains its strength to become better able to move the limb, so the *hydrostatic* resistance to movement in water can play its part in the rehabilitation of the muscle (see figure 15.2).

Figure 15.2 Physiotherapist with patient in a hydrotherapy pool (courtesy of Chartered Society of Physiotherapy)

Archimedes' principle

You must surely have noticed that as you lower yourself into the bath, so the water level *rises*. This is because your body must push aside or *displace* water as you get in.

> The *volume* of water displaced will be equal to the *volume* of your body that is immersed

Hopefully, you will not have filled the bath so full that as you get in water spills over on to the bathroom floor. This, according to 'schoolboy legend' is what is supposed to have happened to the Greek scientist *Archimedes* in the third century B.C.!

Actually Archimedes was more concerned with the *weight* of water displaced when an object is immersed in it and how this relates to the apparent weight loss of the immersed object.

Try this experiment. As before, suspend an object by a thread from a spring balance and note its *weight* in *air*. Now lower the object into a *displacement can* full of water and catch the water which overflows in a weighed beaker (see figure 15.3). Note the apparent loss of weight of the object – the *upthrust* – and weigh the water caught in the beaker.

The *upthrust* equals the *weight of water* displaced

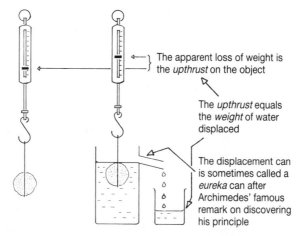

The apparent loss of weight is the *upthrust* on the object

The *upthrust* equals the *weight* of water displaced

The displacement can is sometimes called a *eureka* can after Archimedes' famous remark on discovering his principle

Figure 15.3 Archimedes' principle – the upthrust equals the weight of fluid displaced

Archimedes' principle states – When an object is partially or totally immersed in a fluid, there is an upthrust on the object equal to the weight of fluid displaced.

Note that the principle states *fluid*. A fluid is a liquid or a *gas*. Archimedes' principle applies in any liquid or any gas. Remember it is the *weight* of fluid displaced which equals the upthrust. An object displaces very little weight of air so the upthrust of air on it is negligible – unless of course the object is a balloon or airship.

Archimedes' principle applies to *floating* objects too, such as us in a swimming pool. In this case the upthrust which equals the weight of water displaced also equals the *weight of the object*. A floating object sinks just low enough to displace its own weight of water.

Flotation and density

How far a floating object sinks into a liquid depends on the *density* of that liquid. Density is discussed at length in Volume 1, chapter 1, but briefly *density* is the *weight* of a sample of a substance compared with its *volume*:

$$\text{Density} = \frac{\text{Weight of sample (g)}}{\text{Volume of sample (cm}^3)}$$

By definition, pure water has a *density* of 1 g/cm^3. When an object floats in water, each gram of water displaced is 1 cm^3 of water. This is not so for other liquids.

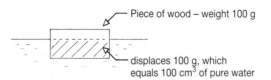

Figure 15.4 Displacement of water by a floating piece of wood

Let us imagine a piece of *wood* weighing 100 grams floating in pure water. It displaces 100 g which equals 100 cm^3 of water (see figure 15.4).

Now let us float the wood in *alcohol* which has a density of 0.8 g/cm^3. 100 g of alcohol has a volume much greater than 100 cm^3:

$$\text{If Density} = \frac{\text{Weight}}{\text{Volume}}, \text{Volume} = \frac{\text{Weight}}{\text{Density}}$$

$$\text{Volume of alcohol displaced} = \frac{100}{0.8}$$

$$= 125 \text{ cm}^3$$

The wood will sink lower in the alcohol to displace 125 cm^3 (see figure 15.5).

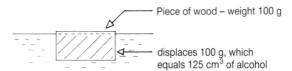

Figure 15.5 Displacement of alcohol by a floating piece of wood

The *salts* dissolved in *sea water* make it *more dense* than pure water. The density of sea water is 1.025 g/cm^3. The same wood block floating in sea water will ride much higher.

$$\text{Volume of sea water displaced} = \frac{100}{1.025}$$

$$= 97.6 \text{ cm}^3$$

The wood will displace only 97.6 cm^3 of sea water (see figure 15.6).

You too will float higher in sea water than in pure water. In the *very* salty water of the Dead Sea in the Middle East, one tends to float on it rather than in it. You cannot swim in the normal way – you have to lie there and paddle yourself along like a canoe! (see figure 15.7).

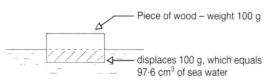

Figure 15.6 Displacement of sea water by a floating piece of wood

Figure 15.7 Bathers in the Dead Sea (courtesy of Royal Jordanian Airlines)

Hydrometer

A hydrometer is a floating device used to *measure the density* of liquids. It uses the principle of displacing its own weight of a liquid. It floats to different depths in liquids of different densities: lower in a low density liquid, higher in a high density liquid (see figure 15.8). The density is read off the scale on its stem. More about the hydrometer can be found in Volume 1, chapter 1.

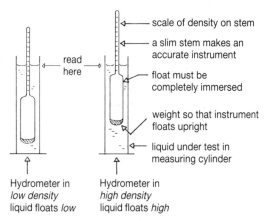

Figure 15.8 A hydrometer measures the density of liquids

An accurate hydrometer is made of glass. It is very *fragile* and expensive and must be handled with great care. It usually measures over quite a small range of density, so a set of instruments is required to cover the full range.

Movement in water

Have you ever run down the beach and straight into the sea? Down the beach is easy. It is still quite easy as you splash through shallow water. But soon you are wading in deeper water and you can then move only quite *slowly*.

Moving very *slowly* through water is relatively easy, the water helps by supporting your weight. But as soon as you try to move *quickly* through water it becomes really *hard work*. This is the value of *exercise* in water. But why should it be so much harder than movement in air?

It is because water is a much *more dense* or 'heavier' substance than air. Because of this, it *presses* in on anything immersed in it much more than air does. This is called *hydrostatic pressure*.

Despite being caused by *gravity*, which means we assume it acts only downwards, hydrostatic pressure actually acts *equally in all directions*. It presses in from the sides and up from beneath too. Hydrostatic pressure also increases the *deeper* one goes in the water. This should not affect us though as normally one does hydrotherapy exercises quite near to the surface!

Water is also much more reluctant to 'move out of the way' when you try to move through it. It is not as 'runny' as air. It has a higher *viscosity*.

When you move a limb in air, the air is pushed aside from in front of the limb and moves round it to fill the space behind (see figure 15.9).

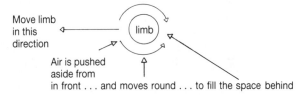

Figure 15.9 A limb moving through the air must push the air aside

Because air has a *low* density and *low* viscosity, it moves out of the way easily, offering very little resistance to the movement. Its presence is not noticed unless you move really quickly.

Now when you move a limb through *water*, the much denser, more viscous water must move from in front of the limb to behind it. If you move *slowly* this happens easily, but if you try to quicken the movement the water cannot move fast enough. It builds up a *high hydrostatic pressure* in front of the limb which offers a very high resistance to the movement – and it is there whichever way you move the limb, unlike gravity and weights which act in *one* direction.

The faster you try to move, the *higher* the hydrostatic pressure and the *harder* the work. The pressure increases in proportion to the speed. This is how an *exercise* in water is *progressed*. To make it harder, you try to move *faster*.

This is unlike exercise on dry land which you can progress by doing it more *slowly* so the weight of the limb offers resistance to the movement.

Exercise in water – hydrogymnastics

While *swimming* is an ideal keep-fit exercise which does involve a multitude of the muscles of the body, it is *general* rather than *specific*.

For figure correction, the therapist will wish to concentrate on those particular muscles which should alleviate the problem and will wish to prescribe a *programme* of exercises rather like those on dry land. These are *hydrogymnastic* exercises.

To start with, the exercises will probably be done slowly, making use of the assistance from the buoyancy effect of the water. These are *assistive* exercises.

They will progress to become more rapid using the resistance to movement in water. These are *resistive* exercises.

The figure correction value of the exercises will come from the increase in muscle tone and the increased strength developed in the muscles (see figure 15.10).

Figure 15.10 A therapist leads water exercises in a level deck pool (courtesy of Champneys at Tring Health Resort)

The exercise sessions will often be conducted with both the client and the therapist in the water. For the most part, the client will need to hold a rail at the pool-side and for certain exercises the therapist will need to support the client gently.

The exercise pool

Most ordinary swimming pools are satisfactory for *hydrogymnastics*, being suitable for both individual and group therapy.

For individual therapy, a smaller pool is adequate. It needs to be about 3 m by 4 m with depths varying between about 80 cm at the shallow end to around 150 cm at the deep end.

It must be lined with a *non-slip* material and have a *secure* pool-side rail set about 15 cm in from the side and just under the water surface. *Steps* into the water to assist the less mobile clients are also an advantage (see figure 15.11).

Figure 15.11 An individual exercise pool

The *water* can be plain or mineralised and would normally be heated to a *neutral temperature* of about 32°C. A filtration and sterilising facility is necessary to prevent cross-infection.

Contra-indications to pool therapy

Despite the therapeutic value of the exercise pool there are a number of conditions which preclude its use:

1 Inflamed joints and limbs. The warmth will alleviate the pain but the injury will still be there and may be aggravated by exercise.
2 Acute infections of the fever type. Danger of chilling.
3 Ear, nose and throat infections. Risk of cross-infection.
4 Weeping wounds and sores. Risk of cross-infection.
5 Contagious skin infections. Risk of cross-infection.
6 Respiratory and heart disorders may be aggravated by the strenuous exercise.

Mechanical impact of water in therapy

The therapeutic value of moving water impinging on the body has long been known and in particular the value of *aerated water* in the *whirlpool bath*. There are also much simpler aerated baths and the *impulse shower*.

The whirlpool bath
– the Jacuzzi

A modern way to relax is to enjoy the warmth and gentle massage of the 'Jacuzzi'. As you bathe you are treated to jets of aerated water from nozzles in the sides of the bath.

Figure 15.12 Client in a whirlpool bath (courtesy of Aquatech Marketing Ltd)

The effects of the aerated bath

The body is gently massaged by the *aerated* water, a mixture of liquid water and bubbles of air. Every part of the skin is impinged by alternately water and air. This results in constantly changing pressure on the skin – almost a gentle tapotement (see figure 15.13).

The physiological effects of the massage are sedative. It relieves pain. The vasodilation of the vessels in the skin and the changing pressure on them results in improved circulation. It cleanses by loosening dirt and skin scales.

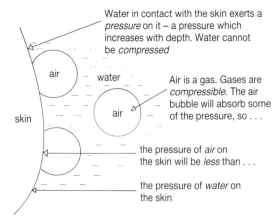

Water in contact with the skin exerts a *pressure* on it – a pressure which increases with depth. Water cannot be *compressed*

Air is a gas. Gases are *compressible*. The air bubble will absorb some of the pressure, so . . .

the pressure of *air* on the skin will be *less* than . . .

the pressure of *water* on the skin

Figure 15.13 The effect on the skin of an aerated bath

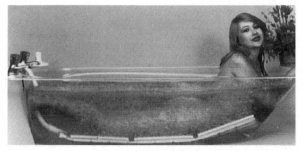

Figure 15.14 A simple aerated bath (courtesy of Health Spa, Peterborough)

Aerating the water

A simple and inexpensive aerated bath uses an *air pump* standing outside a normal bathtub. The air is taken into the water through a hose. The hose may end in a nozzle which is directed on to the skin under water, or there may be a perforated 'duckboard' to fit in the bottom of the bath. The air bubbles come up through the holes in the duckboard and impinge on the body (see figure 15.14).

In the Jacuzzi type of aerated whirlpool bath a special pump mixes *air* and *water* and jets it into the bath through nozzles or a hose.

Although aerated baths were developed in France, they were brought to commercial success by the Jacuzzi Brothers in the USA following their improvisation of an aerated bath from an outboard motor in a tank of water to treat an invalid boy!

The aerating pump is a *turbine pump*. The water is pumped by a rotating *impeller* like a boat propeller. Given the chance, this type of pump will *draw in air*. It does this by *cavitation*.

Let us consider a boat propeller for a moment. If it turns *slowly*, it moves the water but otherwise causes little disturbance. If it turns *fast*, the blades literally 'cut holes' in the water leaving *cavities* inside which is virtually a *vacuum*. Air is drawn down into the cavities to create bubbles which rise again to the surface to leave the foaming wake behind the boat.

This cavitation effect can be shown using a laboratory mixer in a beaker of water. You will see how it draws in the air and mixes it with the water (see figure 15.15).

Obviously for a therapeutic bath, the impeller must be enclosed or the pump must be situated outside the bath otherwise it might very effectively mince the toes!

There are units available which are fitted within the bath either stirring and aerating the water generally producing the *whirlpool* effect or producing a strong jet of aerated water through the bath water (see figure 15.16). There is also a portable pump which stands outside the bath taking its water from the bath through a hose, aerating it and delivering it back to the bath through a second hose (see figure 15.17).

The most common pump system used these days is *installed* outside the bath. It takes water from the bath through an outlet, aerates it and returns it through a series of nozzles fitted low down in the bath tub sides. This system can be installed in a normal bath tub (see figure 15.18).

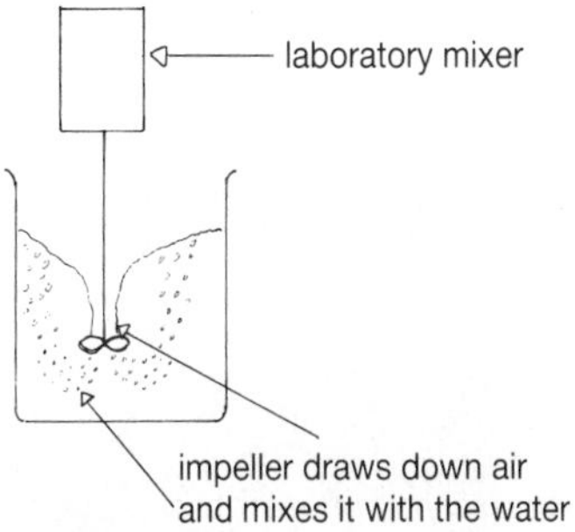

Figure 15.15 A laboratory mixer demonstrates the aeration of the water

Figure 15.16 An in-bath whirlpool pump (courtesy of Jacuzzi Brothers Ltd)

Figure 15.17 Whirlpool bath pump unit to stand outside the bath tub

Figure 15.18 Whirlpool jet installed in a standard bath tub (courtesy of Leigh Stewart Products Ltd)

Figure 15.19 Large whirlpool spa bath for multiple use (courtesy of Champneys at Tring Health Resort)

Figure 15.20 Combined swimming pool and whirlpool complex (courtesy of Aquatech Marketing Ltd)

Frequently found in salons, sports clubs and health centres are larger Jacuzzi baths for use by several persons at a time. Sometimes two baths are used – one warm, one cold, so clients may use the contrast bath effect by alternating between them (see figures 15.19 and 15.20).

Water hygiene

Where clients are involved there is always a chance of cross-infection so attention must be paid to *hygiene* with baths and pools. Recent research has shown that the amount of skin scales and dirt dislodged from the body in a whirlpool bath is *fifty times* that lost in a swimming pool.

The smaller tubs for use by a single client at a time present no real problem. After each client the bath can be drained and sanitised before being refilled with fresh water for the next.

The problem is likely to arise with the larger tubs and pools and particularly those available for continuous casual use by perhaps many clients at a time.

In swimming pools, a filtration and sterilising plant continuously takes water from the pool, filters out any dirt, adds a metered amount of chlorine and returns the water to the pool (see figure 15.21).

Chlorinated water is though not very pleasant. It affects the eyes, the throat and the skin. Peroxides are sometimes added instead or the water might be passed through the *ultra-violet* rays from a ray lamp. These do not have the unpleasant effects of chlorine but also do not have any residual bactericidal effect once the water is returned to the pool.

For aerated, whirlpool baths, chlorine is out. It would be unbearable to be in warm, aerated *chlorinated* water. Many establishments use *no* water steriliser, relying instead on regularly emptying and cleansing the pool before refilling it with fresh water. Obviously this cannot be effective.

There is though an additive called *medifome*. This is a cationic surfactant which acts as a deodorant and steriliser and used in aerated baths produces a milky foam. More recently a metering device has been developed to meter a *bromide* into the water. This is a close chemical relative of chlorine and is similarly effective as a germicide, but it is not evaporated from the water like chlorine so is not so unpleasant.

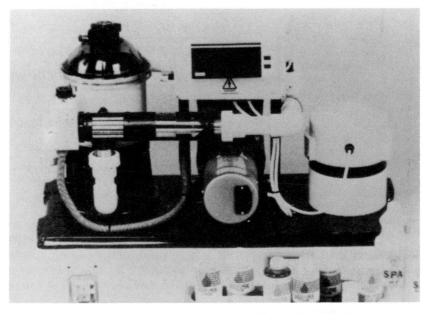

Figure 15.21 Treatment plant for swimming pools and spa baths (courtesy of Aquatech Marketing Ltd)

Self-assessment questions

1 State Archimedes' principle.

2 What is the value of the exercise pool to a physiotherapist treating damaged limbs?

3 Why is one more easily able to float in sea water than in fresh water?

4 What is a hydrometer? What is it for?

5 How does progressing an exercise in water differ from progressing an exercise on dry land?

6 Why do inflamed muscles and joints contra-indicate exercises in the pool?

7 Briefly describe the effects on the skin of an aerated bath.

8 Why is bromide used in preference to chlorine for hygiene purposes in an aerated bath?

16

Exercise and exercise machines

Mechanical principles in health and beauty therapy; the human machine; skeleton and movement; levers and the mechanics of movement; exercises; muscle tone; fatigue; exercise machines; weights and weight machines; rowing machines; exercise cycles; energy, exercise and slimming; posture and figure faults; centre of gravity, lines of gravity and figure diagnosis

Mechanical principles in health and beauty therapy

We are continually being reminded that we are digging ourselves early graves by our 'unhealthy' eating habits and lack of physical fitness. We are encouraged to eat a diet of 'health foods': no sugar, no animal fat, no salt but lots of fruit, vegetables and fibre – and take lots of *real* exercise such as jogging, keep fit, weight training, dance, aerobics and a whole host of sports.

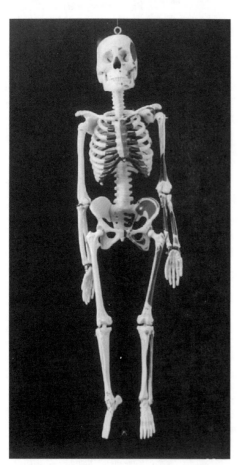

Figure 16.1 A model of a human skeleton

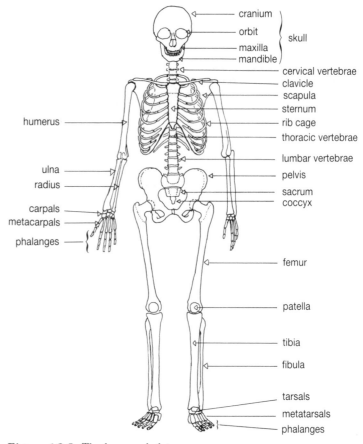

Figure 16.2 The human skeleton

186

There are any number of machines to make our exercise more interesting, more demanding and hopefully, therefore, more effective: rowing machines, exercise cycles, weights, gymnasium machines, the 'multigym'. Do not forget the most marvellous machine of them all – the body itself!

The human machine

Any machine must have a framework or chassis to carry its moving parts. The body has its *skeleton*, an assembly of well over a hundred individual bones, with joints between them which permit a wide variety of degrees of movement (see figures 16.1 and 16.2).

Power for the human machine

To make it work, a machine needs a source of power, an engine or motor. The body has hundreds of motors. These are the *muscles* which bring about the movements at the joints. A motor needs a supply of energy, a fuel. The fuel for human motors is *food*. Figure 16.3 shows some of the hundreds of muscles which drive the movements of the body.

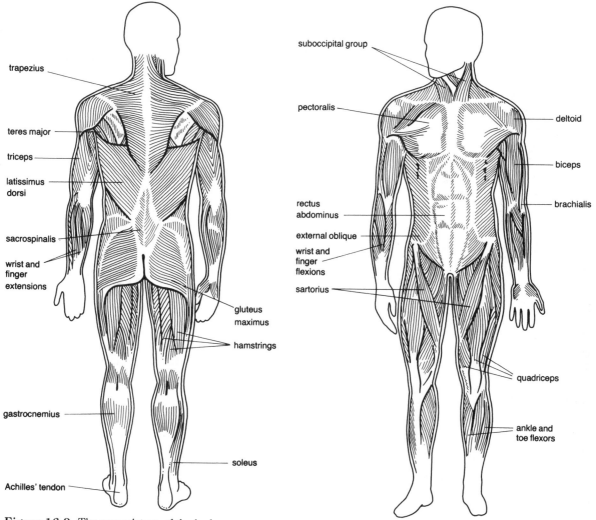

Figure 16.3 The musculature of the body

Why a body requires a skeleton

Only the smallest of animals have bodies which can be self-supporting without a skeleton. A larger animal could be no more than a shapeless 'blob'. Apart from providing this essential framework, the bones are essential to convert the action of the muscles into really *useful* movement.

While a muscle is a reasonably effective means of converting the energy of food into mechanical movement, it does have drawbacks. A muscle *contracts*, becoming shorter and fatter. In doing so it can only *pull*. The extent of a single muscle 'pull' is not very great either; it can produce movement over a very short distance. Once it has contracted and pulled, that is that. It cannot push back again. A second muscle is required to pull the other way to stretch the first one again! The contractile fibres of a muscle are shown in figures 16.4 and 16.5.

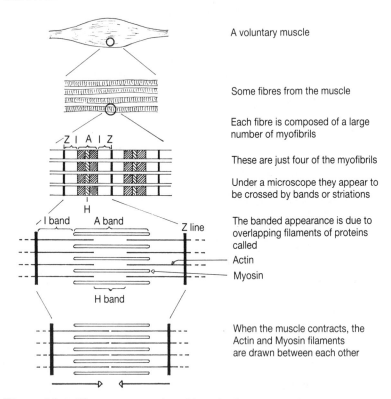

A voluntary muscle

Some fibres from the muscle

Each fibre is composed of a large number of myofibrils

These are just four of the myofibrils

Under a microscope they appear to be crossed by bands or striations

The banded appearance is due to overlapping filaments of proteins called

— Actin

— Myosin

When the muscle contracts, the Actin and Myosin filaments are drawn between each other

Figure 16.4 The structure and working of voluntary muscle

An animal which relies on muscle alone for its movement can move only *slowly*; an earthworm or a snail for example. Muscle is however *very powerful*; much too powerful for most purposes. Have you tried to prise a limpet off a rock or open a mussel shell?

Animals with skeletons forego some of the out and out force of the muscle. By using bones as *levers*, each contraction of a muscle is made to produce a much *longer* movement. By having the muscles arranged to act in opposing pairs, the bones can be moved in both directions. This is the principle of *antagonistic muscles*. It shows very well in the action of the forearm as shown in figure 16.6.

In any pair of antagonistic muscles, usually one acts to bend or *flex* the joint. It is the *flexor* for that joint. The other straightens or *extends* the joint; it is the *extensor*.

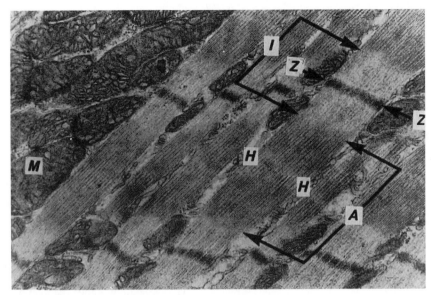

Figure 16.5 Electron micrograph of fibres of voluntary muscle, indicating the A, I, H and Z bands. The mitochondria (M) provide the energy for the muscle (courtesy of Dr A. W. Robards)

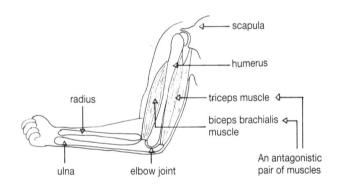

The biceps brachialis raises the forearm
The triceps lowers or straightens the forearm

Figure 16.6 An antagonistic pair of muscles in the upper arm

In the forearm the *ulna* acts as a *lever* to increase the movement produced by the muscle action.

Levers

A lever is in effect a bar. At some point it is *pivoted* or hinged. This point is the *fulcrum* of the lever. At another point hangs or rests the *load* to be moved and at a third point the *effort* is applied (see figure 16.7).

Types of levers

It is usual to recognise three types of levers: *the three orders of levers*. The one shown in figure 16.7 is pivoted at a point somewhere *between* the load and the effort. It is a lever of the *first order*.

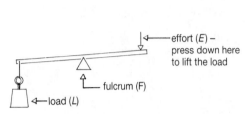

Figure 16.7 A lever of the first order

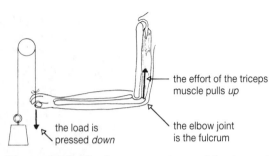

Figure 16.8 The forearm as a lever of the first order

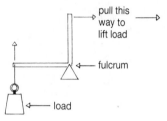

Figure 16.9 An L-shaped lever changes the direction of the movement

You will notice with this type of lever, if the effort presses *down*, the load goes up. The lever has changed the *direction* of the movement. This is most useful in the body to change the *pull* of a muscle into a *push*, for example in pressing down or pushing away with the forearm (see figure 16.8).

An L-shaped lever would change the direction of a movement through a right angle. Figure 16.9 shows an example of this.

A lever pivoted at one end is a lever of either the *second* or *third* order. Which it is will depend on whether the load or the effort is closer to the fulcrum.

If the load is nearer the fulcrum and effort is further away, it is a lever of the *second order* as in figure 16.10.

Applications of levers of the *second order* are not common in the body. An example is rising on to tip-toe (see figure 16.11).

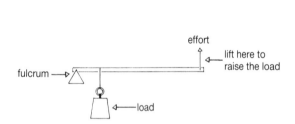

Figure 16.10 A lever of the second order

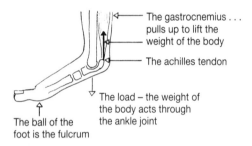

Figure 16.11 Rising on tip-toe – a lever of the second order

If the effort is applied closer to the fulcrum than the load, the lever is of the *third order*. This is shown in figure 16.12.

Levers of the *third order* are quite common in the body. An example is again the forearm but this time *lifting* a load (see figure 16.13).

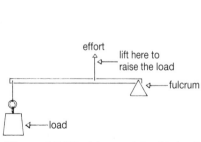

Figure 16.12 A lever of the third order

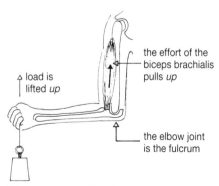

Figure 16.13 The forearm as a lever of the third order

Mechanical advantage or disadvantage – velocity and distance ratio

Now it is time to try some experiments with levers. You will need a bar to act as a lever. Most science laboratories have long rulers with holes at intervals all along them. Failing that a long Meccano strip might do. You will need a firmly fixed pivot such as a stout pin or thin nail held in a suitable support, some weights for loads and a spring balance to measure the effort. Set up the apparatus as in figure 16.14.

Figure 16.14 shows the load and effort *equal* distances from the pivot. The effort will *equal* the load to be moved – at least in *theory* it will, assuming the pivot is without *friction* and no effort is required to move the lever itself. The principles of physics are full of these idealised assumptions!

Note also that if the effort pulls its end of the lever a certain distance *down*, the load goes *up* the *same* distance.

Now let us rearrange things so the effort is *twice* as far from the pivot as is the load (see figure 16.15).

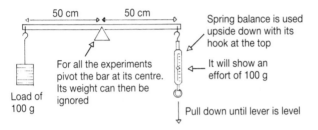

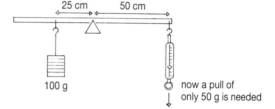

Figure 16.14 Experiment to demonstrate a lever of the first order

Figure 16.15 Mechanical advantage – the load is moved closer to the fulcrum

You will notice that the effort required to move the load is now *halved* . . . Why?

Load × Distance from fulcrum
100 × 25   = 2500

As shown in figure 16.15, this is the *turning force* – it is called a *moment* – trying to turn the lever *anticlockwise*. Now multiply

Effort × Distance from fulcrum
50 × 50   = 2500

This is the *moment* in the *clockwise* direction. If the lever is not actually moving either way:

Anticlockwise moment = Clockwise moment
100 × 25   50 × 50

An effort of a little more than 50 g is here able to lift a load of 100 g. This is called *mechanical advantage*.

A 50 g effort moving a 100 g load may seem like something for nothing. This is not so. Move the effort a distance of, say, 10 cm (see figure 16.16).

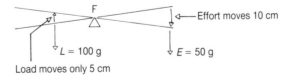

Figure 16.16 Distance/velocity ratio – a 50 g effort moves a 100 g load

Half the effort moves the load only *half* the distance and at *half* the speed:

The *distance ratio* is ½ or 0.5
The *velocity ratio* is ½ or 0.5

Now if you wish, try with the load twice as far from the fulcrum as the effort (see figure 16.17).

If, as now, the effort needed is *greater* than the load moved, the system is working at a *mechanical disadvantage*. What is gained is in the *distance* the load is moved and the *speed* of the movement. The load moves twice as far and twice as fast.

You will remember that we said that *muscles* can pull *too hard* for most purposes but cannot pull far at a time. Using the bones as *levers*, muscles can be made to pull what is still an adequate load over a much more useful distance. Let us look again at the forearm (see figure 16.18).

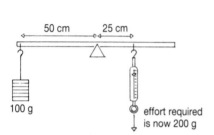

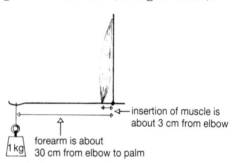

Figure 16.17 Mechanical disadvantage – the effort is closer to the fulcrum

Figure 16.18 Mechanical disadvantage in the forearm

Discounting the weight of the forearm itself, to lift each kilogram in the hand requires a muscle effort of – using moments:

1 kg × 30 cm = ? × 3 cm
? = 10 kg

To lift the 1 kg load requires a muscle effort of 10 kg. But to lift the load 10 cm requires a muscle contraction of only 1 cm. Most muscles work at a *mechanical disadvantage*, but at a *distance advantage*.

Most of you have probably never *strained* a muscle. Fewer too will have *torn a tendon*, but it is amazing how frequently one hears of sportsmen and athletes who have done just that. That is one of the penalties of building up the strength in muscles by athletic training. It makes them so powerful that if the muscles *snatches* and for some reason the limb cannot move, it is possible for the tendon which joins the muscle to the bone to be torn.

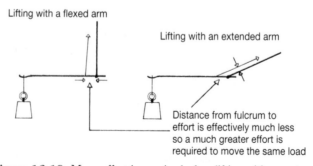

Figure 16.19 More effort is required when lifting with an extended arm than with a flexed arm

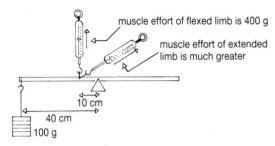

muscle effort of flexed limb is 400 g

muscle effort of extended limb is much greater

10 cm

40 cm

100 g

Figure 16.20 Experiment to show that greater effort is needed when lifting with an extended limb compared with a flexed limb

This is particularly possible with the limb *fully extended* at the *start* of its movement where the muscle pulls at an *angle* to the bone instead of perpendicular to it. This increases the mechanical disadvantage tremendously, as can be seen in figure 16.19.

This can be shown by a bar and spring balance experiment (see figure 16.20).

In all these examples and experiments, the situation is either stationary or slow moving. In most exercise the load has to be *accelerated* and to do this, the muscle efforts involved can be tremendous. For instance, to accelerate a *sprinter* from the starting blocks to over 10 metres per second – over 20 m.p.h. – will require forces from the leg muscles of perhaps several *tonnes*. A tonne is 1000 kg (see figure 16.21).

Figure 16.21 Start of a sprint race (courtesy of Camera Press Ltd, London)

Progressing an exercise

Normally, the initial sessions of an exercise programme will be to establish *mobility* in a movement. Little demand will be made on the *strength* of the muscles. With successive sessions, the exercise is *progressed*, either to increase further the mobility or more likely to develop greater *strength* and *tone* in the muscles.

This is accomplished by making the muscles work *harder* – such as by giving them a greater load to move. The extra load could be *weights* or *exercise machines*, or it could be the weight of the body itself such as in *press-ups, sit-ups* or *pull-ups* (see figures 16.22 to 16.26)

Figure 16.22 Press-ups (photographed by the author at the Telford Racquets and Fitness Centre)

Figure 16.23 Sit-ups with feet under bar (photographed by the author at the Telford Racquets and Fitness Centre)

Figure 16.24 Pull-ups – on to bar

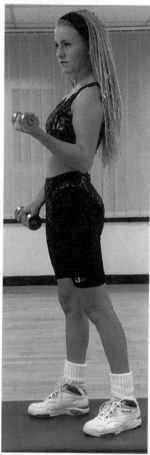

Figure 16.25 Exercise with weights (photographed by the author at the Telford Racquets and Fitness Centre)

Figure 16.26 Exercise with weights (photographed by the author at the Telford Racquets and Fitness Centre)

Starting positions for exercise

The problem with weight is that it acts only one way – *down* – owing to gravity, which means getting the body into the right attitude before starting the exercise. Take for example a *leg-lifting* exercise. If you start it in the *standing* position, the leg starts to move from a hanging position and the early part of the lift is easy, becoming more difficult as the leg becomes more horizontal (see figure 16.27). Starting from a back-lying position the muscles must lift the full weight of the leg straight away, becoming easier as the leg becomes more vertical (see figure 16.28).

These lifting exercises can be very effectively *progressed* by doing them slowly. The weight has then to be supported by the muscles for a much longer time. Try it and see!

Figure 16.27 leg-lifting from a standing position (photographed by the author at the Telford Racquets and Fitness Centre)

Figure 16.28 Leg-lifting from a back-lying position (photographed by the author at the Telford Racquets and Fitness Centre)

Muscle tone and the trim figure

Lest you are getting the impression that exercise is to turn everyone into a Mr Universe or a Miss Universe, it should be stressed that exercise with resistance such as is offered by weights is *not* just to build up *strength* – unless that happens to be your intention. Regularly exercising the muscles helps to give them *tone*.

A muscle lacking in tone hangs loose when relaxed and is flabby to the touch. A muscle with good tone is under slight tension even when relaxed. It is firm to the touch and much more trim in appearance (see figures 16.29 and 16.30).

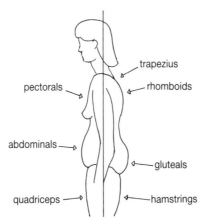

Figure 16.29 Many figure faults are the result of poor muscle tone

Figure 16.30 Figure fault correction by improving muscle tone

Muscle fatigue

If you indulge in strenuous exercise programmes, you will be well aware that as you do your exercises, your muscles will become gradually more reluctant to continue and will start to ache. They will be suffering from *fatigue*.

Should *aerobics* be your scene, you might be encouraged to carry on through the pain threshold and 'go for burn'. In its true sense most exercise is *aerobic* in that it requires energy and the efficient release of energy from food requires a supply of *oxygen*. The process is called *aerobic tissue respiration*.

However in its current usage the term *aerobics* refers to a high-speed, high-intensity exercise routine. In such a routine, the oxygen supply to the muscles cannot keep pace with demand and tissue respiration turns to its inefficient *anaerobic* form. This results in an accumulation of crystals of *lactic acid* in the muscles which makes the movement painful. This is a signal telling you to stop and rest. Carry on and you could risk damaging your muscles.

If in your aerobics you do 'go for burn' you will find that the pain of fatigue passes. You seem to go through the pain barrier and feel 'on top of the world'. Why?

This is your body's emergency 'run away from the charging bull' system at work. Under dire emergencies the muscles produce a hormone called *endorphin* which is a signal to the brain to ignore the pain signals from the muscles. Going for burn is a self-induced 'emergency' and your brain is made to react in the same way. It ignores the pain and the damage being done to the muscles and joints.

The real danger is that the 'high' produced by endorphin is addictive. You can get 'hooked' on aerobics or other really strenuous exercise. It can become an obsession – and like most obsessions, it can be self-destructive. The moral is exercise by all means but *do not* go for burn.

Figure 16.31 An aerobics class in progress.
Source: Sally & Richard Greenhill Photo Library

Exercise machines

While the main purpose of exercise machines and apparatus is to make exercise *physically* and *physiologically* more effective, there is much *psychology* in them too. A kind of love–hate relationship develops. A machine is something physical, something tangible on which you can vent not only your physical strength and energy but also your pent-up emotional energy, your frustrations.

A machine lets you set yourself a *goal* and *targets* along the way and monitors your progress. Ten miles tonight on your exercise cycle without having to leave the house. Eleven miles tomorrow night. Beat both Oxford and Cambridge on your rowing machine!

Between them, the vast array of exercise machines on the market employ a variety of scientific principles to add effectiveness to your exercise:

> Weights
> Pulleys
> Springs
> Hydraulic or pneumatic telescopic dampers
> Friction brakes

Let us look at some of the machines and see the principles at work.

Weights, dumb-bells and bar bells

Many conventional exercises may be progressed by using weights. Holding the weights gives the muscles much harder work to do. But beware. Use only a moderate amount of weight for figure trimming, well within your lifting ability, otherwise the effect could be counter-productive, building for you the muscles and physique of a power-weightlifter!

Weight training equipment comprises various sizes of *dumb-bells* and *bar bells*. The former are available in pairs to be held one in each hand. The latter are bars on to each end of which a variety of weights can be attached to be lifted with both hands – or feet. Figure 16.32 shows a set of exercise weights. Figures 16.33 and 16.34 show just two of the exercises that can be done using the weights.

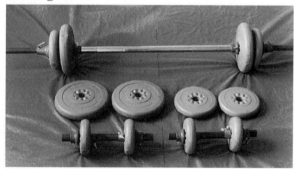

Figure 16.32 Exercise weights

Figure 16.33 Exercise with dumb-bells (photographed by the author at the Telford Racquets and Fitness Centre)

Figure 16.34 Exercise with barbell (photographed by the author at the Telford Racquets and Fitness Centre)

197

Gymnasium machines

The problem with weights is that *gravity* acts only *downwards* so to get resistance in any other direction either the person has to be a different way up, or levers and pulleys must be used to make gravity act in other directions.

The *exercise bench* is a way of getting the body other ways up. Figures 16.35 and 16.36 show exercises on the bench.

Figure 16.35 Exercise on the exercise bench (photographed by the author at the Telford Racquets and Fitness Centre)

Figure 16.36 Exercise with weights on the exercise bench (photographed by the author at the Telford Racquets and Fitness Centre)

Pulleys and *cables* can change the direction of pull for an exercise. Some of the weights used in the machines are very heavy, so care must be taken to ensure that they are positioned well within the framework of the machine and preferably enclosed completely to minimise the chances of accidental injury. Some examples of machines using cables, pulleys and weights are shown in figures 16.37 to 16.44.

Figure 16.38 Pulling at an angle (photographed by the author at the Somerford Physical Therapy Centre)

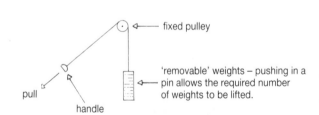

fixed pulley

'removable' weights – pushing in a pin allows the required number of weights to be lifted.

pull

handle

Figure 16.37 Pulling down at an angle

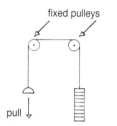

Figure 16.39 Pulling vertically down

Figure 16.40 Pulling down vertically (photographed by the author at the Telford Racquets and Fitness Centre)

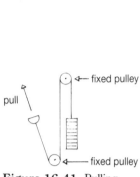

Figure 16.41 Pulling upwards

Figure 16.42 Pulling upwards

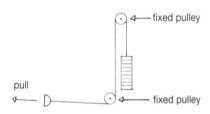

Figure 16.43 Pulling horizontally

Figure 16.44 Pulling horizontally

Note how one machine might be adaptable for a number of different exercises. A factor with *weights* is that the resistance they offer is *constant* throughout the exercise movement. Some exercises demand a *gradually increasing* resistance during the movement. Weights on *levers* use a *ballistic* effect (see figure 16.45).

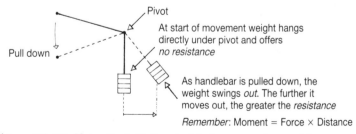

Figure 16.45 Using the ballistic principle in an exercise machine

Figure 16.46 Ballistic weights on an exercise bench

The ballistic lever arrangement can also be used for lifting exercises such as leg-lifting on the exercise bench (see figure 16.46).

Another way of providing a *gradually increasing* resistance to an exercise movement is *springs*. The further you pull out a spring, the harder it becomes to pull. Try the experiment in figure 16.47.

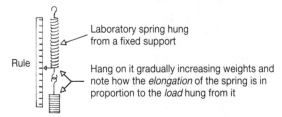

Rule — Laboratory spring hung from a fixed support

Hang on it gradually increasing weights and note how the *elongation* of the spring is in proportion to the *load* hung from it

Figure 16.47 To compare the extension of a spring with the load on it

Figure 16.48 A spring chest expander

Springs are used in the simple 'Bullworker' and frequently in *rowing machines* (see figures 16.48 and 16.50).

Rowing machines

sliding seat   handle bar

spring

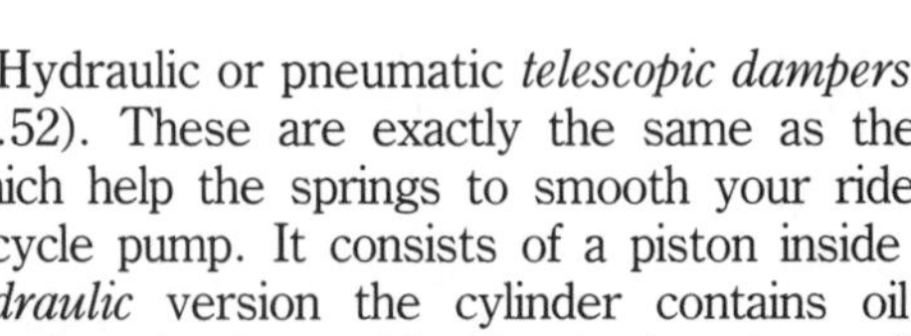

Figure 16.49 A rowing machine using springs

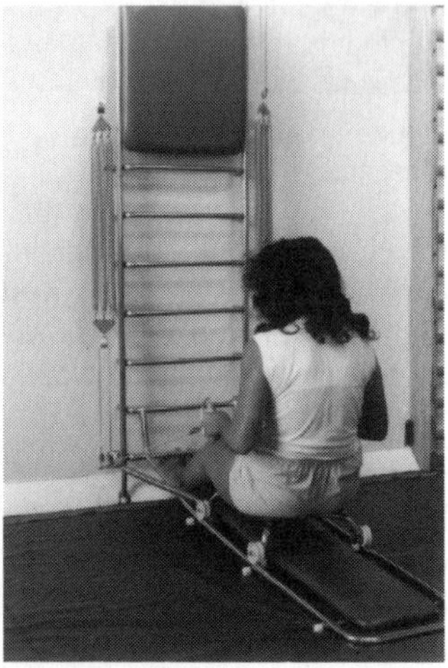

Rowing machines use a variety of means of offering resistance. *Springs* are one way, as is shown in figures 16.49 and 16.50.

Hydraulic or pneumatic *telescopic dampers* might also be used (see figure 16.52). These are exactly the same as the shock absorbers on your car which help the springs to smooth your ride. A damper is made a bit like a cycle pump. It consists of a piston inside a long narrow cylinder. In the *hydraulic* version the cylinder contains oil; in the *pneumatic* version it contains air. A special valve in the piston allows the oil or gas to leak past *with difficulty* on the 'pull-out' stroke so offering the *resistance* to the movement. On the return stroke the piston can be pushed back in easily (see figure 16.51).

There are also rowers which use a strap or cable which winds on a drum. The turning of the drum is resisted by some kind of *friction brake* similar to that on an exercise cycle (see figure 16.53).

Figure 16.50 Rowing machine with springs as part of a multiexerciser (photographed by the author at the Somerford Physical Therapy Centre)

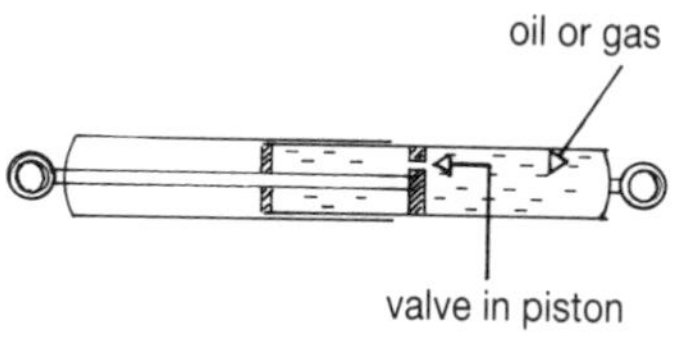

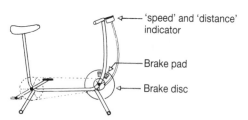

Figure 16.51 A telescopic damper

Figure 16.52 Rowing machine with telescopic dampers (photographed by the author at the Telford Racquets and Fitness Centre)

Figure 16.53 Rowing machine with friction brake (photographed by the author at Westlands Health and Beauty Clinic)

Exercise cycles

On an exercise cycle, resistance to your pedalling is usually offered by means of a *friction brake*. This lets you imagine you are pedalling up a long hill or into a strong headwind. A ride on an exercise bike would not do much for you if it was downhill all the way!

The brake consists of a drum or disc which is driven by the pedals and on to which press the friction pads. Friction tries to prevent the pad and drum or disc sliding over each other. The brake has to absorb all the energy of your pedalling so, like you, it should get quite hot (see figures 16.54 and 16.55).

Figure 16.54 An exercise cycle – with friction disc brake

Figure 16.55 An exercise cycle – with friction band brake

Energy, exercise and slimming

The *fat* deposited in various places around the body is its *reserve of energy*. The trouble is that many people's bodies are reserving far too much energy for their liking and they are *overweight*. It tends, too, to be a reserve that they never seem to need! It is estimated that about *three-quarters* of British adults are overweight: many of them grossly so, restricting their freedom of movement and putting a great strain on the heart.

Exercise is one way people use to attempt to rid themselves of their excess fat, but they are often very disappointed at the slow rate at which it disappears. Some even find themselves putting *on* weight. Exercise makes them eat more!

Measuring the energy – counting the calories

We are all familiar with 'counting the calories' but what actually are they? A *calorie* is a unit for measuring *energy*:

> One calorie of energy will raise the temperature of 1 g of water 1°C

In diets, the calories we count are actually *kilocalories*, units of 1000 calories. We can write them as kcal for short.

> One kilocalorie will raise 1 kilogram of water 1°C

Strictly we should be using units called *kilojoules* abbreviated as kJ. When Système International, the 'new' metric system was introduced, the kilojoule replaced the kilocalorie as the unit of energy. But everybody still uses 'calories'!

Why 'calories' when talking about diet? Food is our fuel. It provides our energy. The trick is to eat just sufficient food each day to provide your daily energy. Then you will not get fat!

How many calories do you need? Well that depends . . . . Table 16.1 lists the daily energy requirements of a selection of 'average' people, as recommended by the Ministry of Agriculture, Fisheries and Food.

Table 16.1 Energy requirements of some 'typical' people

Type of person	Daily energy requirement	
	Kilocalories	*Kilojoules*
Baby – up to 1 year	800	3300
Child – 6 years	1800	7500
Teenage boy	3000	12600
Teenage girl	2300	9600
Moderately active man	3000	12600
Moderately active woman	2200	9200

The problem is that there are remarkably few 'average' people. One '55 kilogram woman' might be eating no more than 700 kcal a day and still getting fatter. Another will be downing 3000 or 4000 kcal each day and staying as thin as a beanpole. Different people need different amounts of food. Some years ago, three categories of people were recognised:

Endomorphs – have a low-energy requirement and tend to put on weight even on a below 'average' diet

Mesomorphs – are the 'average' people

Ectomorphs – can take a high-energy diet without putting on weight. Their bodies, it seems, are well endowed with areas of 'brown fat' cells which literally 'burn off' the excess energy to form heat

The energy requirement of the body is actually at two levels – *basal metabolism* and *external work*. Basal metabolism is the rate of using energy when the body is 'ticking over' in *complete* rest. For our '55 kilogram average woman' the *basal metabolic rate* is about *one* kcal per minute. As soon as she is awake, sits up, stands, walks, climbs, she is also doing *external work*. In table 16.2 are listed the 'typical' energy requirements for some forms of external work.

Table 16.2 Energy used in various kinds of 'external work'

Activity	Energy required	
	kcal/minute	kJ/minute
Asleep, fully relaxed	1	4.2
Sitting	1.4	5.8
Standing	1.7	7.1
Strolling	3	12.6
Brisk walking	5	21
Running	Up to 10	Up to 42
Climbing stairs	9	38

So how much weight *can* you lose by exercise? You must bear in mind that each gram of fat has stored away in it *nine* kilocalories of energy. That is 3600 kcal per pound. That is a heck of a lot of exercise to lose each pound!

Posture and figure fault diagnosis

So far we have considered improving muscle tone and loss of weight as means of figure correction. A third, equally important factor is *correct posture*.

With the person standing correctly, the bones of the skeleton and in particular the vertebrae should be 'stacked' in a *balanced* way so the person can remain standing with a minimum of effort and *no undue strain*. A slouching stance is tiring for the muscles and puts strain on the joints.

Centre of gravity, lines of gravity

The *centre of gravity* of an object is an imaginary point through which the weight of the object appears to act. It is not much use to us in figure diagnosis. What are useful are *lines of gravity*. A line of gravity is an imaginary line drawn vertically passing through the centre of gravity of the body. The weight of the body is distributed *equally* each side of the line.

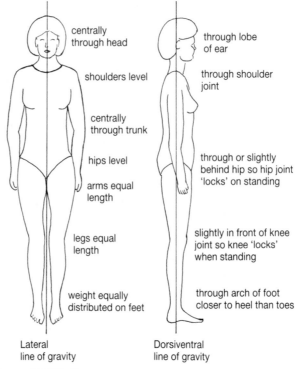

centrally
through head

shoulders level

centrally
through trunk

hips level

arms equal
length

legs equal
length

weight equally
distributed on feet

Lateral
line of gravity

through lobe
of ear

through shoulder
joint

through or slightly
behind hip so hip joint
'locks' on standing

slightly in front of knee
joint so knee 'locks'
when standing

through arch of foot
closer to heel than toes

Dorsiventral
line of gravity

Figure 16.56 Correct posture

In figure diagnosis we consider two such lines of gravity. One drawn vertically and centrally on the *front view* of the body shows the *lateral* distribution of the body. The other drawn on the *side view* gives the *dorsiventral* distribution (see figure 16.56).

Hanging a *plumb-line* in front of the body will give an approximate indication of the state of the posture, but it assumes that the person stands with the weight equally distributed on the two feet and correctly distributed between the ball of the foot and the heel. This experiment will show that this is frequently *not* the case. It will also show up any other defects of posture.

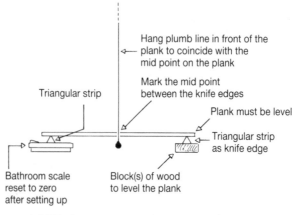

Hang plumb line in front of the
plank to coincide with the
mid point on the plank

Mark the mid point
between the knife edges

Triangular strip

Plank must be level

Triangular strip
as knife edge

Bathroom scale
reset to zero
after setting up

Block(s) of wood
to level the plank

Figure 16.57 Apparatus to analyse a person's posture

You will need a bathroom-type personal scale, a substantial plank of wood about 4 feet long, 1 foot wide and 1 inch thick, a selection of blocks of wood including two 1-foot lengths of triangular section strip, a plumb-line and a 'volunteer' to be diagnosed.

First weigh your volunteer on the bathroom scale. Then set up the apparatus as shown in figure 16.57.

Ask your volunteer to stand on the centre of the plank facing towards the plumb-line. He or she must move slightly to either side until the scale shows *exactly half* his or her weight. The line now coincides with the lateral line of gravity. You can now see how well your 'victim' is distributed to left and right. You will be able to see such figure defects as the head not carried centrally on the shoulders, unequal shoulder level, pelvic tilt perhaps as a result of the legs being of unequal length. It is amazing how many people do not have a 'matched' pair of legs.

Now ask the volunteer to turn to one side to face along the plank. Again adjust his or her position so the scale shows half his or her weight. The line now shows the dorsiventral line of gravity. Once more you can compare with the 'norm'.

Things to do

Collect manufacturers' information literature on the various types of exercise machines.

Self-assessment questions

1   What are 'antagonistic' muscles?

2   Distinguish between a flexor muscle and an extensor.

3   Draw a simple diagram to show a lever of the first order operating in the forearm.

4   Where in the body might you find a lever of the second order?

5   What is a 'moment'?

6   What is (a) mechanical advantage, (b) velocity ratio?

7   State two ways in which a leg-lifting exercise may be progressed.

8   What is muscle tone? What is its importance in figure correction?

9   What is muscle fatigue? Briefly describe what happens in a fatigued muscle.

10   What is endorphin? State two effects it can have on a person who indulges in prolonged strenuous exercise.

11   What is the purpose of pulleys and cables in weight exercising machines?

12   How does the force required to extend a spring change as the spring is extended?

13   State three ways in which the resistance to movement can be produced in rowing machines.

14   What is (a) a kilocalorie, (b) basal metabolism?

15   What is a centre of gravity?

17

The Beauty Salon – Working Conditions and Services

A comfortable salon; working temperature; heating the salon; movement of heat; heating methods; ventilating the salon; humidity; ventilation systems; air-conditioning; thermostats; lighting the salon; adequacy of illumination; avoidance of glare; lighting systems; cold water supplies; hot water systems; drains and drain traps; caring for drains; fire safety precautions; fire extinguishers

A comfortable salon

The whole purpose of beauty treatment is to make the client *feel good* and there is not a hope of this in a cold and draughty salon or one which is unbearably hot and stuffy.

A salon should be maintained at a *comfortable* temperature. The air should be changed frequently, but not so frequently as to create draughts.

The temperature of the salon

What constitutes a *comfortable* temperature depends very much on what you are doing. The Health and Safety at Work Act of 1972 insists that the temperature of a place of work shall have reached a *minimum* of 17°C (63°F) within *one* hour of the start of the working day.

While this *is* a comfortable temperature for someone *at* work, it must be remembered that in a treatment room not everyone is at work! The clients are definitely *not* at work and could quite well be far from fully dressed, so a much higher temperature must be maintained in the client cubicles. A temperature in the range of 20–23°C (68–75°F) is required there.

For the therapist who *is* at work, this order of temperature is rather warm, so she must dress accordingly in a light and airy uniform, usually white cotton. Under such circumstances, she must pay particular attention to her own personal freshness.

In the *gymnasium* or *exercise room* a temperature closer to the statutory minimum is more appropriate. If it is too warm, the clients will want to sleep rather than indulge in their exercise programmes.

Heating the beauty salon

How one heats the salon depends very much on the circumstances of the premises: whether you own it or rent; whether it is new or old. It may be that you must make do with the existing heating system. If, though, it is to be your choice, what heating systems are suitable? It must be economical both to instal and run. It must be effective, clean and easy to control.

Movement of heat

A heating system has to transfer the heat from where it is produced into the room where it is required. There are *three* methods of movement of heat – *conduction*, *convection* and *radiation*.

Conduction is when heat passes through a substance, usually a solid, by being passed from molecule to molecule from the hottest part to the coldest. Metals are good *conductors*. The working parts of heaters are made of metal so the heat can pass easily through. Plastics, wood, textiles and air are poor conductors. They are *insulators*. They are used to prevent the passage of heat. Loft insulation, cavity wall insulation and double glazing all use trapped air to prevent loss of heat from a building and so cut down heating costs.

Convection occurs in fluid substances: liquids and gases. Heat causes the fluid to expand so it becomes less dense and rises. Cool fluid falls to take its place. The movements are called *convection currents*. The heat is carried by the moving fluid. Hot water systems and many room heating systems work by convection.

Radiation is where heat travels as *rays*. It is also called *radiant heat* or *infra-red*. It was considered in detail in chapter 12. Heat radiation is given out by anything hot. It does not necessarily have to be glowing red or white hot. Even the human body radiates several hundred watts of radiant heat and so can contribute significantly to the warmth of a room!

Experiments to show conduction, convection and radiation

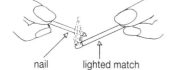

Figure 17.1 The match and nail experiment

The distinction between a conductor and an insulator can be demonstrated very convincingly with a match and a small nail of equal length. Hold the nail in one hand, the match in the other. Strike the match and hold it to the nail. You will put the nail down rather sooner than you might have thought! (see figure 17.1).

How effective is insulation? Take two identical calorimeters – empty cans will do. Wrap one in a piece of thick fabric. Hold it in place with elastic bands. Put a thermometer in each. Fill each with boiling water, then take the temperature in each can every two or three minutes. Note how fast each cools down (see figure 17.2).

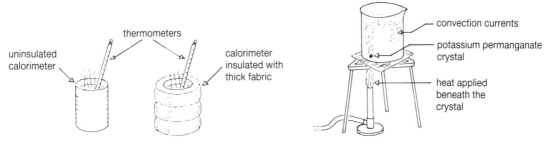

Figure 17.2 The effect of insulation

Figure 17.3 A demonstration of convection currents

To show convection, set up a beaker of water on a tripod. Drop a single crystal of a dye down one side of the beaker; a crystal of potassium permanganate will do. Place a lighted bunsen burner under the beaker right beneath the crystal. Coloured streaks in the water will show the *convection currents* (see figure 17.3).

While everyone knows that red and white hot objects give off heat *radiation*, not many appreciate that cooler, non-glowing surfaces give off heat rays too. How much they do so depends on the nature of the surface. Light and shiny surfaces radiate less than dull black ones. A classic experiment called *Lesley's cube* will show this. You will also need an instrument called a thermopile to

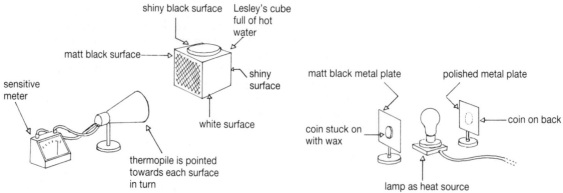

Figure 17.4 Lesley's cube experiment

Figure 17.5 Comparing the heat absorbency of black and shiny surfaces

detect the radiation. It shows its reading on a very sensitive electrical meter (see figure 17.4).

Radiation from each surface of Lesley's cube is – matt black radiates most, then shiny black, then white and finally polished metal radiates least.

How well radiation is *absorbed* also depends on the nature of the surface, matt black surfaces being much better than polished surfaces. The simple experiment in figure 17.5 shows this well.

In this little 'race', the coin falls from the matt black plate first.

Heating a room

A heater heats a room by either *convection* or *radiation*. A *convection* heater causes the air in the room to circulate and the heat is distributed round the room by the moving air. A room heated by convection is heated quite evenly (see figure 17.6).

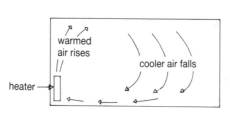

Figure 17.6 Heating a room by convection

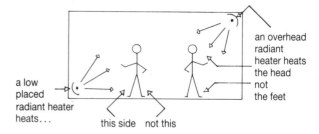

Figure 17.7 Room heating by radiation is uneven

A room heated by *radiation* is likely to be less than evenly heated because heat travelling as rays tends to be absorbed by objects and people rather than by the air in the room. A heater placed low at one side of the room will heat from that side only. Heaters set high in the room will give rise to a hot-head, cold-feet situation (see figure 17.7).

Direct heating

Having decided that heating by *convection* is most effective do you instal *direct heating* with heaters in the rooms, or *central heating*?

Figure 17.8 An electric convector heater mounted on a wall (courtesy of Dimplex Heating Ltd)

Figure 17.9 A gas convector heater on an outside wall with flue ducted outside

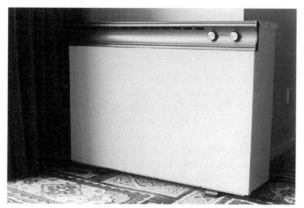

Figure 17.10 An electric storage heater

Direct heating by convector heaters is quick, easy and inexpensive to instal. Choose between gas or electric convectors, or electric storage heaters which use low-cost, off-peak electricity (see figures 17.8, 17.9 and 17.10).

Central heating

Much more expensive to instal but much more controllable is *central heating*. A variety of systems are available. Perhaps the most familiar is a system of *radiators* – actually they are convectors – heated by hot water circulating in pipes from a boiler. The boiler can be fired by gas, oil or solid fuel. All can be completely automatic (see figure 17.11).

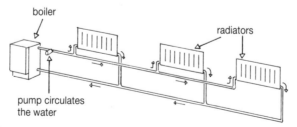

Figure 17.11 A central heating system with boiler and radiators

Figure 17.12 Warm air ducts into a room

Also quite common is a *ducted warm air* system. An electric fan blows air through a gas or oil-fired furnace and then through metal ducts into the rooms (see figure 17.12).

Much less familiar, because nothing is visible, are heated floors or ceilings. They are often installed in office blocks or blocks of flats but have proved less than satisfactory. Floor heating causes hot and tired feet, and ceiling heating heats the head but not the feet. Both forms tend to be expensive to run.

Ventilating the salon

Keeping the salon *warm* is just part of the story. It could be that it is *too warm* already. Maybe there is *too much moisture* in the air and it is forming *condensation* on the windows or even the walls. The air might be starting to *smell* unpleasant. Those present might be feeling tired and listless. They might be yawning a lot. This is due to an excess of *carbon dioxide* in the air.

Air that is too hot, too humid, smelly and too rich in carbon dioxide is *heat stagnant*. It indicates that the *ventilation* arrangements are at fault.

Humidity

Humidity is the moisture content of the air. Humidity is explained more fully in chapter 14 in the pages on Steam baths and Saunas.

The measure of humidity is *relative humidity* or RH for short. Relative humidity expresses the *actual* moisture content of the air as a *percentage* of what it *could* hold at that temperature. It can be measured with a *hygrometer*. Hygrometers, too, are described in chapter 14.

For comfort, the relative humidity should be between 60 and 70 per cent.

If, because of inadequate ventilation, the humidity becomes too *high*, perspiration does not evaporate and a person will feel uncomfortably hot and sticky.

A common fault in centrally heated buildings is that humidity is too *low*. In these warm dry conditions people sweat far more than they realise because there is no perspiration wetness. This results in tiredness, headaches and sore throats due to *dehydration*. Some kind of *humidifying* would cure the problem.

Condensation

In chapter 14, we saw that the *warmer* the air, the *greater* its capacity to hold moisture.

The converse, too, is true. The *cooler* the air, the *less* moisture it can hold. The result of this is that if warm moist air is cooled sufficiently, at a certain temperature it will become *saturated* or fully-laden with moisture. Cooled below this temperature, the air *must* lose its excess moisture as *condensation*. This temperature is known as *dew-point*.

In a building, the windows and the air near them are often cooler than the rest of the room. If they are cooler than dew-point, moisture will condense on the windows, steaming them up and maybe running in rivulets down the glass (see figure 17.13). If the windows have the better insulation of double glazing, the likelihood of condensation is much reduced.

Poorly insulated walls can suffer condensation too, with dire consequences for the decoration. Paint and wallpaper peel away and mould grows beautifully (see figure 17.14).

Figure 17.13 Condensation on a window pane

Figure 17.14 Decorations damaged by condensation

Smells

Everyone would agree that some smells are definitely obnoxious, but even the best perfumes are less than pleasant in excess. Too much smell causes nausea and headaches.

Ventilation systems

Good ventilation must change the air frequently, perhaps several times each hour. At the same time it must not cause draught; people find draughts uncomfortable!

The simplest ventilation is by opening the windows, but there are windows and windows. A simple opening light will probably change the air satisfactorily, but the slightest wind outside will cause a draught.

A better arrangement is to have two opening lights: a hopper type at the bottom of the window and a transom at the top. Then natural *convection* will ventilate the room. At least in theory it will (see figure 17.15). In practice, natural ventilation is often inadequate.

In an attempt to prevent draughts, the lower hopper window should open at no lower than shoulder height, about 1.5 metres from the floor.

Also designed to ventilate without draughts is *Cooper's disc* (see figure 17.16). A circle of holes is cut in the window pane. Over them fits a plastic disc with a similar series of holes. The disc can be rotated to open or close the holes as required.

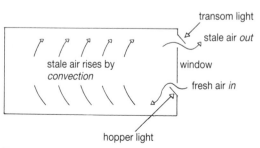

Figure 17.15 Ventilation by natural convection through window openings

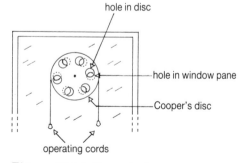

Figure 17.16 Cooper's disc

Forced ventilation

Figure 17.17 Extractor fan in a window

More often than not some form of *forced* ventilation will be required. *Room fans* do little to change the air in a room but because *moving* warm air does at least *feel* cooler than still warm air, they do bring about some improvement in comfort.

The most basic *true* forced ventilation is provided by *extractor fans*. These can be installed in a cut out in a window pane or fitted through a wall (see figure 17.17).

In *very* hot weather, some extractor fans can be reversed to force a draught of fresh air *into* the room.

Ultra-violet equipment, particularly the high-pressure solaria, generates an appreciable amount of *ozone*, which in excess is both nauseating and harmful. Here good ventilation is essential and some form of *ducted* extraction system is appropriate.

Air-conditioning

The ideal is, of course, full air-conditioning. This is a combined heating and ventilation system and is quite expensive to install. Basically, what the system does is to draw stale air from the rooms, cool it to condense out excess moisture, mix it with a proportion of fresh air, heat it to the correct temperature and duct it back into the rooms.

Controlling the temperature

Many heating systems are able to maintain a *constant* room temperature by means of a *thermostat*. This is a device which automatically switches off the system when the required temperature is reached, and switches it on again as the temperature falls.

The main working part of a thermostat is a *bimetallic strip*. This is made of strips of two different metals, brass and a special steel called *invar* bonded together.

Any metal expands when it is heated and contracts when cooled. For the same rise in temperature, brass expands much more than invar, thus causing the bimetallic strip to bend as it is heated and straighten again when cooled. In the thermostat this movement is used to operate a switch which controls the electricity supply to the heating system (see figure 17.18).

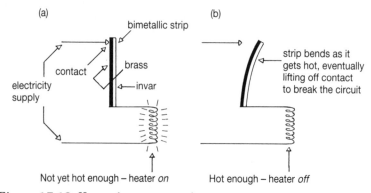

Figure 17.18 How a thermostat works

A thermostat can control oil, gas and solid fuel systems too. It can open or close a valve supplying gas or oil to the burner, or it can open or close a valve controlling the draught to a solid fuel fire.

Lighting the salon

A good standard of illumination is essential for any place of work. Working in inadequate light is likely to lead to eye-strain, particularly when doing detailed work such as epilation or eyelash tinting. It is equally important to consider the comfort of the clients who must not be dazzled by the glare of very bright lamps.

A good working light:

> must be of sufficient intensity
> must be even from all directions
> must not cast sharp shadows
> must not cause glare
> should be as much like daylight as possible

Daylight

The choice of lighting is between natural daylight through windows and artificial light from electric lamps. In the salon it is most unlikely that daylight alone will be adequate. Rooms do not have windows on every side so at best the light will be uneven. For modesty's sake the windows will need to be partially obscured and many clients prefer the privacy of curtained or partitioned cubicles where there is unlikely to be daylight.

Where daylight *is* useful is in the selection and application of colour cosmetics. True colours can only be seen in daylight. For applying make up, having the treatment chair facing a window could be an advantage, but it should not be an unshaded window which faces direct sunlight. This is much too bright – it casts sharp shadows and its glare will dazzle the client.

Artificial light

General lighting in the salon will be provided by ceiling-mounted light units or luminaires. In these the light source will be either *tungsten filament lamps* or *fluorescent tubes*. The working of a filament lamp is described in chapter 1 and that of a fluorescent lamp in chapter 13.

Filament lamps give a light which is very yellow with less blue and green in it than daylight. It is this which makes colour-matching difficult in tungsten light. Filament lamps also give a great deal of heat, so lamps of greater than 60 watts should not be used in small enclosed light units. Ceiling luminaires may contain one or more lamps of 100, 150 or 200 watts each.

Filament lamps are of several types. Plain glass or 'clear' bulbs give a bright glaring light from the filament which unless shaded will dazzle and will cast sharp shadows. 'Pearl' bulbs are made of translucent glass so the filament is not clearly visible. Glare is reduced and shadows are softened. White or 'opal' bulbs reduce glare even more but at the expense of some light output. Internally silvered reflector lamps are for spotlighting displays. They are not suitable for general lighting.

Fluorescent lamps are much more efficient than tungsten lamps. For a given wattage they produce around four times as much light. They also have a working life of 5000 hours compared with 1000 for a tungsten bulb. Although more expensive, their greater efficiency and longer life makes fluorescent lighting more cheaper than tungsten lighting.

The 'colour' of fluorescent lighting depends on the choice of tubes. 'White' tubes produce a harsh white light with more blue in it than daylight. Tubes known as 'warm white' or 'daylight' give a good approximation to natural

Figure 17.19 Fluorescent luminaire

daylight in which most work involving colour-matching can be done satisfactorily.

The long fluorescent tubes, particularly when fitted in luminaires with translucent diffusers (see figure 17.19), will produce a soft even light, free from glare and casting very little shadow.

However, the long straight type of fluorescent units are very 'clinical' in appearance. Recently, major manufacturers have developed miniature fluorescent lamps which fit into an ordinary lampholder (see figures 17.20 and 17.21). They cannot however be used in conjunction with 'dimmer' type switches.

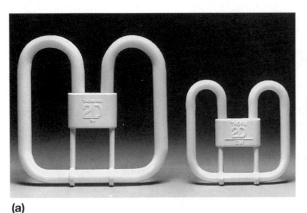

(a)

(b)

Figure 17.20 A Thorn miniature fluorescent lamp: (a) the 25 W and 16 W lamps; (b) in use in a hair salon (courtesy of Thorn Lighting Ltd)

Figure 17.21 Miniature fluorescent lamp to fit standard lampholder

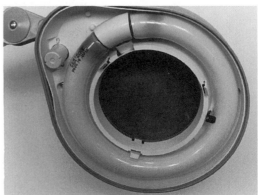

Figure 17.22 Circular fluorescent lamp in an illuminated magnifier

Localised lighting

For detailed work some form of localised lighting is useful to shine a brighter light on the work, but care has to be taken in shining an ordinary worklight on to a client. Its glare will be most uncomfortable. A softer and relatively glare-free light is provided by a circular fluorescent tube as is fitted in the magnifier lamp (see figure 17.22).

The water supply to a salon

Everyone has come to expect, as of right, a constant supply of clean wholesome water to be available at the turn of a tap. The water supplying authority has had to collect the water, clean it and sterilise it, and pump it through the water mains beneath the streets to each of our houses or business premises.

Treatment of water for supplies

The water authority obtains water for supplies by either collecting it in reservoirs in mountain districts, pumping it from wells or boreholes, or pumping it out of the larger rivers.

The water is cleaned by passing it through fine sand in a filter bed. It is then sterilised by adding to it a few parts per million of chlorine. This is to kill bacteria and other germs which might possibly spread such diseases as typhoid, cholera and dysentery.

The preparation of water for water supplies is described more fully in Volume 1.

After cleansing and sterilising at the water treatment works, the treated water is pumped into a covered reservoir at a high point in the district. From there it flows mostly by gravity through the water mains beneath the streets to the consumers, though in some instances the water has to be pumped through the mains so it flows with adequate pressure.

Cold water supply system in a premises

From the water main under the street, water reaches the building through a *service main*. This enters the building from underground and turns up through the floor as the *rising main*. Where the rising main emerges from the floor will be found a *stop-cock*. This tap is to shut off the cold water supply to the building should there be a leak or a burst pipe or while the water system is being serviced. Just above the stop cock there may be a *drain-cock*, to which a hose may be attached to drain the whole system (see figure 17.23).

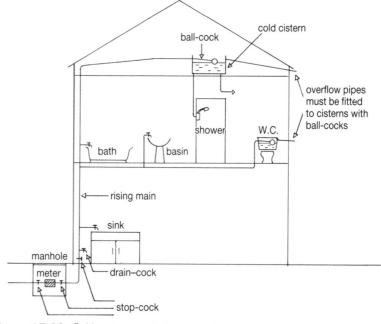

Figure 17.23 Cold water supply to a premises

The water meter and water bills

Outside a business premises, beneath a manhole cover in the pavement, will be found the *water meter* and another stop-cock, the *main stop-cock*.

The water supply to a business will be *metered* and bills will be received half-yearly. The bill is in two parts – a 'standing charge' which is a standard amount each half-year, and a quantity charge of so-much per cubic metre of water used.

The rising main will take water to the cold tap on the kitchen sink and to the cold water cistern in the loft of the building. It will also supply any other cold tap which is to be for *drinking water*. The main purpose of the cold water cistern is to replenish the hot water system. Often though, the cold supply to the bath, wash-basins and toilet flushing cisterns is taken from the cold cistern. Cold water from the cold cistern is *not drinking water*. It has been stored in the open-topped cistern for some time and could well have become contaminated (see figure 17.23).

The cold water supply to the *mixer taps* on showers and shampoo sprays is best taken from the cold cistern so that both hot and cold will be at the *same pressure*. The shower or spray will not then be subject to sudden temperature changes caused by variations in mains pressure. These changes could be dangerous and cause a person to be scalded.

The water tap

One of the most annoying household faults is a dripping tap. The usual cause of this is a worn *tap-washer*. Changing a tap washer is relatively straight-forward if suitable tools are available and the routine is followed carefully. Figure 17.24 shows a tap in section.

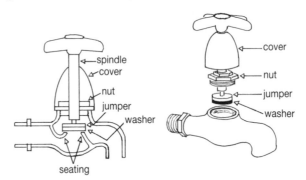

Figure 17.24 A water tap – section diagram and exploded diagram

Changing a tap washer

To change a tap washer, the following routine should be followed. If you doubt your ability to attempt such a task or lack suitable tools it is best done by a qualified plumber.

First turn off the supply at stop-cock.

The cold system stop-cock is just above where the rising main enters the building (see figure 17.23).

The hot system stop-cock is just above the hot water storage cylinder (see figure 17.26).

If a hot tap is to be serviced, the water heating system must be turned off.

Next turn on offending tap to drain any remaining water.

Unscrew the cover to reveal the nut (see figure 17.24).

Using a suitable spanner unscrew nut and remove spindle. It should bring out the jumper and washer with it.

Replace the faulty washer with a new one of the correct type.

Reassemble the tap and turn it off.

Turn on the stop-tap. Test the tap to make sure it works correctly.

The ball-cock

This is an automatic tap which is used to maintain the water level in cold cisterns and toilet flushing cisterns (see figure 17.25). It too has a washer to shut off the water flow. As the water level rises the ball float working through a lever pushes the washer against the seating to shut off the flow. A ball valve, too, can suffer from a faulty washer with the result that the water flow does not stop. In anticipation of such a fault, a cistern *must* have an *overflow pipe* to take excess water safely outside. Because a ball-cock is usually not easily accessible, changing its washer is best done by a plumber.

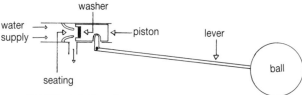

Figure 17.25 A ball-cock

Hot water supply to a premises

The arrangements for the supply of hot water will differ from salon to salon and will depend mostly on the fuel used to heat the water. The choice of fuel is between *electricity, gas, oil* and *solid fuel*.

The other choice is between a *storage system* in which a supply of hot water is stored in an insulated hot water cylinder and an *instant system* where the water is heated instantly when required.

Electricity and gas can be used for both storage and instant systems. Oil and solid fuel may be used only for storage systems. Usually modern storage systems fired by oil, gas or solid fuel will be part of a central heating system.

Storage hot water system

Most salons will have a storage hot water system using an electric immersion heater (see figure 17.26).

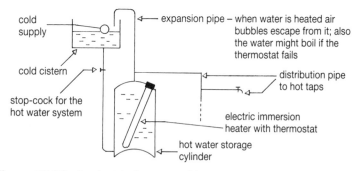

Figure 17.26 An electrically operated hot water storage system

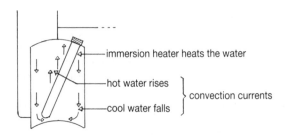

Figure 17.27 Convection in a hot water cylinder

Note how the distribution pipe to take hot water to the taps leaves the *top* of the hot water cylinder and the pipe bringing cold water enters the *bottom* of the cylinder.

Because water *expands* when it is heated, it becomes slightly less dense than cold water and floats to the top. As the immersion heater heats the water, the *hot* water rises to the *top* of the cylinder and any cold water sinks to the bottom. This is *convection* and the movements of the water in the cylinder are *convection currents*. Figure 17.27 shows convection in the hot water cylinder.

Hot water system with a separate boiler

Sometimes a separate boiler burning oil, gas or solid fuel is used to provide hot water. This arrangement is shown in figure 17.28.

If the boiler also supplies hot water to the radiators of a *central heating system*, the water circulating through the radiators gets very dirty and so cannot be used as a hot water supply. In this case an *indirect cylinder* is used. This contains a *heat exchanger coil* through which the 'radiator' water passes and transfers its heat to the water in the storage cylinder (see figure 17.29).

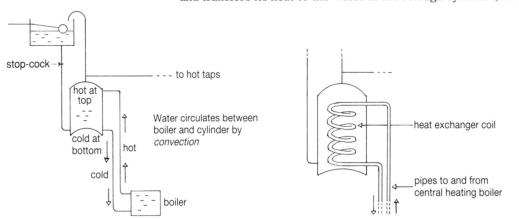

Figure 17.28 Hot water system with a separate boiler **Figure 17.29** An indirect hot water cylinder

Stop-cock in the hot water system

This is situated in the pipe between the cold cistern and the hot water cylinder (see figures 17.26 and 17.28). It is to isolate the hot system if a fault occurs or if it is being serviced.

BEFORE TURNING OFF THIS STOPCOCK – TURN OFF THE SOURCE OF HEAT

Switch off the immersion heater or put out the boiler. Then turn off the stop-cock and open the hot taps to drain the system as far as possible.

Remember that the cylinder and boiler will still be full. If the fault is with either of these, the whole system will have to be drained. This is best left to an expert plumber or heating engineer.

Instant hot water by electricity

The electric instant water heater is most commonly used to provide water at a suitable temperature for a shower or shampoo spray. Often these self-contained units will be in addition to a conventional hot water system.

Inside the very compact unit the pipe which carries the water is surrounded by a *very powerful* electric heating element. Turn on the tap and the movement of the water turns on the heater. Turn off and the heater goes off too. Run the water slowly and it gets very hot; run it quickly and it gets less hot. Figure 17.30 shows an electric shower unit.

Figure 17.30 An electric instant shower heater

Instant hot water by gas

Figure 17.31 shows a gas-fired instant water heater. This type of heater used to be very popular at one time but has become less favoured since most premises now have full hot water systems. Figure 17.32 shows how it works.

Figure 17.31 Gas instant water heater – the Main Medway multipoint (courtesy of Main Gas Appliances)

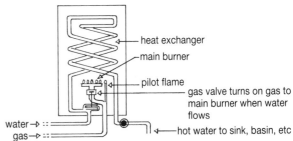

heat exchanger
main burner
pilot flame
gas valve turns on gas to main burner when water flows
water →
gas →
hot water to sink, basin, etc

Figure 17.32 Gas instant water heater

Turn on the water and the main gas burner is ignited automatically from a small pilot flame which is alight all the time. Again the water temperature depends on the rate at which water flows – quickly and it gets less hot, slowly and it gets hotter. Turn off the water and the main gas burner goes off too.

A larger version of this type of heater is the *multipoint*. It is able to supply instant hot water to the normal hot taps on the sink, bath and wash basin (see figure 17.33).

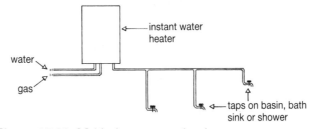

instant water heater
water
gas
taps on basin, bath sink or shower

Figure 17.33 Multipoint gas water heating system

Drains

The waste water from sinks, basins, baths and showers and the effluent from toilets can pose a potential health hazard, as well as being an unpleasant nuisance, unless taken to a sewer through an effective and well maintained drainage system. This waste water will be made safe at a sewage works before being allowed into a river or other watercourse. It must not be disposed of through storm water drains which would take it to the river untreated.

Waste water drains provide ideal places in which germs can thrive. The water is often warm. It contains materials on which germs can feed, materials which tend to stick to the insides of the pipes to provide good living places for the germs. The germs produce unpleasant smells in the drains and if their numbers build up sufficiently they could be the cause of disease.

Drain traps

At the entrance to each drain there must be a *drain trap*. Its purpose is to *prevent germs and smells coming back out of the drain* to cause discomfort and possibly disease. It uses the last water to go down the drain to form a *water seal* which in effect closes the entrance to the drain.

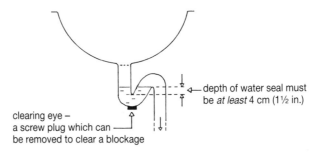

depth of water seal must be *at least* 4 cm (1½ in.)

clearing eye – a screw plug which can be removed to clear a blockage

Figure 17.34 An S-bend siphon trap beneath a wash basin

The simplest form of drain trap is the *siphon trap* or '*S-bend*'. This is fitted immediately beneath the plug-hole of a sink, bath, basin or shower tray (see figure 17.34). Although the purpose of a drain trap is *not* to stop solid objects going down a drain (the grid in the plug-hole is to do that!) it is usually in the S-bend that solids do accumulate eventually to block the drain. Clearing the S-bend of an ordinary siphon trap is a difficult and fiddly process through the tiny clearing-eye, and so it tends to be left until a drain is blocked rather than being done as a part of routine maintenance.

Much easier to clear is a *bottle trap*. Having first placed a bowl beneath, the screw cap is easily removed and its contents tipped out (see figure 17.35).

A toilet bowl or water-closet is in effect a drain trap (see figure 17.36).

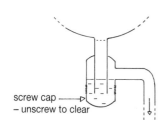

screw cap – unscrew to clear

Figure 17.35 A 'bottle' trap

Looking after drains

Despite the presence of drain traps it is still possible for drains to become smelly and unhygienic. Greasy dirt and unused soaps and detergents may cling to the insides of the pipes, providing a breeding ground for germs. Those in the short length of waste-pipe before the trap may be sufficient to make the drain unpleasant.

Daily use of an *effective* disinfectant or a bleach will prevent the unpleasantness. Not all disinfectants are effective. Some do little more than mask the drain smells with a 'healthy' perfume!

Figure 17.36 A toilet bowl or water closet

Occasionally hot caustic soda solution (sodium hydroxide) may be poured carefully down the drain to remove the accumulation from inside the pipes. Sodium hydroxide is a very **HAZARDOUS SUBSTANCE**. It can cause skin burns.

Toilets in a salon may need attention more than once a day. Use a good-quality special-purpose toilet cleanser or a bleach to cleanse, disinfect and prevent the build up of lime scale and unsightly brown iron stains. Pay particular attention to the flushing rim and the S-bend.

Wash basins, baths and shower trays will all need daily, or more frequent, cleansing using a neutral non-abrasive or soft abrasive cleanser so as not to damage the surfaces.

Fire hazards and fire precautions

Like any other kind of accident a *fire* is something that happens to other people, never to you. But one day it could happen in your salon. How safe is your salon? Has it properly marked emergency exits? Has it suitable fire equipment and has it been regularly maintained? Would you know what to do if a fire did break out?

Under the Health and Safety at Work Act of 1974 you have a duty of care to your clients. If you own or manage the salon, you also have a duty of care to your staff. This involves making sure that the salon is a safe and healthy place in which to be. With regard to fire safety it means that every reasonable precaution should be taken to ensure fire does not break out.

Fire risks include:

1 Flammable liquids. Make sure they are stored away from sources of heat and used with due care.
2 Electrical equipment. Make sure it is in good serviceable condition, including flexes, plugs and switches. Make sure circuits are not overloaded.
3 Drying towels over electric or gas heaters. This must not be done. It could cause the appliance to seriously overheat and set fire to the towels.
4 Careless disposal of cigarettes and matches. Ideally, in a *health* and beauty salon no-one should smoke. If they must, there should be proper ashtrays available.
5 Unsafe upholstery, soft furnishings and decorating materials. When furnishing a salon make sure all materials are of low fire risk.

A salon must have clearly marked emergency exits. If the salon is not on the ground floor, there must be an alternative means of escape to street level apart from the main stairway.

In the event of a fire, the first action should be to evacuate the clients. If the fire is small it can be tackled with an appropriate extinguisher. If not, the staff should also evacuate closing windows and doors, if there is time, and also shut off gas and electric appliances. They should sound the alarm if there is one and call the *fire service* (dial 999). It is important that staff know what to do, and act without panic. The fire service will advise on a suitable evacuation procedure for a salon and this must be rehearsed by regular *fire practice*.

Fire-fighting equipment for the salon

For there to be a fire, *three* factors must be present:

> 1. A flammable material
> 2. A supply of oxygen from the air
> 3. A source of heat to start the burning

To extinguish a fire, one can either cool the burning material with water or smother it to exclude oxygen. For the beauty salon, where a fire could involve flammable liquids or electrical equipment, a water or foam extinguisher is unsuitable.

Suitable extinguishers for the salon are the *carbon dioxide gas* extinguisher, colour-coded black, and the *dry powder* extinguisher, coloured blue. A glass fibre fire blanket is also useful to put out burning clothing on a person or to extinguish small amounts of flammable liquids. The fire service will advise on the positioning of extinguishers and on how to use them. The will also check the equipment periodically.

Self-assessment questions

1   What is a comfortable room temperature (a) for the clients in a beauty salon, (b) for the participants in an exercise class?

2   State the three methods of movement of heat.

3   Distinguish between a conductor and an insulator of heat.

4   Why is a convector heater preferable to a radiant heater for the salon?

5   What is a comfortable level of humidity in the salon?

6   What four things might be wrong with air that is 'heat stagnant'?

7   What is a Cooper's disc? What is its purpose?

8   What is the cause of condensation on the insides of window panes?

9   What is the purpose of a thermostat? What is the main working part of a thermostat?

10   State two advantages of fluorescent lamps compared with tungsten filament lamps for general lighting in the beauty salon.

11   Name two diseases that could be spread by unsterilised drinking water.

12   Where would you find the stop cock for (a) the cold water supply to a building, (b) for the hot water system?

13   What is the function of a drain trap?

14   What is the advantage of a 'bottle trap'?

15   Name two types of accidental fires which should *not* be tackled with a water-type fire extinguisher.

18

Basic First-Aid

First-aid box; first-aid training; accidents in the beauty salon; the unconscious patient; general advice

Even though every precaution may have been taken to ensure the safety and wellbeing of one's clients and staff, people do become ill and accidents do happen. It is therefore wise to be prepared by keeping a fully stocked first-aid kit and becoming proficient in first-aid.

The first-aid box

To conform with the requirements of the Health and Safety (First Aid) Regulations 1981 the first-aid box must contain:

> A selection of individually wrapped sterile adhesive dressings
> A sterile eye pad
> Sterile triangular bandages
> Medium and large sterilised unmedicated dressings
> Safety pins
> First-aid guidance leaflet
> Book, card or forms on which to *record* details of *all* treatments – however trivial

The siting of the box must be shown by the standard sign – a *white* cross on a green background. The person responsible for the box must ensure it is kept clean and fully stocked.

Note that the box contains *no medicines*. These are not now allowed in first-aid boxes nor are first-aiders allowed to administer unprescribed medicines.

First-aid training

Ideally any organisation should have a trained first-aider constantly available. First-aid training is offered in most technical colleges and by voluntary health organisations. It is certificated in the United Kingdom by the British Red Cross Society, the St John's Ambulance and the St Andrew's Ambulance Association (Scotland). Certification expires after three years, at which time first-aiders must take a refresher course and be re-examined.

Even if the beauty therapist is not a trained first-aider, it is essential to know how to act in case of an emergency. The main advice is not to attempt too much and to know where trained or professional help is available. A modern emergency ambulance is crewed by trained *paramedics* and has on board sophisticated first-line treatment equipment. Too much attempted by an untrained person causes unnecessary delay and might make the situation worse.

Accidents in the beauty salon

The kind of accidents likely to occur in a beauty salon are likely to result in cuts, burns and scalds, eye injury, bruises, blisters, fractures and sprains and possible unconsciousness.

Minor cuts can be treated with a sterile adhesive dressing. A more severe cut should have a sterile dressing placed on it and finger pressure applied over it until the bleeding stops. A sterile bandage is then applied. If the bleeding cannot be controlled, the patient should be taken to hospital for the wound to be stitched.

Burns are caused by *dry* heat such as contact with a flame or hot object. *Scalds* are caused by the *wet* heat of very hot water or steam. In either case the aim should be to cool the affected area as soon as possible under running cold water. If blisters do occur they should not be burst. Severe burns should be covered, without disturbing the clothing, with a lightly applied sterile bandage and the patient should be taken to hospital.

Eye injuries are usually the result of foreign bodies in the eye. Attempt to remove the object by pulling back the eyelid and using the moistened corner of a clean handkerchief or wash it out with water in a clean eyebath. If that fails, apply a sterile eye pad and take the patient to hospital.

A fall could result in broken bones. If the person suffers loss of use, swelling and perhaps distortion of a limb, suspect a *fracture*. Do not disturb the patient. Keep him or her warm and send for an ambulance. Do not give food or drink because the patient will probably need a general anaesthetic while the broken bone is set.

Sprains can occur during exercise or from falls. Apply a crepe bandage to the sprain. Keep it cold with water to reduce the swelling. If it is severe a fracture should be suspected. The patient should be taken to hospital for an X-ray examination.

If a person has struck his or her head in a fall, he or she may feel dazed or sick and cold. The person has *concussion*. Get medical help. The person may even become *unconscious*.

Unconsciousness

A person may become unconscious for a variety of reasons, resulting both from an accident or a medical condition. The priority is to deal with the unconsciousness.

The rule is

A B C; AIRWAY, BREATHING, CIRCULATION

Check that the patient has a clear *airway*, that he or she is *breathing*, and that the heart is beating and *circulating* the blood.

Do not leave the patient; get someone else to telephone for an ambulance at once. If the breathing is normal, move the patient into the *recovery position*; turn the body on to one side; move the upper arm to be at right angles to the body with the elbow bent; move the upper leg to be at right angles to the body also bent (see figure 18.1).

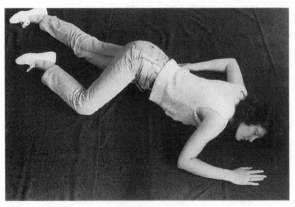

Figure 18.1 Unconscious casualty in the recovery position

Figure 18.2 Mouth to mouth resuscitation demonstrated on a manikin

In this position the patient's airway will remain clear; it will not become blocked with saliva or vomit. Cover the patient and keep him or her warm until the ambulance arrives; do not leave the patient alone.

Mouth-to-mouth resuscitation

If the breathing has stopped or starts to fail, it is necessary to start artificial respiration by the mouth-to-mouth method.

Lay the patient on his or her back and, kneeling by the side, press the head backwards with one hand and the jaw upwards with the other. This opens the airway (see figure 18.2). Then take a deep breath, surround the mouth with your lips at the same time pinching the nostrils closed and gently blow into the lungs until the chest visibly starts to rise. Repeat until natural breathing starts or the ambulance arrives.

Heart massage

If the pulse has also stopped, each breath of artificial respiration must be alternated with *heart massage*. Put your hands palm down one on top of the other and place them on the lower part of the patient's breast bone, and press the bone firmly with the 'heel' of the hand at about one press per second about six times (see figure 18.3). Then give the next breath. Repeat until the ambulance arrives.

CAUTION. Do not practise heart massage on a conscious person. It can seriously injure the chest.

The causes of unconsciousness

Apart from a blow to the head such as might be sustained in a fall, the other accidental cause of unconsciousness is a 'mains-to-earth' *electric shock*. When the current passes through the person's body it contracts all the muscles in its path and holds them contracted. This may prevent the person letting go of the live apparatus and may also stop the breathing.

DO NOT TOUCH THE PERSON. You too will get the shock! Switch off the current at the socket or the mains switch. If this is not possible, wrench the person away using a dry wooden broom handle or a wooden chair. If the breathing has stopped, give artificial respiration until the patient recovers or until help arrives.

Fainting

In a hot stuffy room or after a period lying on the treatment couch or in a steam bath or sauna, a person might feel faint particularly when they try to stand. This is because the blood vessels have dilated, increasing the capacity for blood. If the person has lost a lot of moisture by perspiration, the blood volume may be insufficient to fill the increased capacity so that when the person stands the blood rushes from the head, making him or her feel faint. Sit the person with the head between the knees until he or she feels better.

If the person has become unconscious, he or she should be laid down with the head lower than the feet. The unconsciousness of a faint is usually brief and recovery is quick.

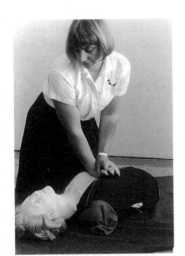

Figure 18.3 Heart massage demonstrated on a manikin

Unconsciousness or illness

Clients are supposed to divulge to you details of any physical or medical condition during their consultations, and these should be noted in their record cards. Remember such information *must* be treated in the utmost confidence. Not always will clients tell the whole truth for fear that it might mean they are refused treatment.

Conditions the therapist should be aware of are diabetes, epilepsy and heart conditions. A *diabetic* might become unconscious as a result of either too little or too much insulin in the blood. In the former case the person has a distinct smell of acetone (nail varnish remover) on the breath. Treat the unconscious person in the normal way.

Epilepsy is a condition in which the person may suffer momentary loss of consciousness for no apparent reason at any time. In its more severe form the person falls unconscious, then after a while the muscles contract jerkily until the person regains consciousness. Do not restrain the sufferer but clear space around him or her to prevent injury. A knotted handkerchief in the patient's mouth will prevent biting of the tongue. After the attack, keep the patient warm and let him or her sleep.

A person with a known heart condition could possibly suffer a *heart attack*, though many seized by heart attacks have had no previous history of heart trouble. The symptoms are severe chest pains spreading to the neck and into the arms, together with the breathlessness and cold sweat of shock. If the person stays conscious, loosen any constricting clothing and send for an ambulance at once. If breathing and pulse begin to fail, commence artificial respiration and heart massage at once while awaiting the ambulance.

A further condition which can suddenly affect the middle-aged and elderly is a *stroke*. This is caused by a blood clot in the brain, starving part of the brain of blood. Depending on its severity it may cause symptoms ranging from the loss of feeling or use of a limb to complete loss of consciousness. Send for an ambulance and treat the unconscious person in the normal way.

General advice

In an emergency:

> Remain calm. Do not panic
> Act speedily but without undue haste
> Do not attempt to do too much
> Send for professional help, indicating clearly what has happened so they can come prepared

Things to do

1 Take a course of training in first-aid.

2 If you work in a salon, find out who is the first-aider, find out where the first-aid box is and find out if the emergency telephone numbers are prominently displayed by the telephone.

Self-assessment questions

1 What is the standard sign for a first-aid box?

2 For how long is a first-aid certificate valid?

3 Distinguish between a burn and a scald.

4 What should be the first-aid treatment for a minor burn?

5 What is the rule for checking an unconscious client?

6 What is the recovery position?

7 Explain briefly how to perform 'mouth-to-mouth' resuscitation.

8 What are the symptoms of a heart attack?

9 What is the purpose of the knotted handkerchief in treating an epileptic fit?

10 What does the smell of acetone on the breath of an unconscious person tell you about his or her medical history?

Bibliography

Further reading in theoretical physics

Reference may be made to textbooks for GCSE and 'A' Level studies. Titles include:

Akrill, T. and Osmond S., *Work Out Physics 'A' Level*, Macmillan, London (1986).
Keighley, H. J. P., *Work Out Physics GCSE,* Macmillan, London (1986).
Keighley, H. J. P. *et al.*, *Mastering Physics*, Macmillan, London (1985).

Simple texts in basic electricity

Burdett, G., *Electricity and Lighting*, Octopus for J. Sainsbury, London (1983).
Chapman, P., *The Young Scientist Book of Electricity*, Usborne, London (1976).

Readings in human biology, anatomy and physiology

The anatomy of the human body is detailed in:

Gray, H., *Gray's Anatomy,* Churchill-Livingstone, London (1980); also in paperback,
  Senate-Studio Editions, London (1994).

General Human Anatomy and Physiology may be studied in:

Arnould-Taylor, W. E., *Textbook of Anatomy and Physiology,* Stanley Thornes, London
  (1988).
Ross, S. J. and Wilson, K. I. W., *Anatomy and Physiology in Health and Illness,* Churchill-
  Livingstone, London (1990).

Human Biology for 'GCSE' and 'A' Level. These include:

Gadd, P., *Human and Social Biology,* Macmillan, London (1983).
Roberts, J., *Mastering Human Biology,* Macmillan, London (1991).
Soper, R. and Tyrell-Smith, S., *Modern Human and Social Biology,* Macmillan, London
  (1982).

Biology for 'GCSE' and 'A' Level. Titles include:

Kilgour, O. F. G., *Work Out Biology GCSE,* Macmillan, London (1986).
Stout, G. W. and Green, N. P. O., *Work Out Biology 'A' Level*, Macmillan, London
  (1986).
Alderson, P. and Rowland, M., *Biology for GCSE*, Macmillan, London (1985).
Ministry of Agriculture, Fisheries and Food, *Manual of Nutrition*, HMSO, London
  (1985).
Kilgour, O. F. G., *Mastering Biology*, Macmillan, London (1983).
Kramer, L. M. J. (Ed.), *Foundations of Biology* (5 volume series), Macmillan, London
  (1979).

Beauty therapy and physiotherapy

Gardiner, M. D., *The Principles of Exercise Therapy*, Bell and Hyman, London (1984).
Colson, J., *Progressive Exercise Therapy*, Wright, Bristol (1983).
Duffield, M. H., *Exercise in Water*, Bailliere, London (1983).
Hollis, M., *Practical Exercise Therapy,* Blackwell, London (1989).
Gallant, A., *Body Treatments and Dietetics for Beauty Therapists,* Stanley Thornes,
  London (1990).
Arnould-Taylor, W. E., *Principles and Practice of Physical Therapy,* Stanley Thornes,
  London (1991).
Githa-Goldberg, A., *Body Massage for Beauty Therapists,* Heinemann,
  London (1991).
Schriber, T. J., *Manual of Electrotherapy*, Lea and Febiger, London (1975).
Wood, E. C., *Beard's Massage – Principles and Techniques*, Saunders, Philadelphia
  (1974).
Scott, P., *Clayton's Electrotherapy and Actinotherapy*, Bailliere, London (1969). [Early
  editions are most useful]
Finnerty, G. B. and Corbitt, T., *Hydrotherapy*, Ungar, New York (1967).

Further reading in hair and beauty from Thomson Learning

Almond, E. (1992). *Manicure, Pedicure and Advanced Nail Techniques.*

Dalamar, P. (1994). *The Complete Make-up Artist: Working in Film, Television and Theatre.*

Green, M., Howson, L. and Palladino, L. (1994). *Professional Hairdressing: The Official Guide to Level 3.*

Nordmann, L. (1995). *Beauty Therapy – The Foundations: NVQ/SVQ Level 1 and 2.*

Palladino, L. (1995). *Hairdressing – The Foundations, second edition: The Official Guide to Level 2.*

Palladino, L. and Hunt, J. (1992). *The Nail File.*

First-aid

Fisher, J., Marsden. A. and Rogers, J., *Save a Life*, BBC Publications, London (1986).

St John's Ambulance Brigade, St Andrew's Ambulance Association, The British Red Cross Society, *First Aid Manual,* 6th Edition, Dorling-Kindersley, London (1983).

Index